Kingsinton House

of the Most Noble & Potent Prince Henry Duke of Beaufort
and Knight of the Most Noble order of the Garter.

1

CHELSEA

The River at Chelsea. Painting by James Webb

CHELSEA

BY

THEA HOLME

TAPLINGER PUBLISHING COMPANY
NEW YORK

First published in the United States in 1971 by
TAPLINGER PUBLISHING CO., INC.
New York, New York

Library of Congress Catalog Card Number: 74–162963
ISBN 0–8008–1440–1

TO
JUDY CAMPBELL

Contents

List of Illustrations

Illustrations 3a, 3b, 5a, 5b, 5c, 7a, 7b, 8b, 10a, 10b, 11b, 12a, 12b, 12c, 13b, 14a, 14b, 15a, 15c, 17a, 17b, 18a, 18b, 19b, 22a, 22b, 24a, and the endpapers are reproduced by permission of the Kensington and Chelsea Public Libraries; 1a, 2a, 9a, 9b, 13a, 15b, 19a, 21a, 23a, 23b, 24b and 27b by permission of the Trustees of the National Portrait Gallery; 1b by permission of the Gordon Fraser Gallery Ltd; 2b by permission of the Trustees of the British Museum; 4 by permission of the Courtauld Institute of Art; 6 by permission of the Victoria and Albert Museum; 8a by permission of the Royal Hospital, Chelsea; 11a by permission of the Trustees of the National Gallery; 20 by permission of William Heinemann Ltd; 21b by permission of the Trustees of the Tate Gallery; 26a and b by permission of the John Lewis Partnership; and 27a by permission of the Slade School of Fine Art.

ACKNOWLEDGMENTS

I am indebted to Dame Sybil Thorndike for her memories of Ellen Terry, and to Mr. Edward Craig for his description of the inside of Ellen Terry's house; to Miss Athene Seyler, C.B.E., for her descriptions of Chelsea in the 1920s, and to Mrs. Jaqueline Hope-Nicholson for her memories of Tite Street in the 1890s.

I should also like to thank Miss Patricia Meara and other members of the staff at the Chelsea Reference Library for all their help, and Mrs. Hester Marsden-Smedley for information about her late husband's work in Chelsea. Sir Zachary Cope supplied interesting details about Charles Haden.

Elizabeth Fortescue Hitchins and Judy Campbell (Mrs. David Birkin) did invaluable pieces of research. Mr. J. V. G. Mallet of the Department of Ceramics, Victoria and Albert Museum, kindly showed me all the fragments of Chelsea china recently dug up in Lawrence Street; and Mr. H. B. Brenan, O.B.E., Assistant Secretary to the Royal Hospital, helped me to visualize the site of Walpole's house and grounds.

I am also grateful to Dr. Patrick Lovett for letting me see his collection of cuttings and photographs relating to Dr. Phene; and to Miss Olivia Walker for allowing me to make use of unpublished notes on the life of her aunt, Dame Ethel Walker. The Hon. Lady Napier, Mrs. H. Nottridge, Miss Marjory Pegram, Miss Dora L. Neale and Mr. F. G. Ferebee all supplied me with interesting memories and anecdotes. Mrs. L. Poole, Archivist to Messrs. John Lewis and Company, gave me photographs and information about the history of Messrs. Peter Jones. Sir John Betjeman and Sir Charles Wheeler have kindly allowed me to quote some of their published works.

I should like, in conclusion, to thank Miss Kathleen Johnston, who typed my manuscript with so much care and attention to detail.

T.H.

INTRODUCTION

'THIS NOBLE VILLAGE'

FOR SOME people Chelsea means a football club; for others a Flower Show, or a Barracks, or a smart place for a wedding. There are also a great many for whom Chelsea means the King's Road, the King's Road on a Saturday afternoon, that curious phenomenon which came into being in the 1960's.

It is difficult for anyone over the age of twenty to explain the fascination which, irresistible as jam to wasps, draws the young in their thousands, Saturday after Saturday, to parade on foot or on wheels, a swarming hurly-burly, bizarrely garbed, among whom a sprinkling of ordinary shoppers pick their way, embarrassed as stage hands who have strayed by mistake on to the scene of a play.

This spectacle confines itself entirely to the King's Road. To turn into a side street is like coming out of a technicolour film into daylight. Eyes and ears take a moment or two to adjust to everyday sights and sounds. The change is less abrupt if you turn into Royal Avenue, for there, under the lime trees, is the show of paintings which, good, bad and indifferent, suggest, perhaps optimistically, that Chelsea is still the artists' quarter. Further down the gravelled enclosure, life goes on as usual: a woman is throwing bread to the pigeons, that particular flock of Chelsea pigeons that inhabits Royal Avenue. A child runs in among them and they scatter and fly up in a huge circle, to swoop down again a moment later in the ceaseless rhythm of town-bred pigeons.

In Burtons Court there is a cricket match, and, seated under the plane trees, a Guards' Band in scarlet tunics are playing Offenbach. Less than five minutes away from the King's Road, we are in another world.

The streets are quiet because it is Saturday and residents are away for the week-end. In Cheyne Walk the wide pavements are almost empty, though the two-way conveyor belt of cars runs ceaselessly along the Embankment—into London, out of London, a monotonous flow to which residents must learn to turn a deaf ear and a blind eye. For here, by the Thames, is the Chelsea which attracted our forefathers—Chelsea Reach, where, on summer evenings, the nobility and gentry came sailing up the river from the City in their gilded barges and pleasure boats, to enjoy food and wine and music in rural surroundings.

Here, for four centuries, the tide ebbed and flowed under a low wall, bordered by a row of elm trees. Painters, from Canaletto to Turner and Whistler, have loved the wide Chelsea reach; and even now the embankmented and workaday Thames has not altogether lost its magic. In winter, when the seagulls whirl and scream over its grey, wind-whipped waters; or on a clear June morning, when the river, smooth and polished as a pond, reflects patches of colour from moored boats and scarlet-lined barges with their cargoes of yellow timber, we may catch a glimpse of the charm that Chelsea has exercised since the days of Thomas More.

The charm was not only aesthetic. People came to Chelsea for their health: in the seventeenth century, ailing noblemen, oppressed by the stuffiness of London, sailed up the Thames to Chelsea to 'take the ayre', and Doctor King, the Rector, noted with pride that 'no village in the vicinity of London contributes more to the ease and recovery of . . . asthmatical and consumptive persons'.

Bowack, writing in 1705, tells us:

'The sweetness of its air, and pleasant situation, has of late years drawn several eminent persons to reside and build here, and filled it with many worthy families of gentry, citizens and others, also the schools with a great number of boarders, especially young ladies, and it has flourished so extremely for twenty or thirty years past, that from a small straggling village, 'tis now become a large beautiful and populous town, having about three hundred houses . . . which is near nine times its number in 1664.'

Chelsea was famous for its fertile gardens. Cherries, plums, medlars, peaches and apricots grew in Thomas More's orchard, and by Charles II's time market gardens abounded. Chelsea strawberries were known for their size and flavour, and at the beginning of the nineteenth century half the vegetables in Covent Garden came from Chelsea and its environs. Vines, mulberries and figs also flourished in private gardens, and their descendants still survive.

Flowers, too, did well, and the King's Road, from Sloane Square to World's End, was famous for its nurseries. In 1777, in a garden on the site of Shawfield Street, Humphrey Richardson Taylor cultivated roses, lavender and other sweet-smelling flowers, and started a perfume distillery which survived till 1852. Even then, though rows of terraced houses were springing up and Chelsea's good air was polluted by smoking chimneys, there were still fields, and the little Misses Thackeray, on their way to visit Mrs. Carlyle in Cheyne Row, walked from Kensington through hawthorn lanes.

A book about Chelsea is, first and foremost, concerned with people. No district of London has housed so many illustrious, brilliant, extraordinary characters. Since Henry VIII's time Chelsea has attracted kings and queens, wits and philosophers, painters and writers; she has also had her eccentrics. There was, for instance, Hortense, the exotic Duchesse de Mazarin, who, after headlong flights across France pursued by a mad husband, finally escaped to England disguised as a man, became Charles II's mistress, and after his death settled in Paradise Row with her menagerie of pets and devoted elderly poet, Saint-Evremond. Here she entertained with threadbare magnificence and cultivated a passion for cleanliness which in those days was thought to be very odd indeed.

Eccentrics are akin to geniuses, and Chelsea has produced a rare number of both. Two characteristics recur: a mania for collecting strange birds and beasts and other rarities, alive or dead; and an inclination for originality in dress. The latter is more common. One remembers with affectionate regret the lady who, only a year or two ago, walked slowly through the streets near Cheyne Walk, dressed in two blankets and leaning upon a broomstick. And also that dapper monocled gentleman known as the Duke of Chelsea, who appeared, regular as clockwork, every evening somewhere near the Cross Keys, in bowler hat, stiff shirt, black coat and striped trousers, with a choice bloom in his buttonhole and a cane in his hand. These were survivors of a vanishing race, genuine originals, of whom many must once have flourished in the district.

Originality of dress is now *de rigueur* in the King's Road, and has in consequence rather lost its meaning, being a fashionable and no longer an individual cult. But it is by no means a modern trend. In the 1880s, when aestheticism was the rage, young ladies dressed as Kate Greenaway illustrations, or in flowing Pre-Raphaelite gowns, danced or drooped along Chelsea streets; and Mr. and Mrs. Oscar Wilde going out to tea—he in velvet, she in clinging white muslin, with a saffron yellow scarf, enormous 'Gainsborough' hat, white stockings and bright yellow shoes—were greeted, understandably, by street urchins with cries of ' 'Ere comes 'Amlet and Ophelia'.

These people were rebels against the stuffy, ugly clothes of their time, and their eccentricity of dress was deliberate. Another butt of the street boys, Walter Greaves, was less conscious of being oddly dressed. The boatman-painter, pupil and protégé of Whistler, survived into the 1920s, when Sir Charles Wheeler remembers seeing him.

'He wore a tall and battered silk hat with square-cut frock coat and concertina-ed pin-stripe trousers. His boots were always immaculately polished—turning up a little at the toe-cap—and his hair oily and ebony black, hanging in serrated locks over his coat collar . . . His coat was greenish-black . . . and was surely made for someone else. The tattered portfolio he invariably carried may also have belonged to another artist— J. McNeill Whistler perhaps—but was always full of drawings of the riverside of earlier days; for when I remember him he was very old with a wizened face and thin, drooping moustache, like those of mandarins painted on Chinese vases. He would hawk around his sketches for a few shillings each . . .'

'We should have been incredulous,' adds Sir Charles, 'if someone had ever said, "There goes a considerable artist." '

It is difficult, in writing of a place so rich in history and in the personalities it has housed, to know where to begin. Chelsea's history stretches back into a past dim enough to be legendary; and, as is the way with all human history, truth and legend are hard to disentangle. In a place favoured by many kings and queens, royal legends abound. Queen Elizabeth I is said to have sheltered from the rain under the Queen's Elm, now commemorated, as is our British custom, by a public house. It is said that the cottage at the south end of Glebe Place (now a nursery school) was Henry VIII's hunting lodge, and one writer went to some pains to speculate upon how that bulky monarch ever got through the door or up the narrow stairs.

Charles II, on the other hand, is said to have ridden a horse up the staircase of Sandford Manor (now part of the gas-works) where Nell Gwynne *is said* to have lived, and where her mother *is said* to have been drowned, when drunk, in the rivulet at the end of the garden.

In the last century it was believed, romantically, that the initials CR entwined over the wrought-iron gates of Rossetti's house in Cheyne Walk stood for *Catherine Regina* (Queen Catherine of Braganza, Charles II's neglected wife; later tenants, the Reverend and Mrs. Haweis, went so far as to re-name the house 'Queen's House'). Now it has been established that the initials were not CR but RC—Richard Chapman, an apothecary of St. Clement Danes, for whom the handsome house was built in 1717. So no queen ever lived there, though no less than four lived in the manor house nearby.

Perhaps the best known and most persistent legend of all—now hotly refuted by every Chelsea Pensioner to a man—is that the Royal Hospital owes its existence to the persuasive tongue of Pretty Witty Nell. This tradition, which has found its way into many histories of Chelsea, has never been completely disproved. For all we know, it may be true, or based on truth. There is, after all, the story about the Romans.

This legend was that part of the Roman army, heading for London, marched across the Thames at Chelsea, and were met by the defenders in mid-stream, where a fierce battle took place. It must have been an uncomfortable battle, particularly for the Romans in heavy cuirasses and helmets, plunging about on the uneven river bed, waist high in swiftly flowing water; but probably their invasion training had included such exercises. The Britons were routed; but a charming tradition has it that their defeat only took place when the Romans called up an elephant, which came stumping out of the Battersea woods: at the sight of this preposterous and terrible beast the defenders of Chelsea fled in confusion.

The main facts of this story, apart from the elephant, are now known to be true. About nineteen hundred years later, when the foundations of Chelsea Bridge were being dug, the workmen unearthed a quantity of skulls and bones, blackened by long burial under the river bed, and with them weapons of British and Celtic origin, Roman swords and spearheads, and a Roman soldier's shoe. Men and weapons had been left where they fell, under the flowing water, and there they might have lain till Doomsday, if they had not happened to be dug up in 1856.

But the Romans did not settle in Chelsea, so have no further bearing on the story. Where should it begin? There is a temptation to focus on a period: say, from Ranelagh to Cremorne; and to concentrate on a limited area. That part of Chelsea that lies along the river between the two pleasure gardens contains the Royal Hospital, the Physic Garden, and the site of Paradise Row; Cheyne Walk and Cheyne Row, the Old Church and Lindsey House. But it also contains the greater part of Chelsea's early history, and the ghosts of her vanished palaces.

It seems impossible to put up barriers, to write of a selected period only and ignore what went before or what followed after—or indeed to write about riverside Chelsea without reference to the rest.

The King's Road, famous today for reasons unconnected with history, has its history none the less, and certainly could not be left out of any account of Chelsea. Part of King Charles II's private road, which extended from Whitehall to Hampton Court, it was long the haunt of highwaymen. On its way east, it was crossed by a rivulet called the Westbourne, which came from Hampstead, ran through Sloane Square and emptied itself into the Thames near Ranelagh. The bridge over the Westbourne, Blandel Bridge, was known from Elizabethan times as Bloody Bridge; and as late as 1748 we read that 'four gentlemen coming from Chelsea, the King's Road, in a coach, were attacked near Bloody Bridge by two highwaymen, but they all getting out of their coach and drawing their swords, the highwaymen made off without their booty'.

The King's Road runs through Sloane Square, the home of the Royal Court Theatre, where first Bernard Shaw and Granville Barker, and later John Osborne and George Devine, made theatre history. This theatre has its link with Ranelagh, for the original Court Theatre was converted from Ranelagh Chapel.

The focus spreads again, for directly north from Sloane Square lies the district once known as Hans Town, which runs up to the border of Knightsbridge. This elegant neighbourhood, designed at the end of the eighteenth century by Henry Holland, has connections with Mary Russell Mitford and Lady Caroline Lamb; with Letitia Landon, one of the first woman journalists—and with Jane Austen, who stayed in Sloane Street and later in Hans Place with her brother Henry.

In Sloane Street, too, was born, lived and died Sir Charles Wentworth Dilke, Member of Parliament for Chelsea and the central figure of a scandal which shook London society in the 1880s. Ten years later another, and worse, scandal broke upon Victorian respectability with the arrest, at the Cadogan Hotel, of Oscar Wilde. John Betjeman imagined the scene:

> To the right and before him Pont Street
>   Did tower in her new built red,
> As hard as the morning gaslight
>   That shone on his unmade bed.
>
> 'I want some more hock in my seltzer,
> 'And Robbie, please give me your hand—
> 'Is this the end or beginning?
> 'How can I understand?'

It will be seen that the writer on Chelsea is faced with a tantalizing wealth and variety of material. In order to be selective, it will be necessary, first of all, to look at some of the earlier buildings and their occupants, who set the stage, as it were, for all that follows.

PART ONE

PLEASURES AND PALACES

CHAPTER ONE

CHELSEA HAS been called the Village of Palaces, and any student of her history must find himself haunted by these ghostly mansions: More's House, Henry VIII's Manor, Shrewsbury House and the rest, of which so few traces remain that in some cases it is difficult to determine precisely where they stood, and only imagination aided by a few old drawings and maps can re-create them. One thing is certain, the term 'palace' is misleading: from the amount of space these buildings occupied, they cannot have been more palatial than a small manor house, and not one is comparable with, for instance, Sion House or Hampton Court. They were modest country residences of royal or noble personages, occupying fertile land with pleasant river views and an unspectacular outlook at the back over fields and trees, towards the gentle slopes of Kensington and Notting Hill.

The only clue to the position of these Chelsea houses is the existence of various pieces of wall, mostly boundary walls containing Tudor bricks, in gardens of Cheyne Walk houses, on either side of the blocks of flats known as Shrewsbury House, at the back of gardens in Paultons Square, round two sides of the Moravian Burying Ground. These old walls, or bits of wall, are incorporated into the modern scene and pass unnoticed, shaken by traffic, backed into by lorries, clambered on by children, doggedly standing up by virtue of good building and force of habit, since the days of Thomas More.

'More,' wrote Erasmus,[1] 'hath built near London upon the Thames side a commodious house, neither mean nor subject to envy, yet magnificent enough; there he converseth with his family, his wife, his son and daughter-in-law, his three daughters and their husbands, with eleven grandchildren . . .'

Thomas More was the first distinguished Londoner to discover the charm of Chelsea and build himself a house there. In 1523, when he was

---

[1] Erasmus, the great humanist, pacifist and scholar, met More on his first visit to England in 1499, and their friendship continued till More's death, when Erasmus wrote: 'I seem to have died myself; we had but one soul between us.' He never visited More in Chelsea: his last journey to England was in 1517.

living in Bucklersbury in the City, he was made Speaker of the House of Commons. He was forty-five, a brilliant and successful man. Part of More's genius lay in creating within his own household, which was a large one, a life of Utopian tranquillity in which every member had a part to play; and the days passed in study, conversation, gardening, music, and —by the influence of its head—regular religious observance. It was for a background to this well organized and happy community that Sir Thomas More bought his Chelsea estate, which lay to the west of the old church. At first, while their house was being furnished, the More family occupied a farmhouse nearby. This was rebuilt in the seventeenth century by Sir Theodore Mayerne, and is now Lindsey House.[1]

The mansion which Sir Thomas More built, and in which he lived for about ten years, is less easily identified, for no trace of it remains. It is only by studying the careful drawing known as Kip's View that one may see where it stood. In 1695, when this drawing was made, More's house was known as Beaufort House, because in 1682 it was bought and rebuilt by the first Duke of Beaufort; but Kip's View is of great value in showing the relative position of the mansion itself to the rest of Chelsea, and to the other buildings on More's estate.

Under the point where Battersea Bridge now joins the Embankment, More had his private landing stage, with a flight of steps from the river, and a wicket gate at the top giving on to grass slopes, from which a handsome pair of gates opened on to the gravel approach to the house. It stood at a little distance from the river—about halfway up Beaufort Street today, straddling the street where, on the right, the Convent chapel now stands. (There is a mulberry tree behind the chapel, which descends from one grown in More's garden.) Of its appearance, we only know that the house was built of brick, on two floors,[2] round an inner court, and that it was, as Erasmus (who never saw it) wrote, commodious.

There was no direct road from London to Chelsea, only rough tracks through the fields, and what is now Belgravia was a bog. It was safer and more comfortable to travel by river, and More kept his own barge. But horses were necessary for longer journeys, and they were stabled at the back of the house, near the top of what is now Milmans Street. These stables, with stalls for twenty-one horses, were left standing after More's house was demolished in 1740 by Sir Hans Sloane. When, in 1751, the

---

[1] See page 53.

[2] From the plan of Beaufort House, at Hatfield, it appears that in 1596 there was 'no floure over ye kitchen', or over the hall: the latter was probably a fine room of some height, with windows overlooking the river.

Lindsey House estate was bought for the Moravian Society, they were converted into a chapel, and the enclosure where they stood became a burying ground. This quiet green place, still bounded on two sides by walls of Tudor brick, remains inviolate, hidden behind and below a vast new tower block—a silent reminder to those who care to look that this is ground which belonged to Sir Thomas More.

His estates were carefully planned. There were gardens 'environed with brick walls' to the north and east of the house, with a kitchen garden on the west, and beyond it the farm with its acres of corn and oats. There were orchards. There was also a small zoo: rabbits, a monkey, a fox, a ferret, and a weasel, for More was fond of animals of all kinds, and liked to watch their habits. He bought exotic foreign birds, and encouraged local ones. 'All the birds in Chelsea,' wrote Erasmus, 'come to him to be fed.' He also tells us how More's monkey sat watching the weasel as it tried to find a way into the rabbit hutches kept at one end of the garden. After a little, according to this account, the hutches fell away from the wall, whereupon the monkey rushed to the rescue, propping them up so success-fully that the weasel slunk away, defeated.

Near the house, the garden was arranged to do justice to the view. Ellis Heywood[1] describes how, after dinner, More conducted his guests 'about two stones' throws into the garden, walked on a little lawn in the middle, and up a green hillock, where they halted to look round them. 'It was an enchanting spot, as well from the convenience of the situation—from one side almost all the noble City of London being visible, and from the other the lovely Thames, surrounded with green fields and wooded hills—as for its own beauty, being crowned with an almost perpetual verdure.'

More is an elusive, a complex and fascinating character. Sir or Saint Thomas, as he is severally designated by Protestants and Catholics (he was canonized in 1935), possessed qualities to inspire reverence, not only as saint and martyr, but as statesman and philosopher. He is now amicably shared between the Churches of England, Scotland and Rome, whose rep-resentatives were present on July 21, 1969, at the unveiling, by the then Speaker of the House of Commons, of his statue by L. Cubitt Bevis. This father of Chelsea sits gazing over the river, in front of the chapel which bears his name, and which he restored in 1528. Across his knees lies the heavy gold chain and Tudor rose given to him by King Henry and relin-quished by him when he was imprisoned. He is wearing the crucifix which he carried with him to the scaffold. At the foot of the statue is More's

[1] A musician, singer and playwright who married More's niece, Elizabeth Rastell.

signature—the signature which he refused, at the cost of his life, to append to the King's Act of Supremacy.[1]

Unfortunately, Chelsea's eighteenth-century benefactor, Sir Hans Sloane, did not find More's house worth saving for posterity. But Sir Thomas is not forgotten, and his life and death are publicly commemorated every July. In the Old Church, where he worshipped, a More Sermon is preached. The Roman Catholics, unable to remember him in his own church, compensate for it by giving up a whole day to him: at their church in Cheyne Row, dedicated to the Holy Redeemer and Saint Thomas More, a solemn mass is held, followed by a procession to the Convent chapel in Beaufort Street. After this the pilgrims, several hundred strong, embark at the Cadogan Pier on river steamers, to make the journey from Chelsea to the Tower.

In the pause after embarkation, the pilgrimage assumes a new character: the atmosphere noticeably changes from one of religious exaltation to a gentle excitement induced by being aboard ship and about to set out on a voyage. The austerities of the morning give way to the demands of the flesh: carrier bags are opened and the welcome lunches unwrapped. On deck, nuns in black plastic mackintoshes pour fizzy lemonade into cardboard cartons. Those of the party who have been foolish enough to come unprovided make a bee-line for the bar, where cups of tea and cans of beer are dispensed, and a stock of sandwiches and cake disappears long before the last of the queue has had his turn.

Then the boats move off, gliding smoothly down the river, a priest at the microphone of each vessel reminding the pilgrims of incidents in the life of the Saint; the narration carefully timed so that the arrival at the Tower coincides with the moment in the story when More disembarked at Traitors' Gate.

The valiant pilgrims, who have been at it for four or five hours now, and have still to visit other places in London connected with More's life and death, proceed to queue up for admission into the fortress which is being simultaneously stormed by hordes of summer tourists; and to make their slow progress through and among the dawdling mob whose objectives are the Crown Jewels and the Bloody Tower, to the gate in the wall which leads to Tower Green. Here, in this pleasant place, where children eat ice creams beside the spot where Anne Boleyn was beheaded, the pilgrims come to a halt outside the Governor's House.

[1] A direct descendant of Thomas More is Kenneth More, the actor, who bears a striking resemblance to the Holbein drawing of his ancestor. He uses 'practically the same family crest, a Moorish head turned sideways'.

Slowly, in parties of twenty, they are admitted and led through the house and down the steps to the cell where Thomas More spent the last fifteen months of his life. It is almost circular, with long narrow slits of windows; the one electric bulb gives a false harsh brightness. In the vaulted roof is a circular carved boss on whose dim shape More's eyes may have lit as he raised them to heaven in prayer. The pilgrims listen silently to the end of the priest's narrative. Through that window Saint Thomas More and his daughter Margaret watched the Carthusian monks and their prior setting out on their way to a death of appalling cruelty at Tyburn—'like bridegrooms,' he said, 'to their marriage.' The enigma of martyrdom is pondered, and the priest is obliged to mention that others are waiting to see the cell. It is a relief to emerge into the sunshine of Tower Green.

When Chelsea Old Church was demolished by a German mine in 1941, the More Chapel alone remained intact, and there it still stands, a part of the restored building: the church where Thomas More, 'with a surplice on his back', worshipped and sang heartily (if a little out of tune) in the choir. 'God's body, God's body, my Lord Chancellor,' exclaimed the Duke of Norfolk, who had come to dine with him, 'a parish clerk, a parish clerk, you dishonour the King and his office.' 'Nay,' quoth Sir Thomas More, smiling upon the Duke, 'your Grace may not think that the King your master and mine, will with me for serving God his Master be offended.' A curious echo of this cheerful rejoinder comes in More's words on the scaffold, that he died 'the King's good servant, but God's first.'

'More,' said his contemporary, Robert Whittinton, 'is a man of an angel's wit;' Erasmus tells us that 'he can make fun of anything', and Roper his son-in-law that in sixteen years in his household he never saw him 'in a fume'. We hear of his gentleness, his humility, his 'marvellous mirth' and 'singular learning'. It was these last qualities which endeared him to his King. Early in More's career as councillor, Henry would invite him to the Palace 'there sometime in matters of Astronomy, Geometry, Divinity and other faculties to sit and confer with him'. Late at night they would climb up on to the leads together, and contemplate 'the diversities, courses, motions and operations of the stars and planets', before whose majesty even King Henry may have felt a little small.

Later, when More was Sir Thomas, and Lord Chancellor, Henry arrived unexpectedly to dine at Chelsea, enjoying the informality of such a visit. Afterwards, as they walked together in the garden, conversing and laughing as old friends, the King flung his arm round More. 'As soon as his Grace was gone,' wrote William Roper, 'I, rejoicing thereat, told Sir Thomas More how happy he was whom the king had so familiarly entertained, as I have never seen him do to any other except Cardinal Wolsey, whom I once saw his Grace walk with arm in arm. "I thank our Lord, son," quoth he, "I find his Grace my very good lord indeed, and I believe he doth as singularly favour me as any subject within this realm. Howbeit, son Roper, I may tell thee I have no cause to be proud thereof, for if my head could win him a castle in France . . . it would not fail to go." '

The family of Sir Thomas More is familiar to posterity from the Holbein portrait group, of which a copy hangs in Crosby Hall, Chelsea. Here they all, including jester, dog and pet monkey, appear. Hans Holbein, who came to England in 1526, brought a letter of introduction to More from Erasmus, and he probably stayed in More's house while he made his careful preliminary drawings of each member of the family before embarking on the large group. The story goes that Henry VIII, on a visit to More, saw some of Holbein's work and exclaimed, 'Is there such an artist alive, and can he be had for money?' The answer was that there was, and he could, for that was what he had come to England for; so Holbein, the first of Chelsea's artists, became in the course of time Court Painter.

In the foreground of Holbein's group sits More's eldest and favourite daughter, Margaret, who was married to William Roper, his father-in-law's first biographer. It is from Roper that many of the little anecdotes come, some probably told him by his wife, who knew and understood her father better than anyone, which illuminate More's complex character and give us momentary glimpses of him as his family saw him. More's second wife, Dame Alice, sits on the extreme right of the picture, with the monkey beside her. She shared her husband's love of animals, and herself kept several little dogs. 'He loveth his old wife as if she were a young maid,' wrote Erasmus, perhaps a little euphemistically. More's two marriages were oddly, deliberately unromantic. His first was with Jane Colt, a country girl; he loved her younger sister, but, said Roper, 'he considered that it would be both great grief and some shame also to the eldest to see her younger sister preferred in marriage before her', so he proposed to Leah, not Rachel, and set himself to educate her, teaching her to read, to converse, to make music. It was a happy marriage, and Jane bore him three daughters and a son, but died four years later. He lost no time in choosing a new wife, a widow seven years older than himself, 'whom in very deed he rather married for the ruling and governing of his children, house and family, than for any bodily pleasure'. 'Yet by his dexterity,' adds Harpsfield,[1] 'he lived a sweet and pleasant life with her,' which cannot

---

[1] Archdeacon Nicholas Harpsfield, a contemporary of Roper, wrote, from Roper's notes, a Life of More.

have been easy, for she was far from meek and had a shrewish tongue which sometimes ran away with her. He cleverly encouraged her to learn to sing and play the lute and virginals, and one day she announced, 'I have this day left all my shrewdness and will begin afresh.' 'Now and then,' said Harpsfield, 'it proved true.'

By her attempts to please her husband, Dame Alice disarms criticism. Her attempts to attract him were less successful. By straining back her hair 'to make her a fair large forehead', and tight-lacing her bodice 'to make her middle small, both twain to her great pain', she only won from him, 'Forsooth, Madam, if God give you not hell, he shall do you great wrong, for it must needs be your own of very right, for you buy it very dear, and take very great pain therefore.'

In his epitaph, which More composed himself some time before his death, he included both his wives, commenting tactfully, 'I know not which is the dearest of the two,' and adding:

> Oh! could religion and the fates agree,
> Together happily might live all three!
> The tomb shall join us, may we meet in heaven!
> And thus by Death, what life denied, be given.

An ideal arrangement, which conceivably might work in a better world than this.

Dame Alice probably enjoyed being mistress of his large household when he was Lord Chancellor and a rich man; but she had no patience with his high principles and did not always appreciate his little jokes. 'Tilly vally, tilly vally, Mr. More,' she would exclaim, and launch into one of her long indignant speeches in a vain attempt to make him see sense. She must have suffered when, in May 1562, her husband—ostensibly on grounds of ill-health (he was suffering from asthma or bronchitis, 'the sure forerunner of old age', as he put it)—resigned the office of Lord Chancellor. He broke the news to his wife in church, in characteristic fashion.

'Whereas,' says Roper, 'during High Chancellorship, one of his gentlemen when service at the Church was down, ordinarily used to come to my lady his wife's pew and say "Madam, my lord is gone," the next holy day after the surrender of his office . . . he came unto my lady his wife's pew himself, and making a low curtsey, said to her "Madam, my lord is gone."'

This graceful little joke did not amuse Lady More. The decision meant cutting down their household: he was now a comparatively poor man. His handsome barge with its eight watermen had to go: he gave it to Lord Audley. His many servants, against their will, were obliged to find other work; even his fool, Pattison, was sent away, to amuse the Lord Mayor and his successors at the Mansion House. More called his family together and told them that they would have to live more simply, descending by degrees, as he put it, to Lincoln's Inn fare, then to that of New Inn, and then to that of Oxford—until they should 'go a-begging, but still keep company and be merry together'.

Fires in bedrooms were given up, as an economy, and the family were obliged to warm themselves by a blazing bundle of dry fern before dispersing to their chilly beds. It must have been particularly galling for his wife, as supplies of food ran low in the winter, and the cold east winds blew through the large draughty house, to know that her husband had refused a large sum of money collected by the clergy out of gratitude for his writings in defence of the Church.

' "Not so, my Lords," quoth he, "I had liefer see it all cast into the Thames, than I or any of mine, should have thereof the worth of one penny." ' He said this because he knew that the whole moral force of his defence would be gone, if he were known to be in the pay of the abbots and bishops. But it was hard on his family. Lady More suffered on account of her common sense, which, try as she would, she could not communicate to her husband. From Roper we have that vivid picture of her rating her husband soundly when she visits him in the Tower.

' "What the good year, Mr. More," quoth she, "I marvel that you have been always hereunto taken for so wise a man, who will now so play the fool to lie here in this filthy close prison, and be content thus to be shut up among mice and rats, when you might be abroad at your liberty and with the favour and goodwill both of the King and his Council, if you would but so as all the Bishops and best learned of this realm have done. And seeing you have at Chelsea a right fair house, your library, your books, your gallery, your garden, your orchards, and all the necessaries so handsomely about you, where you might in the company of me your wife, your children and household be merry, I muse what in God's name you mean thus here fondly to tarry." '

'After he had awhile quietly heard her,' continues Roper, 'with a cheerful countenance he said unto her, "I pray thee, good Mrs. Alice, tell me, tell me one thing." "What is that?" quoth she. "Is not this house as nigh heaven as mine own?" quoth he. To whom she, after her accustomed fashion, not liking such talk, answered: "Tilly vally, tilly vally." ' Poor Mistress Alice, even her tongue was temporarily stilled before her husband's unshakeable determination. His mind, since that silent journey down the river to Lambeth accompanied by Roper, since that sudden cry of release—'Son Roper, I thank our Lord the field is won!'—had been made up. For him there was no alternative.

He went to the scaffold on July 6, 1535, resolute, unswerving in his decision. Illness and long imprisonment had weakened him, and he stumbled as he mounted the shaky steps to the block; but his sense of humour did not desert him. 'I pray you Master Lieutenant, see me safe up, and for my coming down, let me shift for myself.' After he had knelt and prayed, he addressed the executioner, who, perhaps as a mark of his calling, perhaps from genuine feeling, looked glum. 'Pluck up thy spirits, man, and be not afraid to do thy office; my neck is very short; take heed therefore thou strike not awry for the saving of thine honesty.'

Compared with many of the deaths in this pitiless and bloody period, that of Thomas More was merciful: his full sentence, to be hanged, drawn and quartered—a traitor's death—was commuted by the King to beheading. But that was the limit of King Henry's generosity. He allowed More's head to be stuck on a pole at London Bridge, and More's house and lands were seized by the Crown.

During his imprisonment Dame Alice had paid fifteen shillings a week for her husband's board, and that of his servant, at the Tower, and she had been forced to sell some of her clothes to raise the money. Now she was turned out of her home, and, though the King allowed her £20 a year, it was not till 1544, nine years after More's death, that a small house was found for her on the Chelsea estate, for which she had to pay a rent of twenty shillings and twopence a year.

The Great House was given to Sir William Paulet, Comptroller of the Royal Household, and from now on was lived in by a rare collection of illustrious personages, most of them far from saintly. Paulet, like the Vicar of Bray, had the gift of keeping up with the current political and religious trend, and in that dangerous age succeeded in balancing neatly on the razor-edge of royal favour, throughout the reigns of Henry VIII, Edward VI, Mary and Elizabeth. He claimed, in explanation of his success, that he was made of pliable willow, not stubborn oak, and died in his bed at Chelsea, at the age of ninety-seven.

Under Edward VI the pliable Paulet became Marquis of Winchester, and took over the whole of More's estate, including the reversion of the house and land given by More to William Roper and his family, which Roper held, rent-free, for his life. This estate is today commemorated by a sunken garden with lawns and flower-beds and a rather incongruous nude lady awakening from sleep in the centre. It was opened to the public in 1965 and is known as the Roper Garden.

Lord Winchester and his wife lived prosperously (he was Lord High Treasurer) for nearly fifty years in the house which Sir Thomas More built. After Winchester's death the estate passed into the hands of his son, who was obliged to mortgage it, and a good deal else, to pay off a debt of £35,000 to Queen Elizabeth, so Winchester cannot have been as prosperous as he appeared. Three years later the second Earl sold the Chelsea estate for the paltry sum of £3,000, to his stepdaughter, Anne, Lady Dacre and her husband Gregory Fiennes, Lord Dacre of the South.[1] Apart from their fine-sounding name, this couple are chiefly memorable for their magnificent tomb on the south wall of the Old Church, where one may see their recumbent, life-size effigies, carved in alabaster, with their pet dogs at their feet and an infant in ruff and gown on a tiny bier beside her father. Lord Dacre is in full Elizabethan armour; the helmet he wore in life hangs aloft, slightly to the right of the tomb. Lady Dacre was given to works of charity, which she went about in a businesslike way. She founded the Emanuel Hospital in Westminster, where, according to her will, two poor people from the parish of Chelsea might bring up one poor child 'in some good or laudable art or science, where he or she may the better in time to come live by honest labour'.

This charity was subject to one condition: that the tomb of Lord and Lady Dacre be kept clean and in good repair, otherwise the poor of Chelsea would no longer benefit. Regular inspection of the tomb was arranged, and hurried last-minute scrubbings and furbishings took place before Sheriffs of the City of London arrived for this purpose. Mr. Randall Davies describes one such visit in the nineteenth century, when his father, the Rev. R. H. Davies was Incumbent, and as recently as 1901 he tells us that 'Sir Whittaker Ellis paid an official visit, and satisfied himself that no repairs were needed'.

The Dacres, after seeing to it that their name would not be forgotten, both died in 1594, and Lady Dacre bequeathed 'my house at Chelsey, and all the buildings, courts, yards, gardens, orchards, backsides, grounds enclosed' to William Cecil, Lord Burghley, for life, with remainder to his son, Sir Robert Cecil, probably hoping that, in the hands of the powerful Cecils, the house would endure for many generations.

It is unlikely that the great Burghley lived there for more than a couple of years, but it must have been during this time that he went walking up Church Street with Queen Elizabeth. The story goes that as they reached

[1] Lady Dacre's father, Lord Sackville, was a Privy Councillor, and made so much money on the side that he was known as Fill Sack. Her brother, Thomas Sackville, wrote the first English tragedy, *Gorboduc*.

the Fulham Road a shower of rain began to fall and they took shelter under an elm. The shower was heavy, but the leaves were thick and the Queen remained dry. 'Let this henceforth be called the Queen's Tree,' said Elizabeth. So an arbour, or ring of nine elm saplings, was built round it at the expense of the parish, and the Queen's Tree survived into the eighteenth century, when it was replaced by an inn bearing the name of The Queen's Elm. This, in its turn, has given way to a modern public house, but the name remains, and denotes a bus stop.

The younger Cecil spent a great deal of money on alterations to the Great House, then suddenly grew tired of it and sold it, in 1598, to the Earl of Lincoln. The price was £6,000, which the Earl paid reluctantly and in instalments. With each payment he wrote a grudging letter, referring to himself in one as 'an old man, who ought rather to provide for his end, than for any other worldly thing'. Cecil must have regretted selling the house to a man whom his son-in-law referred to as 'this ungrateful miser'. Lincoln was certainly very odd, and must have been a great trial to his family. He kept his wife locked up 'without suffering her either to write or hear from any of her friends, having appointed to guard her an Italian, a man that hath done divers murders in Italy and the Low Countries, for which he fled into England; from whom I protest she has just cause hourly to fear the cutting of her throat'. Or so, at least, her son told Cecil.

Like most misers, Lincoln had a mania that he was on the verge of bankruptcy, and in April 1601, when Queen Elizabeth visited him in Chelsea, he hid, and ordered his servants not to answer the door, for fear he would have to pay for the Queen's entertainment. Sir Robert Cecil was obliged to reprimand him for refusing admittance to the Queen 'in so rude a fashion'. 'For after a great knocking at both gates,' he writes, 'some of your people did not only show themselves within, but some of them looked out of the house over the walls. These things did not a little trouble the Queen . . .' He then suavely but firmly announced that the Queen would dine with the Earl of Lincoln the following Saturday.

'I am sorry,' wrote Lincoln from the safe distance of Tattershall Castle in Lincolnshire, 'I am sorry that the foolish and rude behaviour of base artysants in my house should give cause to my enemies to speak suspiciously of my willingness to do my duty to Her Majesty.' But he followed it up with what Cecil's secretary labelled 'a desperat lettre' in which he complained frenziedly of his poverty and unpaid debts, protesting his readiness to die for the Queen but total inability to afford to entertain her.

In 1615 this miserable old man did die, and the house, which must by now have been rather the worse for wear, went to Lincoln's son-in-law, Sir Arthur Gorges, poet and sailor, and cousin to Sir Walter Raleigh. A West Country man, with the sea in his blood, Sir Arthur was a boisterous, flamboyant character: a minor poet, and a friend of poets. In his youth he was immortalized by Spenser, who referred to him as Alcyon, the jolly shepherd; but after the death of Gorges' first wife he wrote:

> And there is sad Alcyon bent to mourne,
>   Though fit to frame an everlasting dittie,
> Whose gentle spite for Daphne's death doth tourn
> Sweet layes of love to endless plaints of pittie . . .

However, by the time he came to Chelsea Sir Arthur was married again, to Lincoln's daughter, and had served in several naval engagements, including the defeat of the Armada. His portrait in brass may be seen in the More Chapel, kneeling opposite his second wife, with their five daughters and six sons neatly arranged on either side.

Sir Arthur evidently found the Great House old-fashioned and expensive to run, for he quickly sold it, and built himself a smaller one slightly to the south-west, which was called Gorges House.[1] It may be seen in Kip's View, a compact, three-storied building with Dutch gables.

It was Sir Arthur's grandson, another Arthur, who inspired the charming epitaph, also in the More Chapel:

> Here sleepes and feeles noe pressure of ye stone
> he, that had all the Gorges Soules in One
> Here the ingenious valiant Arthur lies
> To be bewail'd by Marble and Our eyes . . .
>
> Live Arthur by the spirit of thy fame
> Chelsey it self must dy before thy Name.

So now More's estate was split up. More's House, with its gardens and about forty acres to the north, were bought by Lionel Cranfield, Earl of Middlesex, Lord Treasurer to King James I. When Cranfield first came to Chelsea he was in high favour with the King, who stood godfather to his son at the Old Church in 1621. The second godfather was George Villiers, Duke of Buckingham, King James's handsome and unscrupulous 'sweet Steenie',[2] his 'sweet child and wife'. 'I, James, am neither God nor an angel, but a man like any other,' he defended himself to the Lords of the Council after bestowing an earldom on Villiers in 1617. 'You may be sure that I love the Earl of Buckingham more than anyone else . . . Jesus Christ did the same, and therefore I cannot be blamed. Christ had his John, and I have my George.'

---

[1] See Chapter Five.   [2] From a supposed resemblance to a painting of Saint Stephen.

His George took full advantage of this fortunate situation, and within five years succeeded in engineering the downfall of Cranfield, and in getting the Chelsea house for himself.

It was now Buckingham House, the property, successively, of those two brilliant rascals, the first and second Dukes. Villiers did not move in at once; but on July 7, 1626, we hear of him feasting King Charles I, who loved him almost as slavishly as had his father; and the following year, before he set out for La Rochelle, he entertained Queen Henrietta Maria. By this time he had begun to fill the house with expensive treasures, and was planning to live there in style. But he never saw Chelsea again: on his return from France, on August 24, 1628, he was stabbed to death at Portsmouth. His death was greeted by the populace with howls of delight.

The widowed Duchess of Buckingham continued to live at Chelsea with her two young sons (the second born posthumously), and she received visits there from the King and Queen. But with the outbreak of the Civil War, Parliament seized the house, which was used as a barrack. As is often the case when a mansion is occupied by soldiers, Buckingham House suffered, 'the walls and wainscot of the house being much pulled down, the windows unglazed, the gardens destroyed, and the whole house much defaced by the soldiery quartered in it'.

After the Restoration the house reverted to the Villiers family; the panelling was mended, the windows re-glazed, the gardens weeded, dug and planted, after which Charles II's Duke of Buckingham moved in, and proceeded to live riotously on his inheritance. His brother Francis had been stabbed to death by the Roundheads on Surbiton Common, but the lucky George escaped, though 'if Oliver had lived for three days longer,' he said, 'I had certainly been put to death.'

This gifted and versatile spendthrift is the subject of Dryden's famous lines in 'Absalom and Achitophel':

> A man so various he seemed to be
> Not one but all mankind's epitome
> Stiff in opinions, always in the wrong
> Was everything by starts and nothing long . . .

The only talent the second Duke of Buckingham lacked was the ability to keep out of debt.

> In squandering wealth was his peculiar art:
> Nothing went unrewarded but desert.
> Beggar'd by fools, whom still he found too late;
> He had his jest, and they had his estate.

In the end he was obliged to take refuge from his creditors in the country, where he died in a tenant's cottage after catching cold from sitting on the ground after fox-hunting. His chief creditor, one James Plummer, got the Chelsea house, and sold it for £7,000 to George Digby, Earl of Bristol, who proceeded to lay out a further £2,000 on repairs and improvements. Unfortunately he only lived to enjoy the place for about four years. In January 1679, John Evelyn wrote in his journal:

'I went . . . to Chelsea, and dined with the Countess of Bristol in the great house, formerly the Duke of Buckingham's, a spacious and excellent place for the extent of ground and situation in good air. The house is large but ill-contrived, though my Lord Bristol . . . expended much money on it.'

He was impressed by the late Earl's collection of Titians and Vandycks and charmed by the rare orange trees in the garden, 'of which she [the Countess] was pleased to bestow some upon me'.

It seemed that the house was fated never to remain in one family. The widowed Countess found it very melancholy there in the winter, and begged Mr. Evelyn to try and sell it for her. He did his best, writing rhapsodic descriptions which rival those of a professional house-agent. '. . . Besides a magnificent house, capable of being made (with small expense) perfectly modish; the offices, gardens, and other accomodations for air, water, situation, vicinity to London, benefit of the river and mediocrity of price nowhere to be paralleled . . .' He wrote first to Sir Stephen Fox, then to the Duke of Ormonde, and finally to the Duke's son, the Earl of Ossory, who was tempted by the description which Evelyn sent him. 'There belongs to Chelsey House sixteen acres of ground, with several large gardens and courts, all walled in and planted with the choicest fruit that could be collected either from abroad or in England . . . The outhousing is very good, ample and commodious, and all the offices supplied with excellent water.' The fixtures included grates, chimney-pieces, panelling, a billiard table, a pair of marble tables, and a 'house clock'.

But it was not till 1681 that 'the sweete place at Chelsey', as Evelyn had called it, was sold, for £5,000, to the first Duke of Beaufort. The diarist evidently had nothing to do with the sale, for he wrote coldly: 'I went to see what had been done by the Duke of Beaufort on his late purchased house at Chelsey; which I once had the selling of for the Countess of Bristol; he had made great alterations, but might have built a better house with the materials and the cost he had been at.'

However, the Duke and Duchess of Beaufort lived there till the accession of William and Mary, when the Duke was obliged, for political reasons, to retire to his country house at Badminton; but the house remained in the Beaufort family, and as late as 1708 we hear of the new Duke and Duchess of Beaufort coming to stay in Chelsea.

The great house, now known as Beaufort House, had undergone many alterations and attempted modernizations since the days of Sir Thomas More; and in spite of being 'ill-contrived', as Evelyn put it, it must, with its long river frontage, have been an imposing and spacious residence, with beautifully laid out gardens, its orange trees and 'snow house', its fruits and flowers of all kinds. It is not surprising to learn from Bowack in 1705 that 'the late Queen Mary had a great desire to purchase it before King William built Kensington', but she was prevented he said 'by secret obstacles'. What these obstacles were we shall never know; but had Queen Mary got her way, Chelsea would still possess a palace, which had once been the home of Sir Thomas More.

As it was, after the death, in 1716, of the Dowager Duchess of Beaufort, nobody wanted it; and ten years later it was still empty when Samuel Travers tried, unsuccessfully, to convert the building into a school 'for educating young men of quality and condition in the principles of virtue and honour, and in useful learning'. But this laudable scheme met with no encouragement, and the old house remained empty. Neglected and falling into disrepair, year after year it became more desolate: the gardens were overgrown with briars and thorns: weeds overran the 'two great forecourts'; the crumbling walls of the banqueting house at the end of the eastern garden reeked with mildew. Rain made its way through the broken tiles into the upper rooms of the house; ceilings began to collapse, and bats flapped about the empty corridors. It was a dying house when Sir Hans Sloane bought it in 1737. He already owned the Manor, and other land in Chelsea, and merely wished to extend his property. He decided to pull the old house down; but for fear lest thieves and vandals should remove or destroy anything of value, he installed a housekeeper to guard the property till arrangements were made for its demolition.

This housekeeper proved to be a man of character, a Quaker named Edmund Howard, who was a gardener by trade. Howard kept a journal, now in the possession of Chelsea Public Library, and here we may read the end of the story of More's house, and also see, through Howard's clear eyes, the man whose name has become a part of Chelsea—Sir Hans Sloane. It is our first meeting with a man who is remembered for his acts of benevolence to posterity: for the founding of the British Museum, for the establishment of Chelsea's Physic Garden, for the gift to the parish of the burying ground on the north side of the King's Road; so it is interesting to learn that at close quarters Sir Hans could be both obstinate and stingy.

Howard must have been badly in need of a job when he took on this one. 'He furnished me,' he said, 'like the Prophet Elijah, with a table, stool and candlestick, also a bed; besides which I had very little, and sent me into this old and desolate place to live and lodge alone.' It needed some courage, for the great empty mansion stood in its grounds, surrounded by high trees, halfway between the Thames and the King's Road, 'where had I been ever so much distressed and called aloud no chance of being heard'. There was talk of a ghost, and a murder committed in the Duke of Beaufort's time, and Howard said that a skeleton had been found in the grounds by labourers employed by Sir Hans to dig gravel.

It is surprising that the poor man got any sleep; but he only admits to being 'twice a little surprised in the night': once by thumps overhead, which he feared to be thieves stealing lead (but did not investigate till next day, when he found that a ceiling had collapsed); and once by seeing a young woman 'clothed elegantly all in white and very comely to behold' standing in the middle of the room where he slept. But this, he assures us, was a dream. He was a reasonable man.

Howard must have grown accustomed to isolation; he did a little gardening; grew and sold lettuces, beans and peas, and he evidently became attached to the ghostly house with its stately main building 'near 200 feet in front' and its 'kitchen, bakehouse, and abundance of other large offices, together with coach-house and stables, etc., adequate to so noble and ancient a palace'; and when, in 1739, Sir Hans talked of pulling it down, he fought hard for its life. 'Board up the windows,' he advised his master, 'mend the sills to keep out the weather and prevent it growing worse.'

Sir Hans, who must by this time have developed a certain respect for Edmund Howard, took his advice and 'consulted one Mr. Sampson, who was Surveyor at the Bank of England, as to the cost of repairs, who said it would cost five hundred pounds; my advice was only to prevent it growing worse that he might wait to see what might offer'.

Several things did offer: some gentlemen thought of building a distillery there, 'and the folks who afterwards built Ranelagh viewed it for a place of public resort, but none of these proposals came to anything'. Meanwhile Mr. Sampson, who had an eye to the main chance and 'knew right well that the receiving of money was to Sir Hans Sloane more pleasant than parting with it', suggested that two friends of his in the building trade might be interested in buying the property, lock stock and barrel, demolishing it and removing the entire fabric. This idea appealed to Sir Hans, and, says Howard, 'a bargain was soon struck'.

Howard, who had taken an instant dislike to Mr. Sampson, mistrusted the whole enterprise. He proved to be right. After Sampson's friends had 'torn the house to pieces, pulled the iron bars out of the windows, and the greater part of the lead from the top of the house, sold and carried off a great deal, and so wounded and crippled the house that it appeared more hideous than before, and would now be madness to attempt to repair it', one of them named Taylor went bankrupt. Sir Hans ordered Howard to lock the gates, for fear the demolition squad should try to take away anything more. Now Howard was in a spot: alone, he was expected to defend the house, which still contained 'abundance of lead and iron stored up in a strong-room . . . and no small quantity remaining where it was originally fixed'. 'I secured and nailed up the front gate,' he wrote, but this was of no avail, for 'they came with a cart and by violence broke open the gate, loaded the cart with what they liked, and drove away. They were so many,' he adds, 'that I could not resist them.' All he could do was to have a ditch dug across the gateway to prevent any more of Mr. Taylor's carts getting through. 'This raised such malice and hatred in Mr. Taylor and his folks that I thought my life in some danger; however, I did the best in my power for my master's interests.'

At length, with the help of lawyers, Sir Hans got rid of Mr. Taylor, 'and the house in its mutilated condition once more came into his hands'.

Its death agonies were prolonged. Sooner than trust another builder, Sir Hans decided that Howard must do the job.

'In vain,' wrote Howard, 'did I plead that I was a gardener, and as such it was not likely I should have sufficient skill in such matters to be fit for so great an undertaking, for there is more danger in pulling down than in building so large a structure; but he still insisted on my doing it . . .'

Howard accordingly set to work, engaging a carpenter and ten labourers to assist him in the extremely difficult and dangerous business of demolishing a house which had been constructed over huge oak girders, thirty feet long, with thick brick walls and high chimney stacks. His organization must have been masterly, for 'no accidents happened worth notice, except one, and then no bones broke'.

So, in this haphazard way, the home of so many illustrious men was torn to pieces, and the materials that went into the making and remaking of it sold piecemeal for as much as they would fetch. It was a lamentable business, which did not reflect well on Sir Hans, who, despite his great learning in the fields of science and ancient history, behaved like a philistine in his attitude to Chelsea's historic buildings.

His final action was to dispose of the handsome gates designed by Inigo

Jones for the Earl of Middlesex. He did not destroy them; but had them removed to Chiswick, and gave them to the Earl of Burlington.[1] Alexander Pope thought the incident worth recording.

> Passenger:
> 'Oh, Gate, how cam'st thou hither?'
>
> Gate:
> 'I was brought from Chelsea last year,
> Battered with wind and weather
> Inigo Jones put me together;
>
> Sir Hans Sloane
> Let me alone
> Burlington brought me hither.'

[1] Lord Burlington's Palladian villa at Chiswick had gardens landscaped by William Kent to give an illusion of the Roman campagna, in the paintings of Gaspard and Claude.

T HE ROYAL barge, resplendent with carved and gilded woodwork and silk hangings, with its team of powerful oarsmen, carried King Henry VIII up the Thames from Westminster, on surprise visits to his 'joyous companion' and friend, Sir Thomas More. The bright clear air, the sparkling river, which produced a wealth of fish, and the happy atmosphere of More's household impressed the King, who must have decided that Chelsea was a good place to live in. As they walked in the garden after dinner, the King with his arm round the Chancellor's neck, Henry may already have had his eye on a piece of land near the river.

In 1535 More was executed, refusing—among other things—to accept the validity of Henry's marriage to Anne Boleyn. Queen Anne, who had counted More her enemy, was playing draughts with her husband when the news came of his death. Henry rose abruptly. 'This is your doing,' he said as he left her: which was perhaps a little unjust. But Anne was already out of favour for having produced a daughter when he wanted a son. And rather less than a year later, the boom of the cannon at the Tower reverberated over the Thames to Chelsea, announcing that Anne Boleyn's elegant head had been struck from her body by a French swordsman.

The following day, May 20, 1536, according to Wriothesley's Chronicle, 'the King was married secretly at Chelsea in Middlesex to one Jane Seymour'.

Henry had already begun to build his Chelsea house. By this time, Sir Thomas More's house and lands were in his possession; but he chose a site further east, as though, by putting the church between himself and More's property, he were exorcizing the memory of their friendship. He had made himself Lord of the Manor of Chelsea, buying out Lord Sandes with the offer of Mottisfont Abbey in Hampshire, one of many religious houses now at the King's disposal. The old Manor House in Chelsea was small and poked away behind the church with no river frontage; the King wanted something better than this, and chose what is now the east end of Cheyne Walk. Here he built his palace, with its gardens to the north and east. The house covered, roughly, numbers 19 to 26, Cheyne Walk, and the garden, numbers 1 to 18, as well as the existing back gardens of all the houses.

King Henry intended this palace for his new bride, who in October 1537 produced the male heir he had so long and so violently desired. But his joy at the birth of a prince was temporarily overpowered by grief for the death, nine days later, of his meek, quiescent queen. Chelsea Manor was now planned as a nursery for the infant Prince Edward and his nurses and attendants—and also to house Anne Boleyn's daughter, Elizabeth, who was now nearly four years old.

No valid picture of this nursery palace has been preserved, but it is thought to have been designed in two quadrangles, the front walls as near to the road as those of the existing houses. The road was then only a narrow track running alongside the river, and a flight of steps led down to a landing stage for the royal barges. Reginald Blunt suggests that the Manor probably looked rather like St. James's Palace, which was built at about the same time, with solid buttresses and castellated walls. It was made of brick, those narrow, tomato-pink Tudor bricks, which may still be found in the garden walls of some of the Cheyne Walk houses. There were casement windows, one of which remained till 1912 on the garden side of number 25's basement, with its original leaded lights, wrought-iron hinges and cockspur handle.

When King Henry built the Manor he had a conduit made from a spring in Kensington, and a pipe laid to bring the water through fields to another conduit somewhere near where Carlyle Square now stands. This supplied the palace, flowing into a vast leaden cistern from which it was drawn. The King saw to it that his gardens, like More's, were designed for both beauty and usefulness. For a start, twenty-nine gardeners and six women weeders were set to work. In November 1538 there were 'delivered to the King's gardener for his garden at Chelsea all such bays, rosemary, grafts etc., as were fit for his Grace's garden'; and at about the same time an order was delivered of twenty cherry trees, five nut trees, five damson trees and two red peach trees—and from the same firm, two hundred plants of damask roses, eleven setts of whitethorn and sixty-four setts of privet, for hedges. Later we hear of mulberry trees and a fishpond. It was a good garden for children to play in, and for lovers to meet in secretly.

Meanwhile, as the garden grew and matured, King Henry married and divorced Anne of Cleves, and fell in love with Katharine Howard, who was unfaithful and lost her head. In 1543, he married Katherine Parr, and as part of her jointure he gave her Chelsea Manor.

A short pink-cheeked North Country woman of thirty, with large eyes and strong brows, Katherine Parr had been widowed before she was sixteen, and then married again to her second elderly husband, Lord Latimer, who died in 1543. So she was experienced in handling husbands; she was also intelligent, a devotee of the fashionable New Learning. Though she was childless, she had a motherly air, and Princess Mary and the younger royal children were fond of her; and this motherliness may have appealed to the King, who, at fifty, was rather the worse for wear and feeling the need, after the emotional shocks of his last marriage, of calm and kind treatment.

At the very moment when Henry's small puffy eye lit upon Katherine Parr she was being courted by Thomas Seymour, younger brother of the late Queen Jane. She was not averse to Seymour's attentions. For the first time in her life she was being wooed by a young man whom she found attractive, for Seymour was ardent, virile, impulsive. 'By God's most precious soul!' he cried as he swore his love (she was left, by her two old husbands, with a very attractive fortune). But the prudent lady was not to be swept off her feet, and when, after deep consideration, she agreed to accept the King's flattering but alarming offer, it was in a spirit of dedication to duty. As she wrote to Seymour after Henry's death, 'God . . . through His grace and goodness made that seem possible which seemed to me most impossible: that was, made me renounce utterly mine own will, and follow His most willingly . . . As my lady of Suffolk saith: "God is a marvellous man." '

By the grace of God and her own shrewdness, Queen Katherine survived the perils and pitfalls of that hotbed of intrigue, King Henry's court, attended him devotedly in sickness and in health, and mourned him with circumspection and probably some regret when he died in January 1547.

Four months after the King's death, Thomas Seymour, now Lord High Admiral, visited her in Chelsea; she must have given him encouragement for he wrote asking for her picture, and ending, 'From him whom ye have bound to honour, love, and in all lawful things obey.' She did her best to remain cool; promised to write to him once a fortnight. But she could not wait so long. 'My Lord, I send you my most humble and hearty commendations, being desirous to know how you have done since I saw you. I pray be not offended with me in that I send sooner to you than I said I would, for my promise was but once a fortnight. Howbeit the time is well abbreviated, by what means I know not, except the weeks be shorter at Chelsea than in other places . . .'

She was in love. But she was aware of her position as Henry's widow, and stepmother to the boy King Edward. She was aware that Protector Somerset, Seymour's brother, had wind of the affair and was violently opposed to it. When Somerset visited her at Chelsea, she wrote, 'It was fortunate we were so much distant, for I suppose, else, I should have bitten him.' She played for time: she must wait two years. But Seymour rode roughshod over her scruples, and within two months they were secretly married. They were obliged to meet by stealth, in the Chelsea garden.

'When it shall be your pleasure to repair hither,' she wrote, 'you must take some pain to come early in the morning, that you may be gone again by 7 o'clock, and so I suppose you may come without suspect. I pray you let me have knowledge overnight at what hour you will come, that your porteress may wait at the gate in the fields for you. By her that is, and shall be, your humble, true and loving wife during her life, Kateryn the Queen.'

In the course of time, through the intervention of the young King, the marriage was accepted and made public. But it was an ill-assorted match. Katherine was accomplished, well-read, religious. Seymour was an ambitious swashbuckler, hot-blooded, and, according to Bishop Latimer, 'a man furthest from the fear of God that ever I knew or heard of in England'. In marrying Queen Katherine he achieved one ambition: he was able to live in greater state than his brother who was Lord Protector. But there were other plums to be had for the plucking. He knew himself to be attractive to women, and here, living in the palace, was the young Princess Elizabeth. He had once applied to the Council for permission to marry her, and had been refused: but now she was fifteen years old, and fair game. It was inevitable that he should take advantage of such a situation.

At first it all seemed innocent enough, chasings and ticklings and bottom-slappings in which Queen Katherine indulgently took part. But then the game became more serious. Seymour, in his nightshirt, paid early morning visits to Elizabeth's bedchamber, sometimes before she was out of bed, when—according to Mrs. Ashley, Elizabeth's governess—'he would put open the curtains and bid her good morrow, and make as though he would come at her; and she would go farther in the bed, so that he could not come at her. And one morning he strave to have kissed her in the bed . . .'

By this time Katherine was pregnant, and in no mood to be amused by her husband's pursuit of Elizabeth. She was aware of the danger of the situation: this kind of intrigue was too near the Throne to be taken lightly. One day she came upon her husband embracing Elizabeth, and without further ado the Princess was removed from Chelsea to Cheshunt. By the Queen's command, the affair was ended. Elizabeth wrote with submissive dignity: 'I was replete with sorrow to depart from your Highness, especially leaving you undoubtful of health, and, albeit I answered little, I weighed more deeper when you said you would warn me of all the evils that you should hear of me.'

Perhaps she had been swept off her feet by Seymour: she was young and he an experienced amorist. But when she heard of the stories that were being circulated about the affair, she wrote angrily to the Lord Protector: 'Master Tyrwhit and others have told me that there goeth rumours abroad which be greatly both against my honour and honesty (which above all things I esteem) which be these; that I am in the Tower, and with child by the Lord Admiral. My Lord these are shameful slanders for the which, beside the great desire I have to see the King's Majesty, I shall heartily desire your Lordship that I may come to Court . . . that I may show myself there as I am.'

Queen Katherine gave birth to a daughter in June 1548, at Sudeley Castle. She survived the birth remarkably well (she was thirty-five, and it was her first child); but four days later she sank back in bed, murmuring, 'Those who are about me do not care for me, but stand laughing at my grief.' 'Why, sweetheart,' her husband protested, 'I would you no hurt.' But she would not be comforted, even when he lay down beside her. 'You have given me many shrewd taunts,' she whispered—but the whisper was overheard, and after her death, it was rumoured that Seymour had poisoned her.

During the lifetime of Queen Katherine, another young girl came to live at the Manor House—Lady Jane Grey. She was only nine years old, and in his relationship with her, Seymour shows at his best, calling himself 'her half-father and more', and awakening gratitude and affection in this studious child, whose parents had no patience with her because she preferred Plato to hunting. Lady Jane, aged eleven, was chief mourner at the funeral of Queen Katherine, and remained in the Seymour household, mouselike, brooding over her studies, till her half-father, who had schemed in vain to marry her to King Edward, was dragged off to the Tower, charged with treason. He was refused a trial, and on March 20, 1549, he went to his death, 'irksomely, dangerously and horribly'. Elizabeth, cured of her infatuation, remarked that he had 'much wit, if very little judgment'; but Lady Jane sincerely mourned him.

Chelsea Manor, which, with everything she possessed, Queen Katherine had left to Seymour, 'wishing it were 1,000 times more', was now granted by King Edward to John Dudley, who had lately become Duke of Northumberland. This reckless, ambitious thruster succeeded in supplanting Somerset as the power behind the throne. Like Seymour, but more ruthless, he played his dangerous, intoxicating game in which Lady Jane Grey, married perforce to his son Guildford Dudley, was one of the pawns. The appalling failure of his plot to oust Mary and Elizabeth and proclaim his daughter-in-law Queen cost him his life, which presumably he had staked on his success. Other, innocent lives were involved, and the tragic Nine Days' Queen passed her husband's headless corpse as she walked in terror and bewilderment to her execution.

Northumberland had failed. Queen Mary was proclaimed, and the Crown took possession of Chelsea Palace and all its rich trappings. Even the Duchess of Northumberland's clothes, of which she owned many, were seized: expensive dresses of French velvet, trimmed with sable or embroidered with gold and silver lace. After a while, however, the Queen was persuaded to reinstate the widowed Duchess in her Chelsea home, and even to restore some of her possessions. So she finished her days in Chelsea, with her green and gold hangings, her Turkey carpet, her chair of state covered in green velvet, and her green parrot which she bequeathed to the Duchess of Elva when, at the age of forty-six, she died.

She asked for a quiet funeral. 'I had ever a thousand fold my debts to be paid, and the poor be given unto, than any pomp be showed unto my wretched carcase . . .' But she was buried with great magnificence, her effigy in wax borne upon her bier, as if she were a Queen. Her monument is in the Old Church, on the south wall of the More Chapel. '. . . wyfe to the right high and mighty prince John Dudley, late Duke of Northumberland, by whom she had yssew 13 children, that is to wete 8 sonnes and 5 daughters . . .' Her sons John and Edward were Earls of Warwick; Robert became Queen Elizabeth's Earl of Leicester. Her eldest daughter, Mary, was the mother of Sir Philip Sidney.

Once again the Manor House was left empty. Then, for a short time, it became the home of yet another Queen, Anne of Cleves, who had remained in England since her rejection, fifteen years before, by King Henry. The poor Flemish Mare with her ungainly figure and 'unpleasant airs' revolted the fastidious King, much as in a curiously similar situation nearly 300 years later the sight and odour of Caroline of Brunswick appalled the Prince Regent. In both cases the unfortunate foreign lady was obliged to face the fact that, to her future husband, she was nothing short of a disaster. Anne of Cleves accepted the situation with humility and some dignity: Henry was obliged, for political reasons, to marry her, but he refused to consummate the marriage, and Anne was given a handsome sum of money and assured that she would in future be the King's sister, with two royal residences at Richmond and Bletchingly, and an income of £4,000 a year. Henry, in his anxiety to be rid of her, was generosity itself. 'Madame de Cleves,' wrote Marillac, 'so far from claiming to be married, is more joyous than ever, and wears new dresses every day.' Her place had already been taken by Katharine Howard.

Anne of Cleves was fond of needlework, and settled down with her little court, leading a dull, safe and blameless life, only stirred into resentment by Henry's marriage to Katherine Parr, who, she declared, was not nearly so good-looking as herself and who, moreover, could not hope to have children, since she had had none by her two former husbands. She also spoke of the new Queen's 'heavy burden'—a reference to Henry's vast bulk—which shows her to have had some spirit.

In 1557, when Henry had been ten years in his grave, Anne of Cleves died at Chelsea. She was given a magnificent funeral, her coffin carried by land from Chelsea to Westminster, accompanied by a hundred torchbearers and followed by a long procession. A contemporary account tells us that at the Requiem Mass at the Abbey 'my lord abbott of Westmynster read a godly sermon as ever was made and then . . . the byshope of London song masse in ys myter'. After the mass she was carried to her tomb, covered with a hearse-cloth of gold. Then there was a splendid feast at the Abbot's house attended by all the mourners, the chief of whom was Lady Winchester, who at More's house had been the Queen's neighbour.

During the reign of Queen Elizabeth I, the Manor was given for life to the Duchess of Somerset, widow of the Protector. Lady Somerset, the proud and jealous sister-in-law of Queen Katherine Parr, was imprisoned in the Tower with her husband in 1551, and, after his execution, married his steward. She was over sixty when she came to Chelsea, and evidently had no qualms about occupying the house so lately lived in by the Duke of Northumberland, who engineered her husband's downfall. She paid the Queen £13 6s. 8d. in rent, and though she did not die till 1588 it seems likely that she moved out in 1581.

The new tenant was Lord Howard of Effingham, the illustrious Admiral who defeated the Spanish Armada in 1588 and after the capture of Cadiz four years later was created Earl of Nottingham. There are records

of visits paid by the Queen to the Lord Admiral and his wife at Chelsea:
in 1587 bell-ringers at Lambeth were paid one and sixpence for their jubi-
lant ding-dong as the royal barge sailed up the river and the bells of St.
Margaret's, Westminster, rang out as she left Chelsea for Richmond. She
usually came to dine, but in January 1600 she spent the week-end with the
Nottinghams. She was accompanied on this visit by Sir Robert Cecil, Lord
Cobham and Sir Walter Raleigh. Unfortunately the accounts of the
Queen's visits are short and meagre: it can only be assumed that she enjoyed them because she went again and again. Perhaps she had an affection for her host, and for the house and garden where she had spent her
childhood and early youth: perhaps the memory of her adolescent infatuation for Seymour and hurried removal had been obliterated by later,
deeper hurts.

Lady Nottingham, her Chelsea hostess, was responsible for one of her
bitterest moments. At the height of her passion for the Earl of Essex
Elizabeth gave him, at his request, a ring which she swore would free him,
if he sent it back to her, 'from any danger or distresse . . . her anger or
enemies' malice could cast him into'. 'After his commitment to the Tower,'
the story continues, 'he sent this jewell to Her Majesty by the Countess of
Nottingham, whom Sir Robert Cecil kept from delivering it.' Essex was
executed because the Queen, waiting in vain for the return of her ring,
refused to save his life. 'But the Lady of Nottingham coming to her death
bed and finding by the daily sorrow the Queen expressed for the loss of
Essex, herself a principall agent in his destruction, could not be at rest till
she had discovered all, and humbly implored mercy from God and for-
giveness from her earthly Soveraigne: who did not only refuse to give it,
but having shook her as she lay in her bed, sent her with the most fearfull
curses to a higher Tribunal.' The story is dramatic, and historians repeat
it shamefacedly; but it may well be true. The death of the Queen occurred
only a month later.

A few months after his wife's death, which he is said to have felt 'ex-
ceeding grievously, mourning in sad earnest', the Lord Admiral married
again. His new wife was Lady Margaret Stuart, daughter of the Earl of
Moray, a prudent match when the thrones of England and Scotland were,
with the accession of James I, at last united; and everything Scottish was
in fashion. There were three children of this marriage, the third, a daughter,
being born when Lord Nottingham was eighty.

The Manor remained in the family throughout the reign of James I,
after which it was granted to the Marquis of Hamilton, Master of the
Horse to Charles I. The Marquis (later Duke) built on a large wing, ad-

joining the Palace on the west, and modernized the front of the Tudor palace to match it. But in the Civil War, the Duke, a supporter of King Charles, was taken prisoner at Preston and executed in 1649. Two years later his brother and heir died from wounds at the Battle of Worcester, and Parliament took possession of the Manor House. With the Duke of Hamilton's lavish additions it was now a fine house, standing in over five acres of gardens; though 'one parcel of land, formerly called the Great Orchard' was ploughed up when Cromwell took over.

Eventually the Duke of Hamilton's trustees succeeded in buying back the property, and in 1657 the manor and Manor House were sold by them to Charles Cheyne Esq., at the sound of whose now familiar name we seem to enter another, calmer age. He came from Buckinghamshire, the only surviving son of Francis Cheyne, of Chesham Bois, and was already living in Chelsea—probably at a house called Blacklands—with his beautiful wife, Lady Jane.

For the first time, the Manor House was occupied by a man who was not an ambitious courtier, who was content to make his home in Chelsea, and who evidently took an interest in local affairs. Mr. Cheyne was not too grand to take his friends for a drink at a local inn, as may be seen from his cash-book, quoted by Mr. Randall Davies: 'December 23, 1669 . . . Spent at ye White Horse with Mr. Rigworth, Challoner, and Uncle Fleetwood 6/–.' The White Horse was at the bottom of Church Lane, nearly opposite the Old Church. Lord Cheyne also went to 'Leverett's feast'[1] at the Magpie and Stump, on the riverside, and belonged to 'ye Chelsea Club' which met at a tavern referred to as Swinden's, which possessed a bowling green. (It may have been the Three Tuns, on the site of whose bowling green Lord Cheyne's son William built Cheyne Row.) His Lordship's entry in his account book states that he lost at bowls, but he does not say how much.

Other entries show that he was a kindly man: 'Given to a distracted woeman 2/6;' and a generous father: 'To Betty, Kate and Will, for play, 7/6,' 'Given to Will for his early rising, 2/6.' And when Will matriculated, in 1671, his father gave him 13s. 0d.

Lady Jane Cheyne was the eldest daughter of William Cavendish, first Duke of Newcastle, who contributed part of his fortune and his considerable military skill to the Royalist cause in the Civil War. After the defeat of Prince Rupert at Marston Moor, the Duke and a remnant of his

---

[1] James Leverett, a retired gardener, who died in 1663, left £4 a year to 'the Churchwardens, Overseers, Constable and Clerk of the Parish for an annual dinner at the Magpie'.

supporters escaped to Holland, where he lived in exile till the Restoration. His daughters, alone at Welbeck with a few servants, were besieged by Cromwell's forces, and bravely held out for several days, while they buried the silver in the brew-house and hid the tapestries and the Vandycks. When at length they were obliged to surrender, the girls (according to one account) were treated 'not barbarously, but much short of due civilities'. Nevertheless, presumably since the place was only occupied by women and children, the Roundheads did not knock it about, but behaved with reasonable restraint; and Lady Jane, at the Restoration, is said to have begged for leniency for her captor.

Lady Jane, cast by nature for the part of a heroine, sold all her jewels to raise money for her exiled father, who was penniless in Rotterdam. But when, in 1660, he was able to return home, he must have recovered part of his estate, and his eldest daughter, whose dowry went to the purchase of the Manor, was wealthy enough to give a generous sum towards the rebuilding of Chelsea Old Church.

The Cheynes decided to live in the old part of the Manor House, and to sell the Duke of Hamilton's new wing, which was a complete house with its own river frontage and with gardens extending across Oakley Street, as far as the grounds of Shrewsbury House. It was bought as a residence for the Bishops of Winchester, and known hereafter as Winchester House.

Lord Cheyne was now able to spend money on the manor, which, after being confiscated by Parliament, must have been in need of repairs. No doubt he replanted the Great Orchard, which had been ploughed up; he took trouble with the garden, and later went in for ponds and fountains— 'Ingenious waterworks invented by Mr. Winstanley,' as Evelyn noted, 'wherein were some things very surprising and extraordinary.' But by this time, Lady Jane, greatly mourned, was dead.

The ordeals she had undergone during her imprisonment at Welbeck, and her father's long exile, must have left their mark, for after some fourteen years of happy marriage she became subject to epilepsy, from which, on October 8, 1669, she died. She was forty-eight. A lyrical sermon on her virtues was preached in the Old Church by the Rector, Dr. Littleton, and 'A person of Quality and a Neighbour in Chelsey' broke into verse:

> Ye Chelsey Fields no more your pleasures boast,
> Your greatest pride is with your lady, lost;
> No more cry up your sweet and healthy air,
> Now only fit for such as breathe despair . . .

and Dryden added, at the end of a eulogistic paean:

Sir Thomas More and his
family. Artist unknown:
based on the Holbein group

Lady Jane Cheyne's monu-
ment, Chelsea Old Church

Photo: Cockcroft

Queen Katherine Parr

The Countess of Shrewsbury
(Bess of Hardwick)

Photo: Freeman

Shrewsbury House

Chelsea Old Church, water-colour by T. Malton, 1788
(The Arch House may be seen to the left beyond the church)

George Villiers, first Duke of Buckingham.
Painting by Rubens

Make much of her, ye saints, for God knows when
Your Quires will ever have her like agen.

No one entering the Old Church can fail to notice the impressive monument erected by her husband on the north wall, which is unusual for several reasons. One is that it was designed and constructed in Rome and shipped to Chelsea in sections. By Mr. Cheyne's orders, the lady was presented 'in her habit as she lived' and the statue, carved in Carrara marble by Antonio Raggi, reclines on a cushion in an attitude of graceful and pious submission, dressed in the fashionable style of her day. Raggi was given a portrait from which to work: it must have been a curious and painful sensation for her husband and children when they first saw this marble image, which apparently was a remarkable likeness. 'The sculptor,' wrote Cheyne's intermediary in Rome, Edward Altham, 'is of the opinion to follow the style of this country in the habilaments of the figure, and as they are represented in the draught so to form them with necklace, pendants, etc., as if alive, without which ornaments very difficultly can be represented the likeness to acquaintance.' Altham had suggested that this might be too lively a presentation of someone who was 'dead or supposed to be upon the bed of languishing', but the sculptor stuck to his guns: 'the custom of this place was to make the figure as like as may be.'

Mr. Altham, anxious that Mr. Cheyne's every wish should be observed, ordered that the lady's head should be crowned with a coronet, as she was a Duke's daughter. But here again the Italians were obdurate. No woman, they asserted, not even one of the Holy Saints, might be represented wearing a crown, but only the Queen of Heaven. Poor Mr. Altham pleaded that 'because the lady was the eldest daughter of a Duke it is very requisite that there should be some sign or token of that honour'. So the sculptor suggested a compromise, and agreed to 'place a crown at her feet as neglected and not esteemed in her life time', and this, Mr. A. hoped, would be agreeable to Mr. Cheyne.

Mr. Randall Davies considers that the architect of the monument was Paolo Bernini, son of 'the celebrated Bernini' who was named by earlier Chelsea historians as being responsible. It was designed with enormous care, to fit into a particular part of the church wall, with a window above it, so that the light should fall behind the canopy, at the right angle 'to render the statue better visible to spectators'. It was shipped to England in thirty cases, leaving Rome on October 19, 1671, and arriving in Chelsea on Monday, January 15, 1672: it is doubtful whether it would be much quicker today. Mr. Cheyne gave the men who carried the cases from the river to the church two and sixpence for drink, which they must have needed. The following day the cases were opened and unpacked, and 'ye carpenter Hodges and three more, for their paines about ye stone cases' were given thirteen shillings and sixpence. Evidently the monument was then erected, and on the Saturday three boys were paid for sweeping up the Church.

In 1681, Charles Cheyne was created Viscount Newhaven, and was married again a few years later. His second wife was Laetitia Isabella, the widowed Countess of Radnor, who had been his neighbour at Danvers House. Lady Radnor had had the misfortune to be married to a curmudgeon—'an old dog, snarling and peevish, and yet fond to a degree to make her mad: and to complete her misery a perpetual resident near her person'—and it must have been a blessing when, in 1685, he died.

Lady Radnor is described in her youth as having been dazzlingly beautiful, 'yet notwithstanding the brightness of the finest complexion, attended with the bloom of youth,' says Anthony Hamilton, 'notwithstanding all that generally kindles desire, she had nothing moving or enticing. However, the Duke of York would gladly have taken up with her . . .' But with her old husband 'a perpetual resident near her person' there wasn't much chance of that. It is to be hoped that her marriage in maturity to Lord Cheyne brought her some happiness, even though it was short-lived, for in 1698 he died. She survived him, moving from the Manor into a house at the corner of Robinson's Lane (Flood Street) and Paradise Row, which is now the western end of Royal Hospital Road.

Lord Cheyne's heir was William, Lord Cheyne, a middle-aged man when he came into his inheritance, and wedded to his country estate in Buckinghamshire. The destiny of the manor never to remain in one family once again manifested itself; for in 1712, when he became Lord Lieutenant of Buckinghamshire, Lord Cheyne sold Chelsea Manor to Sir Hans Sloane and retired happily to the country, leaving one memorial to himself and his family—Cheyne Row, built at his request in 1708.

The arrival of Sir Hans Sloane was the beginning of the end of Chelsea Manor.

CHAPTER THREE

IN THE course of five centuries a quite remarkable number of out-
standing female characters have dominated the Chelsea scene, from
Katherine Parr to Jane Carlyle, from Mary Astell to Mary Quant; and
it is not surprising to learn that members of the Suffragette movement had
a stronghold in the district, and that Mrs. Pankhurst made speeches from
a balcony in Glebe Place.

One of the more flamboyant of Chelsea's great ladies was Bess of Hardwick, who, on marrying George, sixth Earl of Shrewsbury, became the
mistress of Shrewsbury House, which stood on the riverside to the west of
Henry VIII's palace. Its exact position was, for a time, forgotten after its
almost total destruction in 1813, but quite lately evidence has come to
light which establishes where the house stood and what shape it was.

After the demolition, in 1968, of the Pier Hotel,[1] together with adjoining houses in Oakley Street and Cheyne Walk, a vast empty space was left
revealing a long wall of sixteenth-century brickwork, on the other side of
which is the modern block of flats known as Shrewsbury House. (There is
a similar wall about 120 yards to the west.)

But the removal, during this demolition, of some outhouses, showed
that the eastern boundary wall was joined at right angles by yet another
Tudor wall, which runs along the ends of the gardens of numbers 38 and
39 Cheyne Walk, not in a straight line but in a curious shallow zig-zag
which comes to an abrupt end at the corner of number 38's land. What
was this wall?

At the Chelsea Library a plan was discovered, drawn in May 1739 for
the then owner of Shrewsbury House, Edward Butler, Esq., Doctor of
Laws, President of Magdalen College, Oxford, which clearly shows this
zig-zag wall. It was not a garden wall, but the outside wall of a room in
Shrewsbury House, which at this point abutted on to the small piece of
land granted by Henry VIII to the Magpie and Stump Inn. So now we
have rediscovered a small piece of the north-east corner of Shrewsbury
House, and the plan shows that the house faced Cheyne Walk and was
built with two gabled wings of unequal length, projecting southwards

[1] See Chapter 8.

from the main building. It was not, as Faulkner suggests, a quadrangle; there was a gateway on the western side which led to a courtyard at the back, and the grounds extended eastwards across Oakley Street, and northwards across what is now Upper Cheyne Row. Here horses were stabled, and there was a gateway at the south-east corner of Glebe Place, beside the little house mythically known as Henry VIII's hunting lodge.

When Faulkner knew Shrewsbury House, in 1810, it was, he said, 'the most ancient house now remaining in this parish'. But nobody wanted to live in it; it was being used as a 'stained paper manufactory' and was in a sad state of decay. Nevertheless, he was impressed by the principal room on the ground floor, which was, he tells us, one hundred and twenty feet in length—that is to say, the entire breadth of the building between its boundary walls. It was originally panelled in carved oak, 'part of which is still preserved in a small building in the adjoining gardens'. There was another room which appeared to have been a chapel and had walls painted to look like marble. (He mentions a number of portraits, 'in all probability some if its former owners', set into the panelling of the larger rooms, which had regrettably been destroyed a few years earlier.)

There was also an underground passage, explored—and sketched—by Miss Elizabeth Gulston at the end of the eighteenth century. 'I have gotten two drawings of the room and passage,' she wrote to her friend Miss Tate, and described how the entrance was concealed behind a door and led down a circular staircase to a brick passage leading towards the river. (Faulkner mentions a passage leading north, towards Kensington: perhaps it went both ways.) It is unknown for whom this passage was built, but it is one of several in this part of Chelsea, and no doubt they had their uses as escape routes. This might even have been constructed during the visit of Mary Queen of Scots, who was from 1568 to 1584 the Earl of Shrewsbury's prisoner, and a source of growing resentment to his wife.

When Bess of Hardwick married the Earl of Shrewsbury, it was her fourth and most ambitious marriage. In her youth she was dazzlingly beautiful: the poet Henry Constable wrote a sonnet comparing her to the Virgin Mary. She started upon her marital career at the age of fourteen, when she married Richard Barley Esquire, who conveniently died two years later, leaving Bess a rich young widow. Her next husband was Sir William Cavendish, by whom she became ancestress of the Duke of Devonshire, and who left her, at his death, another large fortune. She was still in full bloom, and had no difficulty in finding a third husband, Sir William St. Loo, captain of the Guards to Queen Elizabeth. He, too, died, and his widow became richer than ever.

The Earl of Shrewsbury, who came of a line of powerful and ambitious noblemen, was Earl Marshal of England, and in marrying him Elizabeth St. Loo went up in the world. But it was a good bargain on both sides. She brought him a large fortune, and three magnificent houses, for she was an inveterate builder, and had passed the time during her second marriage by creating Hardwick Hall, Oldcotes and Chatsworth. Her fourth marriage made her mistress of a house in Chelsea which she probably considered rather small, but upon which she doubtless employed her talent for home-making.

Unfortunately, Bess and her fourth husband did not get on. One bone of contention was Mary Queen of Scots, who, on her arrival under arrest in England, was handed to the Earl of Shrewsbury by an embarrassed government who could not decide where to put her. Lord Shrewsbury, a kind man, made Mary welcome, allowing her, though a prisoner, to sit and dine under a cloth of state, as befitted a Queen, and 'sparing no cost for her entertainment; neither could words express the care and concern he had for her' At last Queen Elizabeth, jealous and uneasy, removed her cousin and put her under stricter guard; but after a short interval Shrewsbury begged and obtained leave to take Mary back.

Now the fat was in the fire. Lady Shrewsbury began to resent the attention paid by her husband to the unfortunate but still fascinating Queen. There were quarrels, and finally she accused him of being Mary's lover. This led to a public inquiry, at the end of which Bess was made to declare, on her knees, that the accusation was false. To a woman of her temperament this was an intolerable humiliation, and—in spite of Queen Elizabeth's attempts to make peace—the Shrewsbury marriage broke up. The Earl, sick to death by now of Queen Mary's plots and counter-plots, and worn out by domestic brawls, set out for Lancashire, where the Queen had given him a command, thanking her Majesty heartily for relieving him of two she-devils.

It was ironic, though perhaps not unusual in days when the Tower and the block were never far from the minds of those who concerned themselves with power politics, that Shrewsbury, who had lavished so much kindness upon Queen Mary, was appointed, with the Earl of Kent, to witness the execution of her death warrant.

Bess of Hardwick, had she stuck to building, would be remembered with respect. Unfortunately, she was a schemer. When Mary Stuart first came under her roof, Bess set herself to please the Scottish Queen by relaying scandalous gossip about Queen Elizabeth, her lovers and her vanity. She then, having won Mary's favour by her malicious stories, manoeuvred a marriage for her daughter Elizabeth Cavendish with Mary's brother-in-law, Lord Charles Stuart, which was for some reason conducted in secret. Both parties died a year later, but a daughter survived, Lady Arabella Stuart, who in 1602—at her grandmother's instigation—became a pretender to the throne of England, which can hardly have further endeared Bess to the Queen.

But by this time Lady Shrewsbury was once again a wealthy widow. The Earl of Shrewsbury had died in 1590 and left her the Chelsea house: she was really very well off indeed, and could afford to dispense with her Sovereign's favour. There is a legend that when she was a girl a gypsy told her that she would live to build great houses, and that when she stopped building she would die. In her old age she was forever improving, altering, rebuilding on one or other of her estates. Then, in the year 1607, four years after the death of Queen Elizabeth, there was a long hard frost. All building work was stopped, and Bess of Hardwick died. She was eighty-seven.

Shrewsbury House went to her son William Cavendish, who became the first Earl of Devonshire. He preferred Hardwick and Chatsworth to Chelsea, but after his death his widow lived at Shrewsbury House for a few years. Then following the same odd destiny as its fellow palaces, the house was abandoned by the family who built it and passed from one owner to another till, in 1771, *Lloyd's Evening Post and British Chronicle* announced that it was to be converted into a distillery, 'and buildings erected in the garden behind the house for the feeding of a large number of swine'. By 1810, when Faulkner described it, Shrewsbury House was in the last stage of its downfall. Three years later it was pulled down, leaving one gabled end of the west wing to be used as a butcher's shop and slaughter house, and at the back a large untidy open space where, for over a hundred years, children played, and from where, in the 1860s, young Walter Greaves threw a stone into Carlyle's study window.

'IN THE year 1679 the Honourable William Ashburnham, who was travelling through Chelsea late in the evening in the midst of winter, lost his way and got into the Thames,' writes Faulkner. The tide was high, the water was cold and the Hon. William had lost his bearings; but at this critical moment 'the Church clock struck nine, by the sound of which he was enabled to ascertain his situation, and by this means he saved his life'—and in gratitude he gave a bell to the church, inscribed with his name, and left in his will a sum of money to pay for it to be rung every evening at nine o'clock, from Michaelmas to Lady Day.

The little church by the river was a landmark, not only to benighted travellers: it was the centre of the original village of Chelsea, and appears in innumerable prints and paintings. It was also the oldest building. It is unknown when the first church was built, though there may well have been one here in Saxon times; but in 1157 there was a Norman church, and in 1290 Pope Nicholas IV named it All Saints. Alteration and restoration in succeeding centuries gradually transformed this building, and in 1670 it was enlarged, only the chancel and the two chapels being left intact. This rebuilding was necessitated by the lack of space. Bowack tells us: 'In the year 1667, the Old Church which was much decayed, being too small to contain the Congregation (grown very large by the vast Increase of Buildings about that time in the Town), it was agreed by the Parishioners that part of it should be demolished . . .'

There had evidently been unpleasantness about lack of seating for some time, as Scudamore mentions in 1631 that 'many of the Ancient Inhabitants and their families are too commonly put from their seats, and in a sort excluded from such right and place to serve God in the Church . . . which their predecessors enjoyed'. Ten years earlier there had been a spirited exchange of letters between Sir Edward Cecil, who was living at Chelsea Farm, and Sir John Lawrence, who lived in the old Manor House and owned the Lawrence Chapel on the north side of the church. Sir Edward was a newcomer to Chelsea and evidently had difficulty in finding anywhere to sit when he attended a service, so he had set up a pew for himself at the back of the Lawrence Chapel.

'When I came into the Church,' he wrote to Sir John, 'I found all men accomodated with pues; specialle you and your house; sufficientlie becoming your person and qualitie. I intruded upon no man; but found out an unhandsome neglected corner, imployed for nothing but for the roome of an old rotten chest; seeing every man served, I though it no injury to goe into that poore corner myself to serve God in.'

Sir John had written taking exception to Cecil's use of the chapel, which, he said, belonged by right of inheritance to the lords of the Manor. 'In such a case,' retorted Cecil indignantly, 'there is a similie of a Dogge in a Manger . . . In my mind, those things are given in generall to the parish, speciallie when they concerne groundes that have not been used . . . Therefore I would wish you (Sir) to forbear my pue, and not to vallew yourself at so great a rate and mee so little.'

Sir John, signing himself 'Yo'r loving friend to command', now tried to be conciliatory. 'For my right it stands thus; that many hundred years sithence till King Henry ye 8th builded a nursery in this towne, mine was ye manor house of Chelsey, in that chappell have all my predecessors sate as solely and peculiarly belonging to my house . . . We have a private dore into it with a peculiar locke and key.' Nevertheless, 'as a curtesy, not of right', he would set up a pew for Sir Edward, which he might occupy without charge: 'I thank God . . . my fortunes are not so meane as I need it.'

It looks as if Sir John's chief concern was to emphasize his ancient hereditary rights, though in point of fact they only went back one generation. But the elaborately worded letters came to an end at last, concessions were made on both sides, and Sir Edward Cecil, when he went to church with his wife and daughter, had a pew, free of charge.

In 1667–9 the west end of the nave and the tower, which anyway was on the point of collapse, were pulled down, and the whole building was enlarged westwards. Much that was old and would now be reverently preserved was removed, including the roof, which was wholly rebuilt—'lead, timber, etc., at the sole cost of Lady Jane Cheyne.' Instead of the open timbers there was now a ceiling; there were new pews, and a new tower with a ring of six bells, all paid for 'by the bounty of the inhabitants'. From the west, the church presented a smart up-to-date appearance, worthy of the 'large, Beautiful and Populous Town' with its 300 houses, referred to by Bowack six years later.

But the name 'The Old Church' survived; and survives today, although in 1941 the building was almost completely destroyed by a German landmine, and has been as completely rebuilt. The reconstruction was de-

signed by Mr. Walter Godfrey on the plan of the original building; many
of the old materials were incorporated, and almost all the monuments
which, in their varying styles and periods, contributed such a wealth of
human and historic interest, were meticulously recovered, pieced together,
repaired and replaced. The result is that though the building is for the
most part new, its spirit belongs to the past, and Chelsea's long history is
still woven into its fabric. For on this ground generations have prayed and
praised God, and under it and round its walls their dead still lie, commemorated in the church and churchyard.

'Four hundred years of memory . . . are crowded into that dark old
church,' wrote Henry Kingsley in the 1860s, 'and the great flood of
change beats round the walls and shakes the door in vain but never enters.
The dead stand thick together there, as if to make a brave resistance to the
moving world outside, which jars upon their slumber. It is a church of the
dead. I cannot fancy anyone being married in that church—its air would
chill the boldest bride that ever walked to the altar. No; it is a place for
old people to creep into, and pray, until their prayer is answered and they
sleep with the rest.'[1]

This makes curious reading today, when the church is light and bright,
and generally wears a festal air with its magnificent flower arrangements
for the numerous weddings that take place there. Its cheerful look is em-
phasized by the collection of hand-embroidered kneelers which were made
for the re-consecration of the building in 1958. The kneelers commemor-
ate parishioners of all sorts and conditions, from the first recorded Rector,
Reginald de St. Albans (1289) to Yvonne Green, a young Canadian who
was killed when fire-watching on the disastrous night of April 16, 1941.
They were stitched with loving care and great skill by members of the
congregation and their friends (including several Chelsea Pensioners and
Ernest Thesiger the actor, who was a gifted needleman). They pay
homage to lawyers and scientists, to writers, actors and painters; to
soldiers and sailors, to a carpenter, a brewer and a ferryman: to study them
is to realize afresh the wealth of Chelsea's human history.

The south wall of the chancel survived the bombing, although the More
monument, near the fourteenth-century archway into the More chapel,
was damaged. This memorial was ordered by Sir Thomas during his lifetime, in 1532, and the long epitaph which he composed is framed by
slender pillars bearing up a cornice in the middle of which is his crest, the
Moor's head. Below are his arms and those of his two wives. The epitaph
contains the famous blank where the word 'heretics', following 'thieves

[1] Kingsley was the son of Chelsea's rector.

and murderers'—being those who had cause to dread the Chancellor's punishments—was erased at the request of Erasmus. Beside the tomb a wide arch leads into the chapel which was rebuilt by More, and the capitals supporting this arch are carved with his crest and arms, and the date 1528. Experts consider that Hans Holbein, who was staying with More at this time, designed the capitals. They are curious and unusual for their period, showing the Italian influence which Henry VIII was beginning to encourage. The eastern capital has a design at the top of winged cherubs' heads, each face with a different expression. Below is a shield with More's arms surmounted by his crest. There is also a sword crossed with a sceptre, and a mace. On the western capital there are human heads instead of cherubs', and in the spaces below, a bundle of tapers, two candlesticks, a vessel for holy water and a missal. Thus the two capitals illustrate More's secular and religious life. They show signs of having been thickly daubed with whitewash—as was much of the chancel—in Cromwell's time, and the sharpness of the original carving is blurred.

The Lawrence Chapel, on the north side of the chancel, belonged by tradition to the lords of the old manor, and was originally known as the Lords' chapel. There are few records of the early history of Chelsea Manor. In 1315 it was in the possession of Cecilia de Heyle, and in 1345 her son Richard was 'lord of Chelchith'. In 1368 Robert de Heyle decided to let the whole thing to the Abbot of Westminster for his own lifetime, in exchange for 'a house within the convent for his residence, two white loaves and two flagons of Convent ale a day, and a robe of esquire's silk and £20 a year'. This must have greatly reduced his responsibilities, but left the manor without an heir.

At the end of the fifteenth century Sir Reginald Bray crops up: he was a keen supporter of Henry Tudor's claims to the Throne, and when Henry became King, Sir Reginald became Master of Works, supervising the building of two masterpieces of architecture, St. George's Chapel, Windsor and Henry VII's Chapel at Westminster. Sir Reginald was the second son of Sir Richard Bray, privy councillor to Henry VI: the family, according to Holinshed, came to England with the Conqueror. In any case, he was a distinguished and wealthy man, and Henry VIII awarded him the Manor of Chelsea. Unfortunately, Sir Reginald had no sons, so he bequeathed all his estates including Chelsea to his nephew, Edmund Bray, 'with remainder' to his niece Margery, who married Sir William Sandes. After complicated legal proceedings, the Sandes' won Chelsea Manor (which was promptly taken away from them by Henry VIII in exchange for Mottisfont in Hampshire).

The Brays' monument is the oldest in the church, an altar tomb, knocked about over the centuries, and now built into the north wall of the chancel. It was originally ornamented with brasses of Lord Edmund and his father Lord John (brother of Sir Reginald). The inscription has disappeared but Weever quotes part of it: 'Of your Charitie pray for the Soul of Edmund, Knight, Lord Bray, cosin and heire to Sir Reginald Bray, Knight of the Garter.'

When King Henry annexed Chelsea Manor he had no particular use for the old house because he was building a new one on the river. There is some doubt about its tenancy at this time. There is a possibility that the Lawrence family may have been living somewhere on the estate before their arrival as occupants of the old manor house. They were not, as Sir Thomas tried to suggest, of ancient noble lineage, nor had they been long in Chelsea. Thomas Lawrence, a London goldsmith, was the first of the family to live there, in the sixteenth century, and the manor remained in the hands of the Lawrence family till 1725, though by then the original structure had been pulled down and rebuilt, and the house was, from 1714, the home of the widowed Duchess of Monmouth. She was seventy-four when she came to Chelsea, and lived to be ninety. In her youth she had been one of the beauties of Charles II's court, where she fell for the soft voice and handsome looks of James, Duke of Monmouth, the king's bastard son. After Monmouth's ill-starred rebellion and his subsequent execution, the duchess withdrew from public life; but with the accession of the House of Hanover she was accepted in royal circles, and in Chelsea was visited by Caroline, Princess of Wales, when the church bells rang out a dutiful peal. Between 1712 and 1714 the Duchess's secretary was a young man called John Gay, who spent his spare time writing comedies and farces. Fourteen years later he wrote *The Beggar's Opera*, which, it was said, made Gay rich, and Rich (the producer) gay.

So the old manor house gave way to Monmouth House, which stood at the north end of Lawrence Street where the cottages of Upper Cheyne Row back on to the playground of the Kingsley School. At the other end of Lawrence Street is Lordship Place (or Yard), once the site of the stables and barn of the old manor, which were pulled down in 1662 by Charles Cheyne. In earlier times those unattractive objects, the stocks, the cage and the ducking-stool, stood here, but they were moved (presumably to make room for the stables and barn) to a site nearer the river. In the Court Leet and Court Baron, 1682, it was stated: 'We present that the cage and stocks as they now stand (by the church and the riverside) are a public nuisance, both to the church and passengers, and that they would much more conveniently stand in the Lordship Yard, being the place where they stood formerly.' This was done, and in 1705 Lord Cheyne was 'amerced' for not repairing the cage and stocks and not supplying a new ducking-stool. Perhaps he was averse to these methods of punishment.

Thomas Lawrence of the old manor came from Shropshire; he married a London girl, Martha Sage, whose father was a salter, and they had eleven children. Their charming memorial is in the Lawrence Chapel: between three delicate fluted columns, the goldsmith and his three sons kneel on the left, faced by his wife with a row of six daughters behind her and two dead infants at her side. In the epitaph, apparently composed by Thomas in advance, we learn that only five of their eleven children survived to be 'sole comfort of their mother and my wife'; but with pious resignation the goldsmith winds up:

> Thus Thomas Larrance spekes to tymes ensuing
> That death is sure and tyme is past renuing.

He was succeeded by his second son, John, who married an heiress and spent much of his time at Iver in Buckinghamshire. He also had eleven children, became High Sheriff of the County and was made a baronet. His youngest son, Henry, described on his tomb as a Turky Marchant, is mentioned by Samuel Pepys: '22 December 1660. Went to the Sun Tavern on Fish Street Hill to a dinner of Captain Teddiman's where was (amongst others) one Mr. Lawrence (a fine gentleman, now going to Algiers) and other good company, where we had a very fine dinner, I very merry. Went to bed, my head aching all night.'

On one of his expeditions the Turky Marchant made friends with a Turk called Rigep Dandulo, who subsequently came to England on business and stayed with the Lawrences in Chelsea. Here he won the heart of one of the Misses Lawrence and married her after being converted to Christianity. This was brought about by means of an interpreter, by a local divine, the Rev. Doctor Warmstry, who in 1658 wrote a book about it which he called *The Baptiz'd Turk*.

Henry Lawrence's epitaph in the church runs:

> Here rests ye weary Marchant having tride
> And finding this world's traffic vaine, defide
> That empty triffle. Now he's gone to trade
> In th'other world for gains which never fade.

The goldsmith's eldest daughter, Sara, as well as appearing in her father's memorial, has a remarkable one to herself, in which she is seen in the act of rising from the dead. She is dressed in a loose-fitting shroud,

with the head-piece bunched up on top like a small coronet, which gives
her an odd resemblance to Queen Victoria in middle age. Her arms and
face are raised to heaven, which is represented by stars and clouds carved
on the canopy above, with a dove flying across it.

The Lawrence Chapel, built in the fourteenth century for the private
use of the Manor, had its own door, and continued to be privately owned
till halfway through the nineteenth century. Its release from this anom-
alous situation was brought about by the Rev. Robert Henry Davies, incumbent of the Old Church from 1852 to 1908. This well-loved parish
priest (father of Mr. Randall Davies the Chelsea historian) was determined to incorporate the two chapels, both privately owned, into the
whole building as church property. He succeeded in infecting his parishioners with his enthusiasm, and quickly raised enough money to buy
the Lawrence chapel from its owner, Mr. Rawlins; then, after taking
legal advice, he managed to be first in the field when the More chapel
came up for sale, and promptly bought it, for £100. His memorial tablet
records that he 'secured to the Church for ever the More and Lawrence
chapels formerly held by private owners'.

When the Old Church was restored at the end of the seventeenth
century it became known as St. Luke's, though its original dedication was
to All Saints. It is possible that St. Luke's name came into use out of
gratitude to a benefactor, Dr. Baldwin Hamey, who was one of the 'Noble,
Good and Charitable persons' who contributed to the cost of rebuilding,
and who also gave a tenor bell for the new steeple, which cost him
£106 17s. 0d. Dr. Hamey, a physician, presented this bell to St. Luke,
patron saint of physicians; inscribing it, 'D. Lucae Medico Evangelico
Baldwiney Hamey Philevangelicus Medicus, M.D.' At the same time he
gave the church the small carved and gilded figure of St. Luke which may
still be seen on the north wall of the More Chapel. He was a regular and
devout churchgoer; but brought in his pocket a copy of Virgil, to read
during Dr. Littleton's sermons.

Dr. Hamey was a scholar, a Doctor of Divinity and a Fellow of the Royal
College of Physicians, who worked desperately to save lives during the
Plague of 1665, and retired from London to Chelsea after the Great Fire,
in which, according to his will, he lost many precious possessions, and his
health. He died in 1676, and his monument records that he was 'a beloved
and regretted benefactor of the College of Physicians, being resorted to by
the learned as a light to the profession'.

By this time the new steeple was furnished with 'a good ring of six
bells', and one of these was Dr. Hamey's. Before this, according to the

Church Inventory of 1549, there had been 'three great bells and one lytyll sarvice bell', and these must have been hard-worked, as they had always to be rung when Royalty passed through Chelsea by road or river. In 1597 the churchwardens were obliged to pay a fine of four shillings because the bells were not rung when Queen Elizabeth journeyed from Kensington to Richmond.

The new bells were soon busily ringing, as Faulkner records in a long list of payments to the ringers: 'when the King came through the town', 'when the King came to the Earl of Lindsey's', 'when the Queen landed at Chelsea', 'when the Princess visited the Duchess of Monmouth'—and so on. The Ashburnham bell was added in 1679, under a wooden cupola which was designed to cover the bells, and which appears in many views of the Old Church. It was removed in 1815, when perhaps the bell-ringing for the victory of Waterloo was too much for it (it had already been braced in 1748). Indeed, the vigorous work put in by the Chelsea bell-ringers, who thought nothing of going on for three hours and a quarter, had already given cause for alarm about the safety of the tower. In 1748 a committee was appointed to report on the shaking which had been observed whenever the bells were rung, but 'found the shaking of the steeple was no more than what is common in all steeples, whether they be built of brick or stone, when there is a peal of bells'. Evidently they were right, for in 1815 a surveyor, after a careful inspection, announced boldly that 'he should not fear standing on the top of the tower while the ringers rang a good peal'.

Dr. Baldwin Hamey, when he came to Chelsea, took a house in the area on the south side of the Fulham Road, between Edith Grove and the Queen's Elm, known as Little Chelsea. Here, on the corner of Park Walk, stood the coaching inn, The Goat in Boots, whose name is said to derive from the Dutch 'Mercurius is der Goden Boode'—Mercury is the messenger of the gods. Mercury was a sign used by inns where post-horses were kept; and the original figure of the gods' messenger is believed to have been ingeniously transformed by the artist George Morland[1] into the figure of a goat in top boots, with cutlass and spurs. A crude copy of Morland's painted sign on the side of the present building is all, alas, that remains of the original Goat in Boots.

On the site of St. Stephen's Hospital stood Shaftesbury House, which first belonged to the Rt. Hon. Sir James Smith, and was bought and re-built in 1700 by the third Earl of Shaftesbury. He built a library and culti-

[1] Morland (1763–1804) was generally in a state of financial embarrassment, and painted several inn signs in payment for his entertainment.

vated fruit trees, in particular every species of outdoor vine. Unfortunately the earl suffered from asthma, and finding that when the wind was east the Chelsea air was laden with London smoke, he moved to Highgate in 1706. Shaftesbury House was bought in 1710 by Narcissus Luttrell, who lived there till his death in 1732; he lies buried under the nave of the Old Church, and the stone commemorating him, his wife Sarah and his son, is part of the pavement.

Luttrell was a bibliophile and possessed a vast library which was eyed with critical envy by his contemporaries. ('Nothing,' wrote Thomas Dibdin, the author of *Bibliomania*, 'nothing would seem to have escaped his lynx-like vigilance. Let the object be what it may—especially if it related to poetry,—let the volume contain good, bad, or indifferent warblings of the muse, his invariable craving had stomach for all.') Thomas Hearne, author of *Reliquiae Bodleianae*, writes in his diary after Luttrell's death that he was 'well known for his curious library', adding rather spitefully, 'but tho' he was so curious and diligent in collecting and amassing together, yet he affected to live so private as hardly to be known in private, and yet for all that he must be attended to his grave by Judges, and the first of his profession in the Law, to whom, (such was the sordidness of his temper) he would not have given a meal of meat in his life'.

This was unfair. The diary which Narcissus Luttrell kept after the death of his wife in 1722 shows that he was neither mean nor unsociable, and a few entries are worth quoting as showing the daily life of an elderly gentleman in Chelsea:

'5. November 1722. Rose this morning at 8. So to prayers in Chamber. Then down into garden. Drest after and breakfasted at 10 and being gunpowder plot day I would have gone to Church. But the rain hindered me so did odd things at home . . . To dinner after 3. So into the garden and had a tree dug up. Did business all the evening in the parlour. Supt about 9, up into Chamber after 12. So to prayers and to bed at 2.

'December 2. It being rainy, son and I went with Will Hooper [a neighbour] in his Coach to Chelsey Church. Mr. Stephens the Bishop of Winchester's Chaplain preacht . . . Went again to same Church in that coach, Mr. Shorthouse preacht . . . Called to see Dr. King [the Rector] and staid with him and drank there.

'Down to the Magpie in Chelsey where there was a meeting of justices &c, met about 8 or 10 of us. We settled and chose new Surveyors of the Highways and did other business. . . . We dined there most of us about 3 and broke up about 5 . . . Home after 7 and undrest and read a sermon to family.'

The Magpie is the famous Magpie and Stump on the waterside, the old tavern which was there when Henry VIII bought the Manor, and which retained its small strip of land on his estate, and also its right of grazing one heifer on Chelsea Common. At the Magpie the Court Leet and Court Baron met, and also, less publicly, Jacobite plotters, for whom an underground passage provided an escape route.

The old tavern was rebuilt in the eighteenth century. This building was still standing—and may be seen in views of the waterside by Greaves and others—until, in 1886, it was burnt to the ground. A curious reminder of its existence came to light in 1968. The same demolition which uncovered part of the original wall of Shrewsbury House left bare the high wall of number 37 Cheyne Walk, the first of a row of three designed by C. R. Ashbee in the 1890s. On this naked wall the plan of its demolished neighbour—one of a row of nineteenth-century houses and shops—was stamped: the outlines of roof and chimney-stack, of floors and staircase were clearly visible, while each storey displayed several layers of wallpaper. Wind and rain soon reduced these to rags, and before long it became plain that the original paper on the top floor had been pasted directly on to the bare bricks: that these bricks had at some time been painted blue, and that, most mysteriously, they bore lettering. As the wind obligingly dragged off swags of damp, dirty paper, large, white Roman capitals became visible. Finally, Mr. John Yeoman persuaded the Borough Engineer to send his men to strip off what remained. The writing on the wall was revealed.

THE OLD MAGPIE AND STUMP
SPIRIT STORES.

But the mystery was still unsolved. To have displayed this advertisement, the wall must have been an outside wall. The demolished houses were built in approximately 1840, so the lettering must have been painted before that date. The only possible solution is that the wall was the actual wall of the eighteenth-century Magpie, saved in the fire by the house which had been tacked on to it. When, eight years later, Ashbee came to plan his group of three houses, he designed the first—his own—upon the site of the inn, making use of the existing wall, which he built up to the height he required. Now, all has gone, including Ashbee's tribute to the past in the shape of a carved magpie which supported a bay window on the first floor.

Another riverside meeting place was the famous Don Saltero's, which in Narcissus Luttrell's day was in Prospect Place near the church. Here, after service, Mr. Luttrell 'sat and talked and drunk coffee till 6'. 'What we mean by the pleasures of the City here,' writes Bowack in his eulogy of Chelsea, 'is the good Conversation for which the place is at Present noted, the many Honourable and Worthy Inhabitants . . . living in a perfect Amity among themselves, and have a general meeting every Day at a Coffee House near the Church . . .'

We have already met the first Sir Arthur Gorges, whose brass and epitaph are in the More Chapel. This seafaring flamboyant character had a daughter called Elizabeth, who caused a great rumpus in the proud family of the Stanleys of Derby by marrying their second son, Sir Robert Stanley. Whether this was because she was only a knight's daughter, or because—possibly—she inherited some of the peculiarities of her mother's father, the Earl of Lincoln, history does not relate. We only know that the marriage was said to have been the death of the Countess of Derby. A letter in the Harleian Collection, addressed to the Rev. Joseph Mead, announces her death: 'It is said, of grief she took for Sir Robert Stanley her second son's marriage . . . yet she saw both him and his lady before her death, prayed God to forgive, and left unto him 400L. per annum.'

It is to be hoped that her noble in-laws were mistakenly prejudiced against Sir Robert Stanley's wife (his elder brother referred to her later as 'a most unconscionable woman') and that the young couple, who came to live in Chelsea, had some happiness there. They lived in a house called Brickhills, which Lady Elizabeth Gorges leased to her daughter, on the north side of the King's Road, near Stanley Bridge (now the site of St. Mark's College). Here, three children were born to them, Henrietta, Ferdinando and Charles. The two eldest died in infancy, and in 1632, after only five years of marriage, Sir Robert also died. His monument in the church is vast and imposing, occupying the whole of the east end of the Lawrence Chapel (originally it held the same position in the More Chapel) and calling to mind the remark of Mrs. Carlyle's maid Helen on being shown a Madonna and Child in the National Gallery: 'How beautiful— and how expensive!' It must surely have been paid for by the Derby family, and it is significant that, apart from her coat of arms, there is no mention of the wife of the deceased. Busts of his two dead children are set in medallions on either side of their father, a handsome young man in a curly wig. Above are three urns with, between them, the alabaster figures of Justice and Fortitude holding suitable objects. Over the central urn is an eagle with spread wings, hovering above a nest or cradle, which represents the Stanley badge, an eagle preying on a child. The epitaph begins with the splendid lines:

To say a STANLEY lyes here that a lone
Were Epitaph enough noe Brass noe Stone
No glorious Tombe no Monumentall Hearse
No guilded Trophy or lamp labourd verse
Can dignifie this Grave or sett it forth
Like the Immortall fame of his own Worth . . .

Sir Robert's widow, left with her one surviving child, Charles, now importuned her husband's family for an annuity, and was eventually awarded one by Charles I, which must have been a relief to all concerned. Her mother, Lady Elizabeth Gorges, bequeathed the house, Brickhills, to her, and here this branch of the Stanley family continued to live for two generations. In 1691, the last of the line died, and Stanley House passed into other hands.

It is a curious thing that although Chelsea has been the home of countless artists—painters, writers, musicians and actors—few are buried or commemorated there. One may look in vain for memorials to Carlyle or Rossetti, to Whistler, Turner or Wilde: it must be remembered that although Whistler escorted his mother to the door of the Old Church, he remained outside, as did the others. They were all buried elsewhere. A solitary actor, Henry Mossop, is commemorated: he died in desperate poverty but David Garrick went to his funeral, which was attended by the cream of the acting profession, and conducted with great pomp. There are memorial tablets to two successful artists, William Frend de Morgan (1839–1917), who lived for many years in Chelsea, making his beautiful pottery in Cheyne Row, and writing his novels in The Vale; and Henry James, the great American writer, who died in Carlyle Mansions in 1916: 'a resident of this Parish who renounced a cherished citizenship to give his allegiance to England in the first year of the Great War.'

In the south-east corner of the churchyard stands the imposing monument to Sir Hans Sloane, who 'in the 92nd year of his age, without the least pain of body, and with conscious serenity of mind, ended a virtuous and beneficial life'. Fortunately he did not know what posterity would think of him for pulling down More's house and King Henry's palace. Incorporated in the south wall of the church and conspicuous to passersby is a large slab commemorating Dr. Chamberlayne, who, with others of his family, lived and died in Chelsea. Edward Chamberlayne, we are told in Latin, 'departed into the land of oblivion' in 1703. He was 'an English Gentleman, a Christian, and Doctor of Laws', travelled all over Europe, had nine children and wrote six books. For posterity's sake, 'he ordered some of his books covered with wax to be buried with him, which may be of use in time to come'. But alas for human vanity, the damp and the rats got at them, and when Faulkner wrote, just over a hundred years later, 'gradual decay had totally obliterated every appearance of them'.

Dr. Chamberlayne's eldest son, Peregrine, was a naval officer, and so was his only daughter, Anne, who, 'aspiring above her sex and age', joined her brother's ship and went through a battle against the French, dressed and armed like a man, on June 30, 1690. 'A maiden heroine!' exclaims her epitaph, adding thoughtfully, 'had life been granted, she might have borne a race of naval warriors'. But, unfortunately, after the glories of life at sea she dwindled, like Millamant, into a wife, and died in the attempt to give birth to one naval warrior.

Two Huguenots, Jean Antoine Cavallier and Captain Rieutort, lie here—representatives of a number of French Protestants who settled in Chelsea after the revocation of the Edict of Nantes. A third, Peter de Caumont, Marquis de Cugnac, is commemorated inside the church: he was married to Elizabeth de Mayerne, daughter of the celebrated Swiss doctor, Theodore Turquet de Mayerne, who built Lindsey House on the site of More's farm. The 'little Marquise', his daughter, was married at the Old Church and died at the age of twenty-three.

Contemplation of so many memorials should lead to thoughts of time and mortality. Time is recorded by the tower clock, a copy of the old one made by Edmund Howard, brother of the Quaker who took care of More's house for Sloane. The sundial is likewise a replica of the old one, and bears a Latin inscription, composed in the seventeenth century by the Rector, Dr. Littleton: 'UT VITA FINIS ITA.' This might be translated in several ways, but Mr. Leighton Thomson, the present vicar, offers two alternatives: 'This' (meaning time) 'ends as life ends.' Or, 'As is your life, so will be your end.' Both give food for thought, which is doubtless what the Reverend Dr. Littleton intended.

CHAPTER FIVE

GORGES HOUSE

The first Sir Arthur Gorges inherited More's House through his wife but quickly moved out into a more convenient and up-to-date building on the estate. In November 1599, Rowland White wrote to Sir Robert Sidney:

'As the Queen passed by the faire new House in Chelsey, Sir Arthur Gorge [*sic*] . . . presented her with a faire Jewell.'

And this was the home of the Gorges family till the death of the third ('ingenious valiant') Arthur in 1688. 'Live Arthur by the spirit of thy fame,' cries his epitaph, 'Chelsey itself must dy before thy Name.' But alas, as far as Chelsea was concerned, the name of Gorges did die, for there was no male heir, and the house had to be sold.

It had already been let, in 1664, to the Duchess of Ormonde, who spent the summer there. This is known because she bought some local salmon. At that time, the Thames at Chelsea abounded with fish: salmon, gudgeon, pike, carp and perch, as well as smelts, eels and flounders. Fishermen made a good living, even though the rights and rooms of the salmon fishery belonged to Sir Walter St. John of Battersea House across the river. But in May 1664 these rights were handed over to Charles Cheyne, on behalf of the Chelsea fishermen, for £84. The Chelsea lads lost no time in letting down their nets, and during the first week made a record catch, weighing one hundred and seventy two and a half pounds. Lord Cheyne bought an eighteen-pounder at eighteen pence the pound, and the Duchess of Ormonde got hers, which weighed thirteen pounds, for sixteen pence, which was only twopence a pound more than the price paid by local fishmongers for the rest of the catch.

In spite of primitive sanitation, the Thames was far clearer and cleaner then than it is now; and Faulkner, writing in 1810, assures us that nearly all the species mentioned above were still being caught, and also roach and dace: the scales of these were sold to the Jews, who made false pearls from them.

In 1668, Gorges House was acquired by a dancing master, Mr. Josias Priest, who, with his wife Frank, kept a fashionable boarding school for young ladies, where music and the arts were cultivated. The Priests had a large family of their own, and seven of their younger children were baptized in Chelsea; it was probably this family atmosphere that helped to make the school a success. No doubt the young ladies were instructed in as much learning as was considered necessary; all we know is that they learned 'to japan boxes and to dance'. But the chief claim to fame of Mr. Priest's Academy is that in 1690 the first performance of Purcell's *Dido and Aeneas* was performed there by the girls, 'the words by Mr. Nahum Tate', and a special epilogue written by Tom D'Urfey was spoken by a star pupil, Lady Dorothy Durk.

Josias Priest died in 1734, but the house had been sold long before that, so presumably he had retired. The new owner was Sir William Milman, a barrister. The Milman family was of mixed social status, and in Le Neve's *Pedigrees of Knights* William, knighted in February 1705, is described as 'no gentleman'. This was, presumably, because his father was a shoemaker, and an unsuccessful one at that, who afterwards kept a coffee house. But the shoemaker's son 'having got a little money entred into the trade of Stock jobbing and lived to increase his estate to 20,000'. He died, continues this dispassionate account, '3d day of February 1713-14 . . . a worthless person by the general character of him'. It is hard to see why.

Sir William married three times, but he left Gorges House to his three nieces. They were all married and settled elsewhere, so the house was pulled down, and the land it occupied was let in 1796 for 'a new row of buildings intended to be called Milmans Row'. This became, in the nineteenth century, a very slummy street of dilapidated cottages, which were demolished in 1952 by Chelsea Borough Council. Milmans Street is now part of Cremorne Estate and contains neat blocks of Council flats. The St. George's Home stands on the site of Gorges House, with the Moravian Burying Ground, which was More's stable-yard, to the north of it.

DANVERS HOUSE

To the east of Milmans Street is Danvers Street, which leads from the riverside to Paultons Square. In a builder's yard on the eastern side of Danvers Street is a wall containing Tudor bricks, which may have been the boundary of one of the buildings on More's estate. There is thought to have been a house to the north of this area, which was known in the seventeenth century as Moorhouse, and was probably the one given by More to his son-in-law William Roper. In June 1618, Thomas, Earl of Lincoln (son of the miserly Henry) sold 'the lands called Moorhouse, in Chelsea' to Sir John Danvers, and in 1622 Danvers House was built.

Sir John was so handsome that when he travelled abroad people followed him in the street, gazing in astonished admiration. He was married, in his twenties, to Magdalen Herbert, a woman nearly twice his age, with ten children by a previous marriage. The fifth of her seven sons was George Herbert, the poet and mystic, whose hymns are still sung in Chelsea churches. Isaak Walton writes of Magdalen Herbert's 'great and harmless wit, her cheerful gravity, and her obliging behaviour', which must have contributed to the extraordinary happiness of her marriage to Sir John Danvers.

They spent five tranquil years in their Chelsea house, where they created a celebrated Italian garden, the first of its kind in this country. According to his friend John Aubrey, Sir John had a particular talent for gardening and architecture: the house was 'very elegant and ingeniose', and the gardens 'a monument of his ingenuity'. The greater part lay to the north of the house, towards the King's Road, while to the south the land sloped down to the river, so that, says Aubrey, 'as you sit at dinner in the Hall you are entertained with two delightful Vistos'.

'You did not,' he continues, 'enter directly out of the Hall into the Garden: there was a low semi-circular wall to hinder the immediate pleasure', and you were obliged to turn left or right and descend ten steps, which led to 'a kind of Boscage' of lilacs, syringas, sweet briar, holly and juniper. This 'dark shadie' shrubbery or wilderness opened out on to stately gravelled walks bordered with hyssop and thyme, through which Sir John would brush his beaver hat as he passed, 'which did perfume it with its natural essence and would last a morning or longer'.

The sculptor, Nicholas Stone, was commissioned to make a sundial, and also two figures, the gardener and his wife, done from life, 'both accoutred to their callings', and coloured realistically, for which he was paid £7 apiece. Stone, who was master mason to James I, later designed the gates of the Chelsea Physic Garden.

Lady Danvers died in 1727, after nursing some of Chelsea's first victims to the Plague. She is buried at the Old Church, where John Donne, who had been her friend, preached her commemorative sermon, and, according to Walton, who was there, wept.

Sir John married again twice; but he left no male heir, and very little money, so the house had to be let. Between 1660 and 1685, John Lord Robartes, afterwards Earl of Radnor, lived at Danvers House. This nobleman seems to have been yet another Vicar of Bray, for at the outbreak of the Civil War he fought with Cromwell; but in September 1660, only a few months after the Restoration, he was entertaining King Charles II at his Chelsea house. A year later, when Robartes was Lord Privy Seal, Samuel Pepys went there, and 'found it to be the prettiest contrived house that I ever saw in my life'.

But its days were numbered. Radnor died, Danvers House was sold, and, in 1716, demolished. Already a new street was running through part of the grounds: a stone bearing the words 'This is Danvers Street, begun in ye year 1696 by Benjamin Stallwood' now rests in the garden of Crosby Hall, where it was placed after the lower part of Danvers Street was destroyed during the bombing of 1941. In 1729 an advertisement appeared:

'To be Lett or Sold'. In Danvers Street in Great Chelsea near the Ferry, four new brick houses strong good and well finished with Wainscot done in the best manner . . . Enquire at the corner of the aforesaid street, or at W. Clarkson's who keeps a yard near the Swan Tavern.'

These old houses have all gone: those on the west side were demolished in 1910, when Crosby Hall was moved from the City and reconstructed on Cheyne Walk.

In the early part of the nineteenth century, before Paultons Square was built, Shepherd's Nursery covered the site of Sir John Danvers' ingenious walks and boscages; prim rows of seedlings were reared in the soil that had once nurtured his fragrant borders of hyssop and thyme. Then, in September 1822, gardeners unearthed part of the foundations of the house, together with broken columns and capitals. It was an exciting find, and would have led, no doubt, to others; but Mr. Shepherd decided that it would save trouble to re-bury everything and forget about it. So these relics, and Nicholas Stone's sundial, and the figures of the old gardener and his wife, remain to this day somewhere beneath the grass where children play in the summer, in the centre of Paultons Square.

LINDSEY HOUSE

Although it has been altered and rebuilt, and is now divided into a row, Lindsey House is the only one of Chelsea's palaces which stands today on its original site. It replaced a building on More's estate known as the farm, where More and his family lived before moving into the Great House.

In 1639 the farm was bought by Sir Theodore Turquet de Mayerne, who pulled it down and built himself a handsome house on the site. De Mayerne was a Swiss doctor who lived up to his impressive name by being appointed physician-in-ordinary to four kings—Henry IV and Louis XIII of France, and James I and Charles I of England. History does not relate how many Queens he attended, but he produced in the course of his duties recipes for cosmetics, and a book called *The Compleat Midwife*. Chemist as

well as physician, he horrified the English medical profession by introducing his knowledge of chemistry into his prescriptions, a thing unheard
of at the time. This must have been successful, however, for he was
knighted by his grateful patient, James I, and amassed a considerable
fortune. He lived in Chelsea till 1655, and died at the age of eighty-two, it
is said from the effects of bad wine. The house he lived in, plain but magnificent, had a wide river frontage, and part of it, as it looked in 1707, may
be seen on the extreme left of Kip's engraving, immediately in front of
Gorges House, whose view it must have spoiled.

It was by this time Lindsey House, the property of Robert Bertie, third
Earl of Lindsey and Lord Chamberlain of England, who occupied it for
nearly thirty years; and after his death his widow continued to live there.
But once again one of Chelsea's great houses, built and improved with
loving care, was to pass out of the hands of a family and embark upon a
precarious career of short lets and long vacancies. After being rented
furnished to the Dowager Duchess of Rutland, Lindsey House lay empty
for seventeen years. It then entered the strangest phase of its history, but
perhaps the most fortunate. In May 1750 it was bought by Ludwig Count
Zinzendorff to be a headquarters of the Moravian Brethren. A great deal
of money was spent over the next ten years, on the careful restoration and
alteration of the house to suit the needs of the community; and through
the wise provision of the Moravians its future, after they left, was assured.

John Wesley called the Moravians 'the still brethren'; and it seems
likely that after all they had endured over the centuries they had learned
to be 'still'. Originating in Bohemia at the end of the fourteenth century,
they were one of many Protestant uprisings against the spiritual tyranny of
Rome. They were continually persecuted, and by the middle of the sixteenth century were nearly wiped out: a small remnant escaped to Poland
where they reluctantly joined forces with the Calvinists. The brethren and
sisters who came to Chelsea with Count Zinzendorff were gentle people,
brought up with an unquestioning acceptance of the way of life laid down
for them, and an unquestioning belief in the Bible and in ultimate re-
demption through Jesus Christ.

By Zinzendorff's orders, Lindsey House, together with the grounds of
More's house, which he bought from Sir Hans Sloane, were to be converted into a Moravian settlement, or Sharon, conforming to a standard
pattern, for which plans were drawn up in Germany. Single brethren and
sisters were segregated in houses east and west of the building. But
marriage was encouraged within the community, and there were family
quarters, and school houses for the children. There were workshops where

men and women could earn a living, and both sexes were expected to work on the land and grow food for the community. It was suitable that they should have chosen More's land for their home. Though Protestant and, in his view, heretics, the Moravians with their strong faith and brotherly love were inheritors of the way of life that he upheld.

To the north of the settlement, on the site of More's stable ground, the Moravians buried their dead. The land is divided into four sections, for the single and married of each sex. The stable buildings were converted into a chapel and priest's house, and remain intact today.[1]

Count Zinzendorff, who directed the whole operation, was a man of fifty; handsome, aristocratic, 'witty, cheerful and sociable'. As a young man he had inherited an estate at Berthelsdorff near Saxony, which he set himself to run on Christian principles. When, in 1722, a bedraggled band of two hundred Moravians, fleeing as usual from persecution, sought his help, he established them in a model village, Herrnhut Berthelsdorff, and they in gratitude made him their bishop. He believed that by becoming one with them he would serve the cause of Christian unity which had long been his dream. In his view, Moravians were not a sect, but a people chosen to bind together all existing sects.

But so far as the Chelsea settlement was concerned, the Count's plans never reached completion. On May 9, 1760, Zinzendorff died. It was a disaster for the community. There was no one to take his place. The Moravians, sheep without a shepherd, and penniless, were forced to abandon the Count's expensive plans for the completion of Sharon. They decided to let off part of their land in building plots, and the two beautiful houses, Belle Vue Lodge and Belle Vue House, which stand on Cheyne Walk at the corner of Beaufort Street,[2] owe their existence to this decision. So does Beaufort Street itself, which was cut through the Moravians' land in 1766 and named Beaufort Row. All they kept to the east of Lindsey House was a narrow passage-way which led to the burial ground.

But these economy measures were not enough to support the settlement, and the Moravians were obliged to move. In April 1776, James Hutton their secretary wrote to the Elders' Conference: 'About the same time that this letter will reach you, we shall probably be in our new quarters . . . near to the Elephant, Pimlico, about two minutes' walk from the Palace.'

Once more, Lindsey House stood empty; and only their dead were left behind to remind posterity of Chelsea's connection with the Still Brethren.

---

[1] The small house was lived in, in this century, by Mrs. Gillick, who designed the Queen's head on our coinage.

[2] See page 197.

But the chapel, at the north end of the burying ground, remained in the possession of the Moravians, who continued to worship there. An old out-patient of Chelsea Hospital, James Gillray, father of the caricaturist, was for forty years sexton and grave-digger: then, after burying others, he was finally buried there himself, among the brethren. So was Captain James Frazer, who crossed the Atlantic fifty-six times in their missionary ship, *Harmony*, and died in 1808. Faulkner, wandering round the burial ground about this time, was struck by the Moravians' longevity: many reached their nineties; but an unbaptized Eskimo, placed alone in a corner, died before his time, of tuberculosis.

James Hutton, who was buried there in 1795, deserves a place in Chelsea's gallery of singular characters. He started life as a bookseller, became a Moravian, and travelled all over Germany and Switzerland as a missionary, after which he became secretary to the Society in England. For over twenty years he held the freehold of Lindsey House, and became a well-known figure in the district. He was very friendly with George III. We do not know how or where they met, but it may well have been in Chelsea, for the King was in the habit of visiting the Chelsea Bunhouse with his family, and sometimes they had tea in the garden of Blacklands Farm. Monarch and Moravian must have been a curious pair. Hutton was very deaf, and the King very talkative, an eager and impatient conversationalist with his often repeated 'What, what?' which made Fanny Burney so nervous. The *St. James's Chronicle* for December 17, 1776 noted:

'A new favourite has lately engrossed the King's attention, who bids fair to supplant . . . the facetious Grimaldi in the Royal favours. It is no less a person than the old deaf Moravian, James Hutton.' The chronicler observes that 'a conversation between the King and Hutton must be exceedingly entertaining. Hutton is so deaf that a speaking trumpet will scarce make him hear; and the King talks so fast than an ordinary converser cannot possibly keep pace with him . . .'

But Hutton held his own. At one of his meetings with King George, the young Prince of Wales, a bouncing boy of fourteen, was present. 'After stroking his son for some time, with a father's joy and pride, the King turned to Hutton and said "Is he not a fine boy?" Hutton made no reply. The King, ascribing his silence to his deafness, repeated his question in a louder tone of voice. Hutton still observed the strictest silence. A few minutes later the Prince left the apartment; when Hutton, addressing the King, said: "Your Majesty probably thought that I did not hear the questions you were pleased to ask me. I understood them perfectly. Nor was it from any want of respect or courtesy that I abstained from making a reply; but it is a firm principle of mine, never to praise a child in its presence." '

Lindsey House, after the departure of the Moravians, was gradually divided into seven separate houses and re-named Lindsey Row. Number 98, the central portion of the original building, and the most impressive of the houses, became in 1848 the home of John Martin, the painter, who insisted on calling it Lindsey House, and not number 4 Lindsey Row. In 1817 he had been appointed Historical Painter to Princess Charlotte, Princess of Wales, and her husband Prince Leopold. (The latter had lodged with the Martins on his first visit to England, an impoverished young soldier, in 1814.) Later Martin's work was greatly admired by the Prince Consort, Leopold's nephew, who often visited him at Lindsey House. His canvases, which grew larger and larger, depicted vast scenes of disaster, The Fall of Babylon, The Flood, The Last Judgment, with storm-swept skies and tottering cliffs, and sharp lurid colouring. He was perhaps a little mad, and his brother, William, who died at Chelsea in 1851, must have been very odd indeed. He called himself The Philosophical Conqueror of All Nations, and announced that he had found the secret of perpetual motion. Unfortunately his invention, when exhibited, broke down.

After the Martins came the Brunels, father and son.[1] Now number 4 Lindsey Row is 98 Cheyne Walk, and it was given by its last owner, Mr. Peter Kroyer, to the National Trust. Its neighbour, 97, had, Mr. Kroyer tells us, 'for a variety of reasons remained unoccupied by its succession of owners for 108 years'. So it survived the nineteenth century unaltered, and contains what is thought to be the original staircase of the old house. In 1951 it was repaired by the National Trust, and united to 98, a handsome pair of houses, now divided into flats.

[1] See Chapter 8.

PART TWO

'A TOWN SWEETLY SITUATED'

I N THE seventeenth and early eighteenth centuries Chelsea was at its most beautiful. In spite of a steady increase in population and the building of new houses, the rural landscape was unspoilt; the Tudor palaces still stood among their orchards, and the Thames swept past flowery meadows.

Chelsea was a health resort: the air was thought to be salubrious, and tired noblemen and city gentlemen took little holidays there to restore their jaded nerves. It was also a pleasure resort: 'Hyde Park on the Thames,' Charles II called it; a place for bathing and boating, for fishing and shooting, for sitting on warm evenings beside the river in arbours or on it in boats, eating and drinking and making music.

Samuel Pepys enjoyed an evening in Chelsea, and describes how he and his wife took the actress Mrs. Knipp 'by the coach to Chelsey, and there in a box in a tree, we sat and sang, and talked and ate; my wife out of humour, as she always is when that woman is by'. On another occasion, Mrs. Pepys was left at home: Samuel, with Mrs. Pearce and 'that jade Knipp', drove out together, 'thinking to be merry at Chelsey'. They were bound for the Swan, a tavern overlooking the river on the east of the Physic Garden,[1] but when they got there they found that 'the house was shut of the sickness. So we with great affright turned back'. No wonder, for this was 1666 and the plague still rampant.

But Pepys, who so heartily enjoyed an evening out with somebody else's wife, expressed the deepest disapproval when his patron, Edward Montagu, Earl of Sandwich, went to Chelsea to convalesce after an illness, and fell in love with his landlady's daughter. This young woman, Elizabeth Becke, lived in Paradise Row, where Pepys, suspicious of his Lordship's prolonged rest-cure in Chelsea, paid him a visit. The diarist had nothing but praise for Mrs. Becke's cooking, but was 'ashamed to see my Lord so grossly playing the beast and fool' with her daughter, 'carrying her abroad and playing his lute under her window, and forty other poor sordid things which I am grieved to hear'. For Sandwich, a man in high office, with a long and distinguished military career, this was a lamentable

---

[1] The Swan was converted into a brewery, c. 1780, and the name given to another inn on the west of the Physic Garden.

situation: this 'strange dotage of his upon the slut at Chelsea' seemed to have deprived him of his senses. The young woman, though smart and cunning, was not even pretty. 'She hath not one good feature in her face,' wrote Pepys. His Lordship's long absence from Court and from his official duties were giving rise to rumours, and at last Pepys decided that as Sandwich's secretary and cousin he must write what he called a 'great letter of reproof'. In this he boldly referred to the bad reputation of the house 'wherein your Lordship, now observed in perfect health again, continues to sojourn', and declared that Miss Becke was talked of as 'a common courtizan'. Pepys awaited his Lordship's reception of this letter with trepidation; but either it had its effect or Miss Becke was losing her grip, for ten days later we hear that 'my Lord Sandwich is resolved to go no more to Chelsey'. And so, it is to be hoped, the affair ended; though, rather disconcertingly, we find Lady Sandwich, some six months later, going to visit Mrs. Becke. . . . 'and by and by the daughter came in.' Her Ladyship professed astonishment, declaring afterwards that she had not known that Mrs. Becke had a daughter ('which,' said Pepys, 'I do not believe'), and adding that she thought her 'the most ugly woman that ever she saw'.

The Beckes lived in Paradise Row, that beautiful and lamented line of seventeenth-century houses which ran from Flood Street to Burtons Court along what we now call Royal Hospital Road. L'Estrange, writing in 1880, describes the handsome entrance gates which led through gardens to hall doors flanked with carved wood. The houses were well proportioned with dormer windows, 'and contain good rooms, panelled to the ceilings', and they had long gardens at the back. But even then they had fallen on evil days: many were empty, others were used as laundries or lodging houses, and in 1885, when their leases fell in, the western part of the Row was demolished; the rest, after an unsuccessful plea for their preservation led by Mr. Reginald Blunt, were pulled down in 1906.

The houses varied in size. At the Flood Street end was Radnor House, to which Letitia Isabella, Countess of Radnor, moved from Danvers House, after the death of that 'old snarling troublesome peevish fellow' her husband in 1685. She was described by a contemporary as 'strikingly beautiful' (the Duke of York had made advances to her) 'yet not withstanding the brightness of the finest complexion with all the bloom of youth, and yet with every requisite for inspiring desire, she nevertheless was not attractive'. In spite of this, however, she left Radnor House to become the second wife of Charles (now Viscount) Cheyne, and to live in the Manor House next door.

Part of Paradise Row. Water-colour by George Manson

Hortense Mancini, Duchesse
Mazarin in the character of Pomona

Doctor Atterbury

Two Chelsea figures

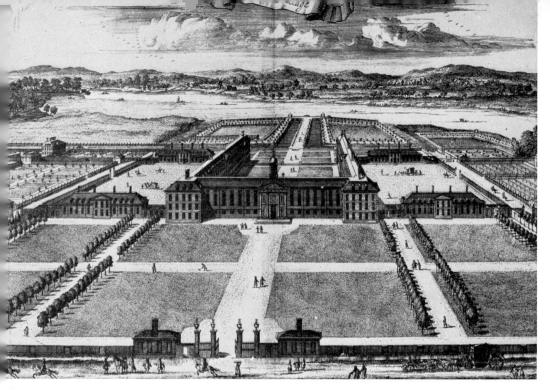

The Royal Hospital. A view (possibly by J. Kip)
showing the river and Battersea Fields

The Royal Hospital, north front, engraving
by T. Malton, c. 1790

Chelsea Pensioner (William Hiseland,
aged 110). Painting by George Alsop

The Chelsea Guard—'Broken with Toils, with Ponderous Arms Opprest'

At the far end of Paradise Row, in a smaller house built by George Norris in 1691, lived Hortense Mancini, Duchesse MaBarin, a woman whose charms were never in question. She had been Charles II's mistress, and during his lifetime had sometimes spent the summer at Chelsea. After his death she left her 'petit palais' in St. James's, and after a short sojourn in Kensington Square, settled in 1694 at number 4, Paradise Row, with the Royal Hospital across the way to remind her of her royal lover, She was hard up, and never paid her rates; but she gave splendid parties offering her guests exquisite meals, immaculately served, after which they tactfully slipped a gift of money under their plates. They also sent her presents of food: Lady Sandwich sent Bath mutton, and Godolphin melons and rabbits.

But it was not for the sake of eating and drinking that the *beau monde* crowded into her house: Hortense Mancini was a fascinating and original woman who after an adventurous life liked to gather round her a *salon* to listen to exchanges of wit and learning, and to enjoy the finest music played by professionals. She is said to have introduced Italian opera into England: she also introduced the game of Basset, at which she cheated with skill and aplomb.

'All the world,' said Evelyn, 'knows her story.' It was, briefly, that her uncle, Cardinal Mazarin, had refused to allow her to marry Charles II when he was a penniless exile; and having let this fish off the hook, arranged a marriage for her with the Duc de la Meilleraye, who agreed to adopt the Cardinal's name and arms. The Duc was unfortunately mad: he thought he saw visions and had the gift of prophecy; sometimes he fancied that he was a tulip. Farmyard sights, he said, were too indelicate for women's eyes, and his wife was debarred from seeing the cows milked. Hortense was gay, wore patches and enjoyed the theatre, so he locked her up in a convent, where she and a girl friend amused themselves by playing tricks on the nuns. At last, in despair, she fled, disguised as a boy, and hotly pursued over Europe by the Duc and his emissaries. In 1675 she managed to reach England, where her cousin was the Duchess of York. Her beauty and extraordinary story delighted King Charles; she was installed in a house at St. James's, and, to the rage of Louise de Kerouaille, the reigning favourite, became the King's mistress, with an allowance of £4,000 a year.

After the death of Charles in 1685, and the accession of James II, her position was difficult: and on July 15, 1689, Narcissus Luttrell noted in his diary: 'Commons address to be presented to his majestie, that the Dutchesse of Mazarin be speedily commanded to retire beyond the sea.'

But she stayed, supported by her friends, and by the devotion of her fellow exile, Charles de Saint-Evremond, who had since 1662 enjoyed a sinecure under King Charles as Governor of Duck Island in St. James's Park, and who was now, like herself, unemployed. When she settled in Chelsea, Saint-Evremond was in constant attendance: she was forty-six, he seventy-eight and her slave.

'A man can never be ridiculous in loving you,' he wrote. 'A Minister of State renounces his politics for you, and a philosopher his morals . . . The power of an exquisite beauty justifies all the passion which it is capable of producing . . . I will tell you, without fear of being ridiculed for it, that I love you.'

He wrote poetry for her, he lent her money; he arranged the music for her parties, he even tried to be clean to please her, though this was impossible:

> Old Evremond renowned for wit and dirt
> Would change his living rather than his shirt.

When Governor of Duck Island he kept chickens in his bedroom, and allowed ducks and other creatures to roam over his house, declaring that 'when we grow old and our own spirits decay, it reanimates one to have a number of living creatures about one'.

And here at least Hortense, who on the whole treated him abominably, was in sympathy with him. The menagerie with which she surrounded herself at Paradise Row included a number of little dogs with endearing names like Little, Rogue and Chop, and a cat called Monsieur Poussy. She had a tame sparrow on whose death Saint-Evremond composed an elegy, a starling called Jacob and a bullfinch known as Boulé. She also had more exotic pets, brought by admirers returning from abroad. 'The Duchesse Mazarin,' wrote Saint-Evremond to a friend on his travels, 'can hardly conceive how a Caravan can return without bringing home with them Monkeys and Parrots.' 'If you return,' he adds, 'bring Monkeys and Parrots. If you go to Rome, bring Pardons and Beads.'

The last request was more to the point, for the lovely Duchess was dying. Only a year before this, Ninon de Lenclos had written: 'Everyone that comes from England speaks of the Duchesse Mazarin's beauty;' yet in 1699, beset by money troubles and with little heart for entertaining, she tried to economize by giving up wine and drinking beer and spirits, which were cheap.

'Don't lose your hopes, Madam,' wrote Sainte-Evremond from the country; 'for your Troubles and Difficulties will have an end. Leave off Beer, drink your Wine . . .'

Her troubles and difficulties did indeed have an end. Evelyn, recording her death in his Diary for June 11, adds, 'She is reported to have hastened her death by intemperate drinking of strong spirits.'

Her husband, who had failed to capture her alive, now paid her debts in order to get possession of her dead body.

'The corps of the Dutchesse of Mazarine is shipt off for France,' wrote Evelyn, 'in order to be interred with her Ancestors.' But far from having her interred, the Duc had her embalmed, and apparently carried her about with him wherever he went.

Her neighbour in Paradise Row, Miss Mary Astell, was prompted to point a moral. In *Some Reflections upon Marriage, Occasioned by the Duke and Dutchess of Mazarin's Case* (published anonymously) she wrote: 'One can't help wishing that so much Wit and Beauty, so much politeness and address, had been accompanied and supported by more valuable and lasting qualities . . . An ill husband may deprive a wife of the comfort and quiet of her Life; may give her occasion of exercising her virtue; may try her patience and fortitude to the utmost; but that's all he can do. She herself only can accomplish her ruin.'

Mary Astell had no husband, good or ill: perhaps she had frightened off her suitors by being so clever, which was at that time considered neither attractive nor quite the thing. Little is known about her background, beyond the fact that she was the daughter of a merchant in Newcastle-on-Tyne, and this place of origin suggests that she may have been sister or aunt to a coal merchant named John Astell, who, early in the eighteenth century, was appointed Comptroller of the Coal Yards at the Royal Hospital. When she came to Chelsea she was twenty, and she lived there for nearly fifty years. She was far from idle. In Newcastle she had been given a good education, exceptionally good for a woman. But she was exceptionally clever: she had mastered mathematics, logic and philosophy, and could read the classics, both Latin and Greek. Today, many professions would be open to a woman of her ability: in her own time she was a phenomenon, a joke, and became a poverty-stricken old maid. She had ideas about the emancipation of women, and that was not only ridiculous, but risky, like being a Jacobite. But she was deeply in earnest, and unafraid. In 1694 she wrote *A Serious Proposal to the Ladies*, in which she suggested the formation of an Anglican community of celibate females: a paradise without serpents. Deploring the frivolity of her female contemporaries, she proposed to teach her fellow celibates to be not only as lovely but as wise as angels.

Poor thing, she was doomed to failure. An admirer, Lady Elizabeth

Hastings, offered her ten thousand pounds towards the Community; but withdrew the offer after being dissuaded by Bishop Burnet. Such a thing, he said, smacked of popery, and was highly dangerous. Then a young Irishman of twenty-seven, Jonathan Swift, satirized her Proposal in the *Tatler*. 'A clique of ladies of quality gave out that "virginity was to be their state of life during this mortal condition", and joined to establish a nunnery; but before long a party of rakes gained admission, and . . . made themselves so agreeable that soon the whole company were walking round the garden hand in hand . . .' This was thought very amusing.

Mary Astell is said to have lived at times on bread and water and a little small beer. It may have been asceticism, it may have been poverty—nobody seems to have bothered to find out. She was no recluse: she enjoyed entertaining. But when she was busy writing she would throw up her window and call out, 'Mistress Astell is not at home.'

Dr. Francis Atterbury, a notable preacher, politician and theologian, lived at this time in Chelsea, and was one of the few men (Evelyn was another) to appreciate Mary Astell's intellectual powers. In 1706 he dined with her, and at her request sent her a copy of one of his sermons, which she returned with a page of trenchant comments. 'Extraordinary,' said Atterbury, 'considering they come from the pen of a woman . . . There is not an expression that carries the least air of her sex.' But even he cannot help recoiling slightly. A woman should not be so clever. It is ill bred. 'Had she as much good breeding as good sense, she would be perfect,' he wrote. 'But she is now and then a little offensive and shocking in her expressions . . . I dread to engage her.'

Apparently undeterred by her failures, she pursued her ambition, to advance the education of women. It was a laudable object, for women were for the most part abysmally uneducated, and even though England was quite successfully governed by two females, Queen Anne and the Duchess of Marlborough, men were still chary of allowing the sex to use their brains. At last, after years of effort, Mary Astell succeeded—with the aid of the faithful Lady Elizabeth Hastings and Lady Catherine Jones[1] who put up the money—in founding a school for daughters of Chelsea Pensioners. This establishment, which later became part of the School for Soldiers' Daughters, was her memorial. She died of cancer two years later, after a long and agonizing illness, during which she insisted that her shroud and coffin should be placed beside her bed.

[1] The youngest daughter of the Earl of Ranelagh.

MARY ASTELL'S FRIEND Dr. Atterbury lived in Church Lane, now Church Street, and the oldest of Chelsea's thoroughfares. Till the King's Private Road was opened to the public in 1830 Church Lane was the only way into Chelsea by coach. An old posting house, the White Horse, stood on its western side, opposite the old church, and adjoining the Arch House, which straddled the road, at right angles to the river. Both these buildings dated from the sixteenth century. The inn was noted for the mysterious winged figures carved on either side of its entrance—benevolent or malevolent according to your state of mind—and its sign bore the date 1509. When you turned into Church Street from the river walk you left the spaciousness of the waterside with its noble estates, and found yourself in a quiet street lived in by professional men and their families, as it is today.

At the top, on the eastern side, the rectory stood in its gardens of nearly three acres, surrounded by a high wall. Dr. King, the rector in Dr. Atterbury's time, was not living in the rectory because it was unfit for habitation. His predecessor, Dr. Adam Littleton, the great Latin scholar, unfortunately died insolvent, 'leaving his widow,' wrote Dr. King rather unkindly, 'who had brought him a large fortune, in mean circumstances, and an object of compassion'. The house and outbuildings were in a shocking state, and Dr. King was obliged to spend a great deal of money on repairs. Meanwhile, he rented number nine, Church Lane. Bowack, the historian, paid £14 a year for a house there; Dr. John Arbuthnot, one of Queen Anne's many physicians-in-ordinary, who was also physician to the Royal Hospital, lived there; so did John Martyn, F.R.S., a famous botanist, who married Dr. King's daughter. It was a very respectable street.

On April 24, 1711, Jonathan Swift wrote from Bury Street, London, 'I design in two days, if possible, to go to lodge at Chelsea for the air.' He was suffering from pains in the head, partly, he thought, from missing the horse exercise he was accustomed to in Ireland. He took a lodging in Church Lane, and on arrival wrote in his *Journal to Stella*: 'I got here with Patrick [his servant] and my portmantua for sixpence, and pay six shillings a week for one silly room, with confounded coarse sheets.'

There are no eulogies from Swift: Chelsea in his eyes was far from being an earthly paradise, even though it had been the home of Thomas More, a man 'of the greatest virtue this kingdom has ever produced'. Nothing pleased him. He had looked forward to pleasant country walks: the day after his arrival was so wet that instead of walking into London, he was obliged to take the sixpenny stage, which started at the White Horse at the bottom of the street.

'I lodge,' wrote Swift, 'over against Dr. Atterbury's house; and yet perhaps I shall not like the place the better for that.'

There is some uncertainty as to where Dr. Atterbury's house was. Mr. Randall Davies is positive that it was not, as Alfred Beaver and others thought, the Arch House, but a house higher up the street. It might even have been the large old house which stood where Paultons Street now leads to Paultons Square, and which is mentioned by every Chelsea historian, though nobody has the faintest idea what it was or who lived there. Its date, according to Faulkner, was 1641, and it was called by various names: Essex House, Queen Anne's Laundry, Church Place. It is a house of mystery, in which Henry Kingsley housed his humble family in *The Hillyers and the Burtons*: in the mid-nineteenth century, when he was writing, the once magnificent house was let out in tenements, and soon after it was demolished.

'An ambitious and turbulent priest attached to the House of Stuart,' wrote Horace Walpole of Atterbury, who was an avowed Jacobite. At the death of Queen Anne, who made him Bishop of Rochester, he is said to have offered to go in his lawn sleeves to proclaim King James III at Charing Cross; but he was evidently dissuaded. In 1722 he was shut up in the Tower for openly helping the Pretender; but at the time of Swift's visit his activities were confined to secret plottings. He was glad to welcome the Irish cleric to Chelsea.

On May 1 Swift wrote: 'I have just now a compliment from Dean Atterbury's lady, to command the garden, library, and whatever the house affords; but the dean is in town with his convocation.' The following day it was 'terrible rainy', and by the evening Swift was glad to avail himself of Mrs. Atterbury's invitation. 'She would needs send me home some veal, and small beer, and ale.' Later we find him dining with the Dean and sitting with him till one o'clock.

The Dean of Carlisle also tried to be helpful, sending his chariot to carry Swift to church in the rain. Unfortunately he had to tip the coachman two shillings, so the kindness was overlooked.

When the weather improved he started walking into London. It took him, he said, less than an hour. 'It is two good miles, and just five thousand and seven hundred and forty-eight steps.' He left his wig and his best coat at Mrs. Van Homrigh's, so that he could change when he reached town and make himself into a 'spark' before dining with the Lord Treasurer and other important people. On May 25 he wrote, 'It was bloody hot walking today; and I was so lazy, I dined where my new gown was, at Mrs. Van Homrigh's, and came back like a fool, and the Dean of Carlisle has sitten with me till eleven.'

Walking back in the evenings he passed along Pall Mall, which was crowded, he said, with a prodigious number of young ladies taking good exercise, as he wished Irish ladies would do. He seems to have been innocent of the dangers at night on the road to Chelsea. Returning by moonlight at one in the morning, he encountered a sailor and a parson fighting in the road: presumably the sailor was out to rob the parson, but Swift was not worried about that. 'I had no money in my pocket, so could not be robbed.'

It was a hot summer. Swift, tired of walking, found that he could travel to London by public boat. This was cheap and pleasant—but 'there is never a boat on Sunday, never!' The nights were warm, so in his nightgown, shirt and slippers, with a napkin borrowed from his landlady tied over his head, Swift marched down Church Lane to the river. Then, handing his clothes to his servant Patrick, he plunged into the water and swam about. Perhaps, like Carlyle, who was also a bathing enthusiast, he found cold water beneficial to his liver.

But Chelsea could not please him. He visited the celebrated Chelsea Bun House, and bought a bun. It was stale. He writes of the 'sweet scent of the flowery meads' of Chelsea during the hay harvest; but adds that the 'haymaking nymphs are perfect drabs', and he has never seen so many dirty straw hats. On July 4 he wrote, 'This day I left Chelsea for good,' and though he went back twice to visit the Dean of Carlisle, he never stayed there again.

Opening out of Church Street on the eastern side is Justice Walk, an alley which leads into Lawrence Street, at the head of which was once the old Manor House, and then Monmouth House. There is some uncertainty about how the name Justice Walk originated: it was at one time an avenue of lime trees, and a Justice of the Peace, Mr. John Gregory, is said to have walked there. It seems more likely that Sir John Fielding, who lived for a time in Monmouth House, was the 'justice'. But further confusion has been caused by a persistent legend that a Court House stood here, on the site of the Wesleyan Chapel built in the 1830s. A curve in the pavement opposite suggests that at some earlier period carriages drove in at this point to a stable yard. The Judge's carriage? But this may well have been the way in to the stables of Monmouth House. So the origin of Justice Walk and its Court House (with cells down below where the Wine Cooper now stores his bottles) remains among Chelsea's many unsolved mysteries.

Another is the precise origin of the Chelsea China factory. During 1970 workmen digging in the back garden of number 15, Lawrence Street unearthed some fragments of china, and the new owner of the house, Mr. John Casson, called in experts from the Victoria and Albert Museum, who identified them as Chelsea porcelain. An organized dig on the site produced a vast quantity of fragments which were taken to the Museum to be washed and, as far as possible, identified. The china was for the most part neither painted nor glazed, and evidently consisted of throw-outs from the Chelsea Manufactory; but most pieces were identifiable, some even to an untrained eye: part of the lid of a pineapple tureen, the fluted base of a vase, a delicately moulded handle attached to part of a cup.

This discovery has established the long-disputed position of the china works, which must have occupied the west side of Lawrence Street, between Monmouth House and Justice Walk. The house on the further side of Justice Walk was originally a pub called the Prince of Wales, under which, at the beginning of this century, Reginald Blunt found 'some remains of cylindrical, dome-topped brick structures', which he claimed were kilns. Mr. J. V. G. Mallet of the Victoria and Albert Museum is dubious about this. He is also dubious about the often-repeated story that the great Dr. Johnson used to go to the china works, accompanied by his housekeeper carrying a basket of provisions, and settle down for the day to make china. The proprietors put everything at his disposal except their secret recipe for china paste, which was unfortunate, as his models invariably broke in the firing. It is a pity that this picture of Johnson has to be turned with its back to the wall, for this is one of the nicer Chelsea legends, and has lost nothing in the telling. Alfred Beaver writes in *Memorials of Old Chelsea* that the sad experiments 'resulted in nothing but injury to his eyesight, which, much to his annoyance, Reynolds has perpetuated in one of his portraits'. And all the time it was another, quite obscure, Dr. Johnson, about whom we do not care a fig.

The first proprietor and manager of the works was Charles Gouyn who came to Chelsea about 1745, and the china with the triangle mark was produced during the next four years. In 1749 Nicholas Sprimont was engaged as manager. Born at Liège in 1716, he was the nephew of a silversmith, Nicholas Joseph Sprimont, to whom he was apprenticed. He came to England to follow his trade, and in 1742 he married a Kensington girl, Ann Protin. When he decided to change his medium from silver to clay he brought his wife to Chelsea, where they lived in Prospect Place, between Lawrence Street and the old Church. Sprimont is the chief genius of Chelsea porcelain. His early work was influenced by his training as a silversmith, and some of his china vessels, teapots for example, were designed on the same lines as silver ones. During the twenty years when he was there the Chelsea factory became increasingly famous. After 1758, when the owner, Sir Everard Fawkener, died and Sprimont took over, the products gradually changed in character. The simplicity and gaiety of the early (raised anchor and red anchor) groups were replaced by the elaborate elegance of the later (gold anchor) period.

The early Chelsea porcelain was made from an exceedingly fine, soft paste, which formed translucent patches or 'moons' after being fired. Now Sprimont introduced bone ash, which eliminated the moons, but the china lost its silky texture. He also introduced a new colour called Mazarine, a beautiful rich deep blue, which was used a great deal, with lavish gilding. Thus the original character of Chelsea was changed, some experts say not for the better, by the introduction of French influences. This difference may be seen by comparing two groups, 'The Music Lesson' modelled by Louis Roubiliac from a Boucher painting, 'Le Mouton Favori', between 1763 and 1765, and 'Nurse and Child' made ten years earlier. In the former a shepherd is teaching his love to play a pipe; a pet lamb lies in her lap while another one gambols with two dogs at their feet and a tree spreads its blossoms behind them: the scene is brilliantly coloured and alive with detail.[1] In the earlier group a swaddled infant is being suckled by a homely lady wearing a flowered skirt. The figure relies upon its graceful lines and charming attitude for beauty but has not the sophisticated elegance of 'The Music Lesson'. The Nurse was produced in 1755, which must have been a vintage year as it also saw the creation of 'Leda and the Swan' and a superb cock and hen. Chelsea was also producing 'porcelain toys'—scent bottles, étuis and patch-boxes, and for dandies there were Chelsea cane-handles and seals.

The Chelsea China Works was patronized by Royalty: George II, foreseeing an English Meissen, is said to have helped the factory in its early

---

[1] The owner of this group, wanting to buy a second-hand car, put it up for sale, hoping that it would raise between £50 and £100. It went for £3,250 (in 1929). *Apollo*, January 1944, p. 122. A replica is in the V. and A.

days by importing materials and workmen from Saxony. His second son, William Augustus, Duke of Cumberland, the victor of Culloden, displayed a surprising interest in porcelain which he passed on to his nephew, George III. In 1763, King George and Queen Charlotte ordered a dinner service from Chelsea as a present to the Duke of Mecklenburg-Strelitz. It cost £1,200: 'dishes and plates without number,' wrote Horace Walpole to Sir Horace Mann, on March 4, 1763, 'an epergne, candlestick, saltcellars, sauce-boats, tea and coffee equipages'—but he adds, 'I cannot boast of our taste; the forms were neither new, beautiful, nor various.'

In 1769, Sprimont, by now a wealthy man but in poor health, retired to the country, and the business was taken over by William Duesbury, who came from Derby, but was working with the Chelsea factory as far back as 1751. The Chelsea Library has a copy of his Account Book between this year and 1753, when he seems to have been employed making small details such as flowers, and doing repairs. Some extracts give an idea of the variety of these jobs.

For purpleing the Quishng (cushion), large pugg Doggs	6d
2 pair of squerrills to repair	2/-
1 pair Gardinars	3/-
1 Doussan (dozen) of Tewlips	2/-
A Dancing man Repaired this bill is gone in this is not payd	
1 pair of Chelsey phesants to repar	
3 pair of torcks (Turks) and torkises	15/-
2 pair of Jupetors and Junose	6/-

Duesbury was proprietor of the works for ten years. Then, in 1779, 'the leases of the premises being expir'd', he offered the stock for sale at Christie's but orders continued to be fulfilled. Five years later, the china works finally closed, and a workman left in charge wrote to Duesbury:

'Lawrence Street, Chelsea, Feb. 18, 1784,—Sir, I wright to inform yow how we are pretty forward in the pulling Down of the buildings at Chelsey.' He adds, 'I wish you would lett me no if yow will have the mold of the Large figur of Britannia sent to the Ware hous or Broake.'

Apparently many of the Chelsea moulds were destroyed: others were removed to Derby, where William Duesbury continued to work. But Chelsea was dead. The lovely birds and beasts, the flowers and harlequins, the tureens modelled like ducks and peacocks, ceased to be made—cast and painted with such exquisite skill by men who gave their lives to the work for wages totalling a few shillings a day. Only the failures, broken up and thrown into the ground, remain to tell us where this flourishing industry once stood.

Monmouth House, at the head of Lawrence Street, consisted in fact of four houses, of which the Duchess of Monmouth had occupied the two on the eastern side. In 1749 Tobias Smollett came to Chelsea, hoping that the good air would benefit his young daughter, who was suffering from tuberculosis. He occupied the central house on the western side. This optimistic, hot-tempered, generous Scotsman began life as a surgeon's mate in Ogle's West India Squadron. In Jamaica he met and married a creole lady who brought him a modest fortune in property and slaves. He brought his wife to London, where he set up in practice as a surgeon, and between patients (they were not frequent) began to write. His first successful novel, *Roderick Random*, appeared the year before he moved to Chelsea. In *Humphry Clinker*, written more than twenty years later, he describes his 'plain yet decent habitation which opened backwards into a very pleasant garden'. According to this account, every Sunday Smollett threw his house open 'to all unfortunate brothers of the quill, whom he treats with beef, pudding and potatoes, port punch, and Calvert's entire butt beer'. But his guests appear to have been badly behaved and ungrateful, which must have been poor consolation when he found himself running into debt. Like his fellow writer Leigh Hunt, who lived, a hundred years later, close by in Upper Cheyne Row, Smollett was harassed by duns and obliged to borrow money. 'I have since paid one hundred and twenty pounds to different tradesmen,' he wrote, 'from a small remittance we have received. We have granted ample power to Tom Bontein to sell our negroes in the West Indies.'

In 1763 his daughter died. She was fifteen, and his only child. He decided to turn his back on Chelsea, and he and his wife set off for France, 'overwhelmed by the sense of a domestic calamity, which it was not in the power of fortune to repay'. Nevertheless, he continued to think kindly of his seven years 'retirement' at Monmouth House, and his Chelsea friends of the club and coffee-house—'a set of honest phlegmatic Englishmen, whom I cultivate for their integrity of heart and simplicity of manners', which is an interesting side-light on the Chelsea gentry of this time.

Blind Sir John Fielding, the Presiding Magistrate at Bow Street and brother of Henry Fielding the novelist, was Smollett's neighbour at Monmouth House. He was a keen social reformer, and devoted himself to a plan to avert crime by drafting pauper boys into the Navy. The life at sea evidently benefited these lads, to judge from a newspaper report of 1757:

'Yesterday above 100 stout Boys went from Mr. Justice Fielding's to the Royal Exchange, to be reviewed by the Marine Society, from thence they went to the Sign of the Ship, and dined together; and in the Evening they attended the above Magistrate to Ranelagh-House, where Acis and Galatea was inimitably performed to a most numerous, polite and brilliant Audience . . . The Boys were placed in the Galleries, and gave great satisfaction to their kind Benefactors. After the first Act they expressed their Thanks by Three Cheers and marched off to Portsmouth in great Spirits.'

This great and good man also concerned himself with the totally inadequate fire precautions in force in the mid-eighteenth century. Fire engines consisted of water tanks on wheels, drawn and operated by Thames watermen, who were paid sixpence for a chimney on fire, and two-and-sixpence for a house ablaze. It seems that, nearly a hundred years after, London had learnt few lessons from the Great Fire. Sir John campaigned against bonfires in the streets on the Fifth of November, asserting that 'Seldom a bonfire is made but several lives are Lost'—a statement which has a familiar ring today. He also suggested that it might be a good idea if fire brigades were equipped with ladders. This became compulsory in 1774: it is odd that no one had thought of it before.

Sir John Fielding was deeply concerned at the increase of crime and violence in London, and he set out to find a way of breaking up the robber gangs that infested the city and its outskirts. As Hogarth shows us, poverty and drunkenness went hand in hand, and were the chief causes of crime. Gin was dirt cheap and could be sold without a licence, so every slum had its gin shops where those intent on robbery could put fire into themselves for twopence. Chelsea had a bad name both for drunkenness and crime. Chelsea Common, north of the King's Road, was a notorious haunt of highwaymen, and the Five Fields—the Eaton Square district—was so dangerous that many Londoners, like Richard Steele, preferred after dining in Chelsea to stop the night and return by daylight.

The newspapers were full of accounts of robberies.

'On Sunday morning last about 8 o'clock Mr. Rogers of Chelsea crossing the Common in order to go to Kensington was knocked down and robbed by two Footpads who robb'd him of his money and beat him in a barbarous manner and then made off across the Fields towards Little Chelsea.'

'A Gentleman was knocked down at Half-an-hour past Eleven on Wednesday night, on the Back of Chelsea College Wall by two Footpads who robbed him of Four Guineas and a Half, a Five-and three-penny Piece and Six Shillings in Silver, and after wards broke his Sword about him because he had not his Watch with him.'

Sometimes the violence was more serious, and rewards were offered for the capture of the criminals.

'On 16th April, 1765, Mr. James House Knight, of Walham Green, returning home from London, was robbed and murdered on the highroad in the vicinity of Little Chelsea. A reward of £50 was offered for the discovery of the murderers. On the 7th of July following, two Chelsea Pensioners were committed to prison charged with this murder, on the testimony of their accomplice, another Chelsea Pensioner.' This was an ugly affair. The two Pensioners were found guilty and hanged, after which their tarred bodies were hung on gibbets in the Fulham Road, the scene of the murder, where they remained for some years, objects of horror and warning to passers-by.

Earlier in the century the Royal Hospital had been called in on the side of the law. In 1715, in an effort to protect the woefully undefended public, a Patrol was formed of Pensioners, who took turns to man the sentry boxes which were set up at intervals on the road between St. James's and Chelsea. The Patrol consisted of two Sergeants, four Corporals and twenty Privates, who were issued with stout shoes and stockings, and hooded cloaks made of Devonshire Kersey, to keep them warm and dry. They did their best, poor old men, bravely shouldering their muskets with bayonets fixed, but the thieves were undaunted, and in March 1716 attacked the Patrol, killing one Pensioner and wounding another, who was afterwards awarded three guineas by the Chelsea Board for his 'good behaviour and sufferings'.

After this the Patrol was strengthened by the addition of six more Pensioners and three more sentry boxes, and a guardhouse was built at Ebury Farm; but the thieves were undeterred. Lord Stanley and his brother, in a post-chaise, were held up by four footpads, with whom they fought, Lord Stanley wounding one of the men 'on the back of the head with a scymetar'. 'The two ruffians at the heads of the horses then went to the assistance of their comrades, when the postillions driving furiously on, the Nobleman and his brother escaped unhurt.' If you were a nobleman in a post-chaise, and possessed a 'scymetar', you had certain advantages over the ordinary citizen. Smollett, for instance, was robbed of his watch and money while sitting in the stage coach from Chelsea to London.

In 1783, the Governor of the Royal Hospital reported to the Board that the number of men he could muster were 'not enough to clear the Roads and prevent Robberies', which, he said, were become so frequent and daring as to be alarming.

But by this time Sir John Fielding had got to work: he initiated a patrol which became known as the Bow Street Runners. There were mobile, well organized and vigilant: forerunners of the Police Force. They succeeded in inspiring respect among thieves. 'Some robberies having been committed within these few days in the King's private road, and the environs of Chelsea, on Monday night some of Sir John Fielding's people went in search of the offenders, and one of them was soon after attacked by two ruffians armed with pistols and a cutlass, but *perceiving their mistake*, the robbers endeavoured to make off; they were, however, apprehended.'

It was the beginning of a new era. Soon it would be possible to walk from London to Chelsea at night, unarmed and unmolested.

CHAPTER THREE

I N CHARLES II'S REIGN a number of discharged soldiers, battered and maimed in wars at home and abroad, roamed the country, homeless and destitute. Many, unable to scrape a living, died. The pretty story that Nell Gwynne drew the King's attention to the plight of the old soldiers and begged him to provide them with a home is now discredited; but someone did draw his attention to it, and his son the Duke of Monmouth sent him from France a detailed description of l'Hôtel des Invalides, which Louis XIV had built for his disabled soldiers.

The plan for constructing a hospital at Chelsea seems to have originated with Sir Stephen Fox:[1] in 1681 Evelyn noted that he dined with Fox, who proposed to him the purchasing of Chelsea College[2] from the Royal Society, 'to build an hospital or infirmary for soldiers there'. A year later, Evelyn writes: 'This evening Sir Stephen Fox acquainted me with His Majesty's resolution of proceeding in the erection of a Royal Hospital.' The King had bought the land for £1,300, and promised to settle £5,000 per annum on the Hospital, and to build 'to the value of £20,000'.

Unfortunately King Charles ran short of money. He wrote to the Archbishops of Canterbury and York telling them that 'out of a tender and deep compassion of ye sad and deplorable condition of so many loial and brave men . . . [we] have . . . resolved to found and erect at Chelsey (in a place very proper for such a design) a perpetuall hospital, in which more than 400 aged or otherwise disabled soldiers may at present (and so successively ye same number for ever) be lodged and supplied with ye necessary supports of life suitable to their respective conditions.' The Archbishops, invited by the King to raise funds through an appeal to the richer patrons of each diocese, were dubious. 'Hatred and contempt we may get,' wrote York to Canterbury, 'but no money.'

---

[1] Fox, a Tory, was father of the first Lord Holland, and grandfather of the great Whig, Charles James Fox.

[2] Chelsea College, built in James I's reign, was intended as a theological college for the study of the Scriptures and the reinforcement of the Protestant faith 'against the pedantry, Sophistries and novelties of the Jesuits and others . . . that draw towards Popery and Babylonian slavery'. The building was never completed, and during Cromwell's rule was used as a prison. In 1666 it was taken over by the Royal Society, who considered building an observatory there.

But the money had to be found, for the plan was by this time under weigh. Sir Stephen Fox set about raising money, and was, said Evelyn, 'himself a great benefactor'. Perhaps there was a reason for this.

Fox, an ardent Royalist, had fought at the battle of Worcester, and helped Charles escape after the disastrous defeat. As a reward, Charles on becoming King made Sir Stephen the first Paymaster General of the Forces. While he held this office Fox, an astute man, succeeded in making a considerable income on the side. At this time the troops were paid at long and irregular intervals, and often suffered considerable hardship. Fox offered to make them regular payments out of his own pocket, charging them a shilling in the pound for the service. This plan worked well, and it has been reckoned that he made an annual profit of over six thousand pounds. So he had, as Evelyn put it, 'gotten a vast estate by the soldiers', and may have felt that he owed them something in return.

After dinner, as they sat over their port in Sir Stephen's study, he and John Evelyn drew up plans for the running of the Hospital. There would be, they decided, 'a governor, chaplain, steward, housekeeper, chirurgeon, cook, butler, gardener, porter'. There must also, said Evelyn, be a library, 'since some soldiers might possibly be studious'.

In 1682 a foundation stone was laid, and building began.

Originally a mathematician and astronomer, Sir Christopher Wren had in twenty years won an unchallenged position as architect of the new London which had risen from the ashes of the Great Fire, with St. Paul's as its centrepiece and the City Churches its chief ornaments. His design for the Chelsea Hospital is dignified and curiously simple, relying for its beauty upon repetition of the same pattern of roofs and chimneys and windows, their symmetry divided by the central Doric portico crowned by a cupola.

'The Royall Hospitall at Chelsey is pleasantly seated on a plane of gravell overlooking the Meadowes and the River Thames, which lies to the South, and having the prospect of the City and a pleasant view of the Country on all sides. It consists of a large Courte built on three sides, the fourth side next to the Thames lying open to the gardens and Meadows.'

So Wren began the description of his project, which accompanied his drawings and scale model. His eye took in the whole scene, and his design was completed in his mind to fit into the landscape. More land was needed in front of the building, to make an impressive approach; a piece of ground known as Burtons Court was bought from Lord Cheyne and, to save money, let to a farmer, Thomas Franklyn, for six years. The progress of the work was constantly being held up owing to shortage of money, and it was eight years before the main building was finished. By this time it was known that there would be considerably more than four hundred In-Pensioners, and more accommodation would have to be added, but the money was used up and King Charles was dead.

Fortunately for the Hospital, King James was better off than his brother; he was anxious, moreover, to promote his own popularity, and the idea of being a benefactor to the soldiers pleased him. As the queue for admittance grew longer after the defeat of Monmouth's rebellion, he decreed that all soldiers eligible for the Hospital should at once be paid a pension in proportion to the extent of their wounds, till the building should be ready to receive them.

As it turned out, this was not for another seven years. In 1692, under William and Mary, the Royal Hospital was at last finished, furnished, supplied with a Governor and staff, and every detail of its administration arranged. A committee composed of Lord Ranelagh (Paymaster General and Treasurer), Sir Stephen Fox and Sir Christopher Wren had been commissioned for this work, and to plan the catering, to appoint gardeners, a barber and a launderer, and to organize the lighting, which consisted of candles, lamps and lanterns (no candles were allowed in the men's rooms). The place was heated entirely by coal fires, and an allowance of coal doled out, which must at times have been inadequate. Coals were issued throughout the winter, from which the Pensioners were expected to keep back a small supply for use when needed during the summer. This led to a murder.

In 1801, violent quarrels arose between two old soldiers, one wanting to use up the fuel they shared during the cold season, the other insisting on economy. Efforts were made to stop the quarrels, but without avail. Finally the improvident one burst open the door of his neighbour's room brandishing a pistol and insisting that they should fight a duel. The other, knocking the pistol out of his hand, refused, whereupon the aggressor without further ado shot him through the heart. He was tried for murder, and though his conduct 'previous to this unhappy affair' had been exemplary, was hanged.

The food was good: 'one sees as good Meat at Dinner as one can buy for Money,' wrote one visitor. Firkins of salt butter were bought at fivepence a pound, and supplies of Gloucester cheese at threepence. Bread (wholemeal) was baked on the premises, and beer (seven and sixpence for a thirty-six-gallon barrel) was supplied with meals. The sick in the Infirmary were given wine.

The first Pensioners' uniform consisted of 'a red cloth coat with Brass

Buttons lined with blue Bays [baize] and false sleeves' with a large cypher of the King and Queen on the back, and blue kersey breeches. Their hats were black tricornes bound with gold tinsel, and they wore blue woollen stockings and buckled shoes. The uniform varied slightly according to rank, and changes were made over the years, such as the elimination of William and Mary's cipher and the introduction, in 1703, of waistcoats 'of blew Cloth lined with white fustian' for officers, and 'Blew Kersey lined with white Hessens linen, with Brass Buttons' for the lower ranks.

Officers, upon admission, all became Ensigns, regardless of their status in the Army, and received three and sixpence a week. Light Horsemen were next in importance, being paid two shillings a week and addressed as 'Mr.'. Sergeants were also paid two shillings, corporals and drummers tenpence and privates eightpence. After 1719, when disabled officers were awarded half pay, few officers applied for admission to the Hospital.

Many of the old soldiers must have enjoyed the regular meals and healthy surroundings, and some took on a new lease of life. One of these was William Hiseland, a veteran who, when he was admitted, 'had served the Crown upwards of eighty years, and signalised himself in a gallant manner at Edgehill Fight against the Parliament Army; was also in the Wars in Ireland under King William; and likewise served His Grace the late Duke of Marlborough through all his Campaigns in Flanders'. At the age of a hundred this valiant Pensioner married, and spent the next twelve years going to and fro (married In-Pensioners have to meet their wives outside the Hospital). He then died, though it is hard to see why, for according to his tombstone, 'His Complexion was fresh and florid, his Health hale and hearty, his Memory exact and ready. In Stature he exceeded the Military size. In Strength he surpassed the prime of Youth'. His portrait, painted in 1730 by George Alsop, hangs in the Great Hall.

Military discipline obtained. Regular hours were observed, as in a barracks. The gates were locked at 10 p.m., and anyone returning after this hour was shut up in the guardroom for the night. The Pensioners were also expected to perform certain military duties: as has been seen, they formed a patrol for the protection of citizens against robbers.[1] They also manned their own guardhouses, one at each side of the Hospital, and one at the entrance to Burtons Court.

Nobody knows why this spacious piece of ground is called Burtons[2] Court, though Alfred Beaver tells us that there was a Sir Edmund Burton

[1] In 1759 they were ordered to be in readiness 'in case of an Invasion' which, however, did not materialize.
[2] The apostrophe is generally omitted.

living in Chelsea in Edward VI's reign, and suggests that this may have been the site of his house. The land today is divided into two: on the west is the cricket ground bordered by plane trees; on the east an enclosure with lawns and gravel paths, where Chelsea dogs and children frisk, under escort. For this privilege their parents or owners pay an annual subscription to the Royal Hospital, and dogs (but not children) are subject to military discipline, biters and brawlers being smartly shown the gate, and refused readmission by the porter.

In 1687 the Burtons Court porter was named, by an odd chance, Button. He lived in the eastern of the two lodges, and was given an impressive green livery. His duties seem, for the most part, to have been inside the main building, which in those days was not divided from Burtons Court by a road. He was expected to 'open and shut the Gates every morning and evening, attend in the kitchen when the meat was taken in, cut up and served, attend at the Cupola during Divine Service, that the Congregation may not be disturbed by idle persons or Dogs; to prevent people begging in the Hospital, idle persons or Vagrants loitering about in the Stair Cases and Passages, Boys and Children making a noise or disturbance in the Courts, and to take care that the Walls are not defaced or Windows broke'. It was no sinecure, but Button stayed the course for thirty years.

In spite of damage suffered in the two wars of this century, the appearance of the Royal Hospital has changed hardly at all, and, the subject of so many prints and paintings, is easily recognized today. The building we pass in a 39 bus—'that magnificent hospital,' as Bowack called it—was described by Narcissus Luttrell as 'that stately fabrick'. A hundred years or so later we find Samuel Rogers referring to it as 'Chelsea's glorious pile', while Carlyle, more restrained, and possibly more apt, considered that it was 'quiet and dignified and the work of a gentleman'.

Though the front remains so little changed, there is a difference at the back, where Wren designed formal gardens on three levels, divided by balustrades. In the lowest garden two canals, separated by a gravel walk, ran at right angles to the river, and were stocked with fish and water birds, a pleasant whim of Wren's, which provided problems for later generations. The canals became choked with weeds, grew muddy, overflowed, and got filled up with unpleasant refuse, including dead dogs. But the general effect, seen from the river, with young trees planted on either side, was impressive. In the centre of Figure Court, from which the gardens descended, was set the equestrian statue by Grinling Gibbons of the Hospital's founder. A rather unfamiliar King Charles, wearing neither wig nor moustache, sits astride his horse in the dress of a Roman general. He still commands a fine prospect to the south, but the gardens no longer run down to the river: the busy Embankment with its constant flow of traffic cuts across the lower expanse, which is a public garden. Here, in the early summer, the Chelsea Flower Show, which used to confine itself to Ranelagh garden, now spreads its enormous tents, and milling crowds flock from far and wide to see the prize blooms.

The Royal Hospital was officially opened to Pensioners on March 28, 1692, and should have been ready earlier. The central building, planned by Charles II, took eight years to complete, and was finished in 1689. The enlargement, under James II, consisted of the addition of the two wings to east and west, with their quadrangles, which became known respectively as the Light Horse and Infirmary Courts. Under William and Mary a further £60,000 was spent—more than had been sanctioned by either previous monarch; and the buildings for which it was used appear relatively humble, a laundry, a bakehouse, a coal store, garden sheds. Two summerhouses were designed by Wren—one at each end of the river wall, and an 'Elabritory' where the apothecary attached to the Hospital could manufacture his pills and potions. It was placed far from the other buildings on account of the unpleasant smells that issued from its chimney. But £60,000 was a large sum to spend on outbuildings.

However, any uncertainty as to the destination of the rest of the money fades when one remembers that Lord Ranelagh had the spending of it and was at this time engaged in building himself a house on the east side of the Hospital—a handsome house, as befitted the Paymaster General and Treasurer, and designed, like the Hospital, by Wren.

This fantastic character held his important post from 1685 to 1702, when he was found guilty of gross fraud and dismissed. He died ten years later but his name lived on in the famous pleasure gardens which opened on his Chelsea estate. He was forty-five when he first came to the Hospital, a handsome, plausible Irish rascal, who had been obliged, in 1680, to leave Ireland for good. 'Few trusted him,' wrote Bishop Burnet,[1] 'though everybody loved his company.'

Ranelagh's charm must indeed have been extraordinary, for in spite of shady transactions when he was Chancellor of the Irish Exchequer, he was made Vice-Treasurer of Ireland in 1674, and given an earldom three years later.

It is perhaps fortunate for him that one of his daughters became Charles

[1] Bishop of Salisbury, a friend of Ranelagh's uncle, Robert Boyle, who lived in little Chelsea.

II's mistress, for in 1680 an action was brought against him in Ireland for embezzlement of public funds: he owed £76,000, and was obliged to leave the country for good. In England, unemployed and penniless, the Earl managed to pull strings at Court, and in the course of time succeeded in landing an annuity paid out of the Irish revenue, and in getting the action against him suspended 'for the present' by the King's intervention.

It seems odd that a man with such a record should be appointed Paymaster General and Treasurer to the Royal Hospital, but this was brought about in 1685, through the agency of Laurence Hyde, Earl of Rochester and Lord Treasurer, who was a distant relation of Ranelagh's.

'My dear Lord,' Ranelagh wrote . . . 'I return you a thousand thanks for my Paymaster's place and a hundred thousand for the place you are pleased to give me in your good opinion, and having thus given you a hundred and eleven thousand thanks, I subscribe myself, which I am sure I am, Your Lordship's etc., Ranelagh.'

It was perhaps as well that his arithmetic did not affect his appointment

Ranelagh had a strong aversion to submitting accounts, but was evidently clever at handling people, and a good administrator. 'He had great dexterity in business,' said Burnet; and in consequence the appointment was not as disastrous as it might have been. Moreover, for the first four years he was obliged to work with Wren and Fox. It was not till Fox's retirement, for political reasons, at the accession of William and Mary, that Ranelagh began to have a free rein. When he was appointed in 1685, his salary was £2,000: he now asked for a rise. £3,000 a year, he told King William, was what the Treasurer of the Navy received, 'who had not halfe so much Buisnesse'. He also suggested that he should keep back the sum of £6,911 which happened to by lying about, to pay for his travelling expenses on an official visit to Salisbury. The extraordinary thing is that the King agreed.

It was lucky for Ranelagh that William III was obliged to spend a great deal of time abroad, and so the Paymaster was able to devote himself to the building of his own house at public expense, without fear of losing the king's favour. It may also have been lucky that the first Governor of the Hospital, Sir Thomas Ogle, was a feeble old man, prematurely aged. He reached the rank of Lieutenant Colonel at sixty-four, and after his appointment to the Hospital, resigned his commission and settled down to lead a quiet life. In 1702 he lost his greyhound and offered ten shillings reward for its recovery. Six months later, perhaps from grief at its loss, he died. It seems unlikely that his presence at Chelsea caused the Earl of Ranelagh a moment's uneasiness.

His lordship succeeded in nominating a crony, Ralph Cook, to the post of Deputy Treasurer, which must have made it easier for him to cook the accounts. When Ranelagh House was completed, Ralph Cook inherited the large suite of rooms which Ranelagh had occupied in the central bay of Light Horse building.

Ranelagh House stood in its own grounds, which lay to the east of the Royal Hospital. It was built, like the Hospital, of brick with stone facings and slate roofs, and with the symmetry of design displayed in all the buildings. It was intended to be the official residence of the Treasurer, so to some extent Ranelagh was justified in lavishing public money upon it, but it is significant that the coat of arms over the entrance was his own. A contemporary description (1691) tells us that the house was 'very fine within, all the rooms being wainscotted with Norway oak, and all the chimneys adorned with carvings'. These carvings were later attributed to Grinling Gibbons, but were in fact the work of William Emmett, who did the carving in the Chapel and Great Hall of the Hospital, and who was paid (by the Hospital) £150 for this extra piece of work.

Ranelagh now turned his attention to the garden. He was determined to make it magnificent, productive and decorative, using as much land as he could reasonably appropriate. In 1690 he petitioned the King for a long lease of the land, and was granted one for sixty-one years at a nominal rent of £15 7s. 6d. per annum. He then got to work on his garden, and a gardener called Philip Buffler planted an orchard for him, which cost £189 (paid from Hospital funds), and which contained a wide variety of delicious fruits, as well as sunflowers and roses. By this time his lordship had laid out an elaborate flower garden, with 'vastly agreeable walks, small pools, tolerable plants and many charming pots of flowers and statues'—including one of King William. He also built himself a laundry, a large aviary and a 'bathing house'.

By this time his expenses had increased, for he had married a second wife, the Dowager Lady Stawell, who as Lady Margaret Cecil had been one of Kneller's 'Beauties of Hampton Court'. He was determined to ensure that the house and grounds should remain in his family, and accordingly wrote to the King in 1697, describing himself as 'a great sufferer by the late war in Ireland, having lost nearly £12,000 in rent, and his castles of Roscommon and Athlone being utterly ruined; his mansion in Dublin being pulled down' etc., etc., and petitioning for 'the inheritance of his house att Chelsea . . . that he may be thereby enabled to make such a Settlement thereof as may preserve the same in his Family'.

Unfortunately, King William was abroad, and the Treasury Commissioners were not moved by Ranelagh's pitiful appeal. The petition was set aside 'till His Majesty's return'.

Meanwhile, Godolphin's place as head of the Treasury Board was taken by one Charles Montague. Ranelagh invited him to stay. Montague, a recent widower, was entertained lavishly, and his attentive host showed him 'many pleasing objects to divert melancholy'. He could hardly have helped being impressed by Ranelagh's well-ordered house and grounds, in which 'the very Greenhouses and Stables (adorned with Festoons, Urns, etc.) have an Air of Grandeur not to be seen in many Princes Pallaces. And which way soever a Man turns his Eyes, he views such Elegancies as fills him at once with Delight and Wonder'. Moreover he probably believed his host's claim that the whole thing had been created at his own expense.

Four months after this visit, in November 1698, the Treasury awarded Lord Ranelagh a grant in perpetuity of all the land on his Chelsea Estate, subject to a rent of £5 a year, to be paid to the Royal Hospital. He had succeeded in appropriating about one third of the entire Hospital property.

On January 1, 1701–2, Luttrell wrote in his diary, 'It's discoursed the Earl of Ranelagh, Paymaster to the Army . . . will be discharged.'

However, six months later he wrote, 'The Earl of Ranelagh has had his commission renewed for continuing Paymaster to the Army.'

But Ranelagh's luck was running out. In 1702 King William, who had been his ally, died. Parliament decided that it was time to make an enquiry into the finances of the Royal Hospital, and though it was found that the Paymaster was incapable of producing any comprehensible accounts, it was also discovered that for some six years a number of Out-Pensioners had not received their pensions, 'near five thousand pounds or thereabouts—most of which, if not all, is owing to the inhabitants of Westminster and Chelsea, who have supported them ever since the year 1696'. This was the beginning of a melancholy history of corruption and dishonesty, which was brought to light during the next two years. In 1704 the Committee of Public Accounts found Lord Ranelagh guilty of gross fraud. But long before this, in December 1702, he had resigned from his post as Paymaster General. In February 1703 he was expelled from the House of Commons; but with characteristic resilience only five months later he applied to Godolphin, the Lord Treasurer, signing himself 'the unfortunate Richard, Earl of Ranelagh' and asking for a job as he had 'had the misfortune to loose all his employments after many years' service'.

Somehow he managed to get on the right side of Queen Anne, who made

him a Governor of her Bounty for the help of poor clergy. It is to be hoped
that the poor clergy were better served by him than the poor Pensioners.
And then, unbelievably, he was appointed a Privy Councillor, although by
now it was known that his Army accounts showed a deficit of £72,000.

He was very hard up, and wrote a number of begging letters, referring
to himself as 'poor old Ranelagh'. He tried, unsuccessfully, to sell his
Chelsea house, and then tried to retrieve the sum of £3,250, which he had
taken some years before from his daughter's marriage portion because he
disliked her husband, and put in trust as a legacy to the Chelsea Pensioners. Finding that he could not get at the money, he decided to make a
grand gesture. The income of £200 was to be used, he ordered, to buy
overcoats once every three years for all the Pensioners (except officers and
Light Horsemen, who presumably did not need them) at a cost of £1
apiece.

The balance from this legacy was to be devoted to 'drink money' every
Founder's Day: five shillings for a Light Horseman, four shillings for a
Sergeant or Matron, three shillings for a Corporal or drummer, and two
shillings for a Private. So perhaps, after all, the name of Ranelagh was
kindly remembered once a year after January 5, 1712, when he died.

Although its generations of inmates have fought in wars which are now
history, there is a timelessness about the Royal Hospital which gives it a
monastic dignity, a feeling of endurance. 'For ever,' said King Charles of
his plan to lodge old soldiers at Chelsea. Now, after nearly three hundred
years visitors see it as a working community, with a way of life which has
changed very little. Pensioners today are probably warmer, better lit and
more comfortably housed than in the past; they eat their meals in the
Great Hall (as Wren intended they should), and not brought round half
cold on trolleys to their rooms, as for generations they did. They draw
their pensions from the nearby post office, and wear, except for best,
practical navy blue uniforms instead of the decorative scarlet coats of
tradition; but otherwise there is little outward change. Like the Knights
of Windsor and the Yeomen Warders at the Tower, the Chelsea Pensioners are a British institution.

The Hon. Lady Napier, who has lived in Chelsea for many years, spent
part of her youth at the Royal Hospital, where her father, Field Marshal
Sir George White, V.C., was Governor between 1906 and 1912. She remembers visiting the Infirmary with her family every Sunday, when 'one
old soldier aged a hundred always had a good story ready—a different one
each week—about his valour in the field. He may have laid it on a bit
thick, but we always enjoyed listening'. Another young girl, now Mrs.

Hyacinth Nottridge, remembers shaking hands with an old man who had fought at Balaclava and ridden in the charge of the Light Brigade. Generations of Chelsea children have been fascinated by the old men in their red coats, and links in time must often have been forged: in the 1880s Oscar Wilde's son Vyvyan had tea with a Pensioner who had been a drummer boy at Waterloo, a battle which, to listen to one of the old men who conduct visitors round the Hospital Museum, is still as clear in some minds as if it had been fought yesterday.

U NTIL A year or two ago there was a half-ruined building on the west side of the Royal Hospital, behind where the new Military Museum now stands. This fragment was all that remained of the Hospital Infirmary, which was bombed in the 1940s. It was designed by Sir John Soane as part of his scheme for additions and alterations on this side of the Hospital early in the nineteenth century. In the Soane Museum Sir John's drawings show that the Infirmary was built on the site of Walpole's house, and that the southernmost part of the original house was left untouched inside. The large room on the ground floor became Ward 7 of the Infirmary, and is described by L'Estrange, in 1880, as having 'a splendid white marble mantelpiece and Greek mouldings on the transverse beams of the ceiling'. 'Everything,' he adds, 'speaks of former grandeur, and rightly, for this was the drawing room of a mansion of great renown, in which the great Sir Robert Walpole received his guests.'

Firmly encased in yellow brickwork by Soane, with its elegant windows altered to conform with his general, rather dull, design, this was all that remained of the Whig leader's summer residence. Walpole had been Paymaster of the Royal Hospital in 1714, and again in 1720, and in acquiring this site for his house he displayed the same astuteness as did Lord Ranelagh: he is even thought to have used some of Ranelagh's questionable methods of paying the builders. But in this case there was a house already there, erected by William Jephson, Secretary to the Treasury, in 1697. Sir Robert, in his lavish way, engaged Vanbrugh, the architect of Blenheim, to alter and enlarge this building. He also required him to design the gardens, which he added to, buying an extra piece of land on the west from his neighbour, Sir John Gough. There was already a river wall, with a gazebo at the western end, built by his predecessor; Vanbrugh designed an octagonal summer house at the other end (about where number 23, Embankment Gardens now stands). This decorative building had a pillared porch, and its roof was topped by a golden pineapple. It must have been a pretty sight from the river, and appears in many views.

There was also an L-shaped 'greenhouse' or orangery, part of which is now converted into the Hospital library. It was joined to a second rather larger orangery or pavilion designed by Wren, and here in August 1729 George II's Queen, Caroline of Ansbach, with her son Frederick, Prince of Wales, and his brothers and sisters were entertained to dinner by the Walpoles.

Elaborate preparations were made. A special outdoor kitchen with twenty fireplaces was built in the stable yard, and from there sweating servants had to carry the sumptuous dishes all the way to the orangery, which meant going through the coal yard and past the bleaching ground, bakehouse and wash-house—nearly two hundred yards; but as it was August perhaps the food did not get cold. Fruit for the dessert, said the *Monthly Chronicle*, was collected a week ahead from all over London.

'After Dinner,' the report continues, 'Her Majesty and the Royal Family retir'd to the (Octagon) Banqueting House on the river to drink Tea; where were several Barges of fine Musick playing all the Time. After which they returned to the Green House, where the illustrious company were entertained with a ball, and afterwards supp'd in the same place.'

It was a corrupt age, of which Peachum, the receiver of stolen goods in *The Beggar's Opera* sings:

> The priest calls the lawyer a cheat,
> The lawyer beknaves the divine,
> And the statesman, because he's so great,
> Thinks his trade as honest as mine.

Sir Robert Walpole probably thought his trade as honest as most: in politics, honesty was indeed his trademark. He looked honest, with his brown doglike eyes and beaming bucolic countenance. He cultivated his country-squire personality, spoke with a Norfolk accent, and every week-end flung his twenty stones astride an unfortunate horse to ride off to Richmond Park and chase deer, after which he slept in the arms of his mistress, Molly Skerrit. He ate and drank hugely; yet beneath this coarse exterior was a brilliant mind.

'No man,' wrote Hervey, 'ever was blessed with a clearer head, a truer or quicker judgment, or a deeper insight into mankind; he knew the strength and weakness of everybody he had to deal with, and how to make his advantage of both.'

His critical and fastidious son, Horace (who may not have been his son at all: Lady Walpole was unreliable), writes of him with surprising and rather touching devotion:

'Strawberry Hill, August 26, 1785 . . . On *this* day, about an hundred years ago . . . was born the wisest man I have seen. He kept this country at peace for twenty years, and it flourished accordingly. He injured no man, was benevolent, good-humoured . . . Yet was he burnt in effigy . . . and so traduced, that his memory is not purified yet!'

Walpole came to power with the House of Hanover, and 'governed the country with bad Latin' during the reign of George I, who spoke no English and his Minister no French. The Prince of Wales, that angry little man who became George II, detested Walpole and damned him for a rogue and a rascal. Walpole, for his part, referred to the Princess of Wales as a fat bitch. Fat she was—the Hanoverian kings liked large women—but Walpole was to change his opinion of her when she became queen. She was wise, clever and enterprising: she designed the Serpentine. In her young days she enjoyed being rowed about the Thames at Chelsea by the local watermen, and she once boarded a west-country barge, making friends with the sailors, and sharing their meal of bread and salt pork, for which she paid handsomely.

When George II succeeded his father, Walpole remained in office: the king could find no reason to sack him, and Caroline wished him to remain. He became her devoted servant and confidant, and before long the Tories were singing:

> You may strut, dapper George, but 'twill all be in vain;
> We know that 'tis Queen Caroline, not you that reign.

The King, like his father, spent a great deal of time in Hanover; in 1729, Queen Caroline was appointed Regent during his absence, and much of the business of state was conducted at Chelsea between Walpole and the Queen. Perhaps because of this, Walpole was nicknamed 'the Chelsea Monarch'.

Irascible, cruel and constitutionally incapable of fidelity, George II adored his large blonde wife and consulted her on everything, even the choice of his mistresses. Hervey records the famous scene on Caroline's death-bed when, in response to her entreaty to him to marry again, the King with tears streaming down his scarlet face, blubbered, 'Non! J'aurai—des—maîtresses.' To which the Queen made no other reply than: 'Ah! mon Dieu! çela n'empêche pas.'

His mistresses had been the subject of many lengthy letters which he wrote to the Queen from Hanover. In 1735 he acquired a new one, Mme. Walmoden, and Caroline was treated to a series of rapturous descriptions of every detail of her charms, the presents he had given her, and the really very trifling sum for which he had won her affection. 'I know,' he told his wife, 'that you will love the Walmoden, because she loves me.'

This was more than Caroline could bear. She confided in Walpole, who in his wisdom reminded her that she was no longer young, and if she wished to preserve her power over the King, her only course was to accept the situation with dignity. She took his advice.

Perhaps with the idea of cheering her up, shortly after this the Walpoles gave another banquet for the Queen. Caroline shared Walpole's interest in art: she had excellent taste, and it was she who found hidden away in an old bureau at Kensington Palace about a hundred Holbein drawings, now part of the Royal Collection. To please the Queen, Walpole had some of the best of his own collection of paintings taken down and hung round the walls of the Summer House where they dined. (After his death his grandson and heir sold Walpole's pictures to the Empress of Russia: 'the most signal mortification to my idolatry for my father's memory,' said Horace Walpole, 'that it could receive.')

If her gouty feet were up to it, the Queen may have been taken to see Lady Walpole's grotto, in the lower part of the garden. Grottoes were the fashion, as Gothick ruins were to become later, and Queen Caroline herself had one; so had Alexander Pope. They were artificial caverns, their walls covered with shells, curious stones, tiny mirrors and bits of brightly coloured glass. Lady Walpole had evidently spared no pains to make her grotto celebrated and when it was reported that she had received a present of shells from the Channel Islands, the *Gentleman's Magazine* published a sarcastic poem:

> Whilst patriots murmur at the weight
>   Of taxes that support the State;
> See how the isles obeisance pay
>   To W–l–p–le's most auspicious sway!
> Each little isle with generous zeal
>   Sends grateful every precious shell;
> Shells in which Venus and her train
>   Of nymphs ride stately o'er the main . . .
> To make the W–l–p–le grotto fine
>   And rival grotto Caroline.

Lady Walpole's grotto has long disappeared, buried under Chelsea Embankment. The summer house in which she entertained Queen Caroline was pulled down in 1809; the octagon was removed in 1871 to make way for the new road.

All trace of Walpole's lavishly planned house and garden has now vanished. Only the name, Walpole Street, remains to jog our memories. We may remember his peccadilloes, his Miss Skerrit at Richmond ('How happy could I be with either,' wrote John Gay, of Walpole, his wife and his mistress: he was happy with both, and when Lady Walpole died he married Molly Skerrit); his extravagance—he died owing £40,000—and his high-handed and not over-scrupulous handling of the Royal Hospital accounts. But Walpole should also be remembered as a statesman who brought his country 'twenty years of peace, and credit, and happiness, and liberty'.

After Walpole's death the house was let for a short time to the Duke of Newcastle,[1] a nervous personage who married late in life. Horace Walpole chose a time when the Newcastles were away to pay a nostalgic visit.

August 5, 1746: . . . 'I went t'other night to look at my poor favourite Chelsea, for the little Newcastle is gone to be dipped in the sea. In one of the rooms is a bed for her Duke, and a press-bed for his footman, for he never dares lie alone, and till he was married, had always a servant to sit up with him.'

In 1759 the house was taken by Mr. George Aufrere, an art collector who placed a statue of Neptune by Bernini inside the octagon summer house. Mr. Aufrere had his lease extended to 1825, and when he died in 1800 left the house to his son-in-law; but meanwhile the Royal Hospital began to require more space for the increasing numbers of Pensioners and of wounded men from the American War of Independence.

The Duke of York, Commander-in-Chief of the Army, was informed of the Hospital's need to expand, and the matter was put into the hands of his secretary, Lieutenant Colonel Gordon. Numerous suggestions were afoot. In 1805 Samuel Wyatt, Clerk of the Works, suggested that the Governor's wing should be converted into rooms for 120 Pensioners and that the leasehold of Walpole's House should be bought for the Governor. Sir David Dundas, the Governor, was in favour of this, and wanted to buy the grounds of Ranelagh as well 'either for a military hospital, or extension of the Royal Hospital, and for preservation from other buildings'. Nothing came of this, but in November 1808 the lease of Walpole's house was suddenly bought by the Treasury: it was rumoured that the young Princess Charlotte of Wales, a girl of fourteen, was to occupy the house. But nothing came of this either, which was a pity, for the Regent's daughter, an independent and original character, might have been happy in Chelsea. Then Dr. Benjamin Moseley, the Hospital Physician, suggested that Walpole's House should be converted into an infirmary, and the Chelsea Board applied to the Treasury for possession of house and grounds. There were delays, and meanwhile Colonel Gordon, the Duke of York's secretary, had been making his own arrangements. By the time that the report came through that Walpole's House could be made into an

[1] Thomas Pelham-Holles, first Duke of Newcastle, Secretary of State, 1724–54.

Infirmary, Colonel Gordon had leased the gardens, and had engaged an architect to build him a house there.

The matter came up in Parliament; a member said that it 'bore the appearance of a scandalous job', and the Treasury authorized an enquiry. But fortunately for Gordon this scandalous job coincided with another. It had lately been discovered that the Duke of York's mistress, Mary Ann Clark, had been carrying on a successful traffic in army appointments; and the Royal Duke was obliged to resign his post as Commander-in-Chief. In the circumstances, it was felt that an inquiry into his secretary's lease would be ill-timed and might prove embarrassing to all concerned. So Colonel Gordon built his house, which is still there. The architect, Thomas Leverton, was a follower of the Adam Brothers, and Gordon House is a pleasant, dignified building standing back at the head of a short drive, surrounded by lawns and trees. Its river view has been cut off by Chelsea Embankment, but it still has the air of a country house.

Colonel Gordon became a Major General and a Commander of the Bath, and entertained the Emperor of Russia and the King of Prussia at his villa in 1814. But he is not kindly remembered at the Royal Hospital.

THE YEAR 1742 saw the defeat of Walpole and the rise to power of Pitt: the beginning of a new era. On May 24 of this year Ranelagh Gardens were opened to the public.

Lord Ranelagh's house, with its beautiful grounds, had been sold in 1733 to Lacy, the patentee of Drury Lane Theatre, who planned, to the consternation of the Royal Hospital Board, to make it a place of public entertainment. However, he ran out of money, and by the time the gardens were opened, nine years later, a company had been formed, of whom the chief shareholder was Sir Thomas Robinson, M.P. Noted for the length of his speeches in the House of Commons, 'the knight of the woeful countenance' was about to go off and govern the Barbados for five years; but on his return he became Director of Entertainments and became known as 'Ranelagh's Maypole and Garden of Delights'.

When the gardens opened, Lord Ranelagh had been dead for thirty years. But his name was to live on, and throughout the eighteenth century the very word suggested pleasure, even if that only consisted in staring and being stared at. 'Yes, Sir,' said Dr. Johnson to Boswell on their first visit, 'Yes, Sir, there are many happy people here. There are many people here who are watching hundreds, and who think hundreds are watching them.'

There were other entertainments, of course. You could partake of 'fine Imperial tea, coffee, punch and other refreshments', you could listen to music; on certain evenings you could dance and watch fireworks, and if you had a fancy for disguise, there were masquerades, for which the tickets cost from half a guinea to two guineas. The great advantage in an English summer was that you were not obliged to spend the evening out of doors. There was the Rotunda.

This building was thought to be a masterpiece of architectural ingenuity, and is described enthusiastically by everyone who has recorded his impressions of Ranelagh. It was, naturally, round, and was designed by William Jones, architect to the East India Company, in imitation of the Pantheon at Rome. Outside, it was like a smaller and more elegant Albert Hall, and it was built, for economy, entirely of wood. The interior was illuminated by thousands of naked lights, and the refreshments were pre-

Sir Robert Walpole.
Painting by Jean Baptiste Van Loo

Caroline, consort to George II.
Painting from the studio
of Charles Jervas

Walpole's Octagon Summer House, showing the Red House,
Battersea, in the distance. Water-colour by Elizabeth Gulston

The back of Monmouth House. Water-colour by Elizabeth Gulston

Interior of the Rotunda at Ranelagh. Painting by Canaletto

View of Ranelagh, showing the fountain, the canal and the Rotunda.
Ranelagh House is at the top on the right

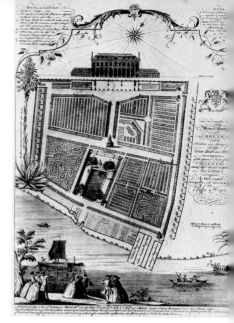

A ticket for Ranelagh

Plan of the Physic Garden,
dated 1751

Water Gate of the Physic Garden.
Water-colour by J. Fugé

pared over open fires, but nobody seems to have bothered about risks of
that sort. When you entered, the effect was magical, as we learn from the
heroines of two contemporary novels, *Evelina* and *Humphry Clinker*. The
first tells us that 'the brilliancy of the lights, on my first entrance, made me
almost think I was in some enchanted castle, or fairy palace', while Miss
Lydia Melford, in the same vein, goes into greater detail: 'Ranelagh looks
like the enchanted palace of a genio, adorned with the most exquisite per-
formances of painting, carving and gilding, enlightened with a thousand
golden lamps . . . crowded with the rich, the gay, the happy and the fair;
glittering with cloth of gold and silver, lace, embroidery and precious
stones.' But it was not only fictitious young ladies who went into raptures:
a gentleman from abroad was quite overcome:

'It is impossible to describe, or indeed to conceive, the effect it had on
me, when, coming out of the gloom of the garden, I suddenly entered a
round building, illuminated by many hundred lamps; the splendour
and beauty of which surpassed every thing of the kind I have ever seen
before.'

'Everything,' he continues, 'seemed here to be round; above, there was
a gallery divided into boxes; and in one part of it an organ with a beautiful
choir, from which issued both instrumental and vocal music. All around,
under this gallery, are handsome painted boxes for those who wish to take
refreshments.'

This visitor was struck by the variety of the assemblage of people who
promenaded slowly round and round under the chandeliers. 'An English-
man, who joined me . . . pointed out to me, on my enquiring, princes and
lords with their dazzling stars, with which they eclipsed the less brilliant
part of the company.'

Anybody who had a shilling could get into Ranelagh, and Horace Walpole, who was at the opening night, wrote that there was 'much nobility
and much mob'. Later in the century, Samuel Rogers speaks of 'persons
of inferior birth' mixing with 'the highest nobility of Britain' at Ranelagh.
By then the price of admission had gone up to half a crown.

At first Horace Walpole did not think much of Ranelagh; he preferred
Vauxhall. But soon the little slender man with his curious tiptoeing walk
began to be seen more and more at the Chelsea gardens, in his dress of
ceremony, usually lavender or grey, the waistcoat embroidered with a little
silver, his spindly legs clothed in partridge silk stockings and his feet in
gold-buckled shoes.

By June 1744 he was going 'every night constantly to Ranelagh, which
has totally beat Vauxhall. Nobody goes anywhere else; everybody goes

there. My Lord Chesterfield is so fond of it, that he says he has ordered all his letters to be directed thither'.

Ranelagh was not only patronized by the nobility: the Royal Family were often there: the King had his own box, draped with crimson damask, and 'the floor,' said Walpole, 'is all of beaten princes . . . You can't set your foot without treading on a Prince of Wales or Duke of Cumberland'. It was very democratic, and very successful. But by 1760 we find a fashionable lady complaining that there are too many tradesmen's wives at Ranelagh; and it gradually became the thing for the aristocracy to arrive late, at an hour when 'persons of inferior birth', who had to work next morning, were obliged to go home to bed.

The thoughtful management provided a variety of entertainments. From the start, Ranelagh was celebrated for music: there was a large orchestra in the Rotunda, and many noted singers and musicians were heard there. In the intervals, on fine nights, the company could stroll along tree-bordered paths, past lawns and shrubberies, to the river, the scene illuminated by lamps in the trees. Small orchestras, chiefly of wood-wind instruments ('the hautbois in the open air is heavenly,' said Evelina) were concealed in the gardens.

Ranelagh reacted to historical events. In 1749, in celebration of the Peace of Aix-la-Chapelle and to please the King, who enjoyed fancy dress parades—in Hanover he had pranced about after his wife's death dressed as a sultan with a magnificent agrafe of diamonds in his turban and Mme. Walmoden as his sultana—the management advertised a Jubilee Masquerade in the Venetian Manner. 'It had nothing Venetian in it,' said Horace Walpole, who of course was there; but he found it very pretty.

There was a thoroughly English maypole, decked with garlands, round which people in fancy dress danced to old-fashioned rustic music. All the musicians in the gardens were disguised, 'some like huntsmen with French horns, some like peasants, and a troop of harlequins and scaramouches in the little open temple on the mount (overlooking the river). In deference to Venice, there was 'a sort of gondola' on the canal, filled with more musicians, and all round the outside of the rotunda were little shops in imitation of the Piazza San Marco, filled with expensive nicknacks.

Inside the amphitheatre, which was elaborately decorated with huge fir trees in tubs, orange trees with small lamps in each orange, and below them a mass of auriculas, growing in pots, there were booths for tea and wine. There were also gaming tables, though gaming was not officially allowed, and dancing, in which about two thousand people took part. 'In short,' said Walpole, 'it pleased me more than the finest thing I ever saw.'

The 1761 season opened with a bang. It was a year of victories abroad, and at home there was a new king, a Royal Wedding and a Coronation; as Horace Walpole put it, the country was ruining itself in gunpowder and skyrockets.

By this time, the great Doctor Arne[1] was in charge of Ranelagh's music, and in honour of the King's marriage to the sadly plain Princess Charlotte of Mecklenburg-Strelitz, he composed a serenata called 'Beauty and Virtue'. Dr. Arne reigned at Ranelagh during the 1760s, when many fine singers and instrumentalists were heard there. The Italian operatic style was in fashion when Ranelagh opened, but, chiefly thanks to Arne, English singers and composers came into their own again at Ranelagh and the other London pleasure gardens, which have been called 'the nurseries of English song'. It was Handel who first used the tenor voice instead of the Italian castrato, and John Beard, who sang at Ranelagh, was Handel's first tenor. Dr. Arne's illegitimate son, Michael, the composer of 'the Lass with a Delicate air', performed at Ranelagh, and so did Charles Dibdin, the composer of *Lionel and Clarissa*, and Arne's successful pupil, Charlotte Brent, who had just played Polly Peachum at Covent Garden. In the prosperous season of 1764, after the Peace of Paris, Charlotte Brent had a benefit night, in which Handel's *Samson* was performed, conducted by Dr. Arne.

In the same season, a concert was given 'for the Benefit of a Public useful Charity'. 'In the Course of the Evening's Entertainments,' the advertisement ran, 'the celebrated and astonishing Master MOZART, lately arrived, a Child of 7 years of Age, will perform several select Pieces of his own Composition on the Harpsichord and on the Organ, which has already given the highest Pleasure, Delight and Surprize to the greatest Judges of Music in England or Italy, and is justly esteemed the most extraordinary Prodigy, and most amazing Genius that has appeared in any Age.'

It is a pity that Horace Walpole was not present to record his impressions of this concert. Master Mozart was in fact eight and a half. He spent some fifteen months in England, and for seven weeks lived with his family at a doctor's house in Fivefields Row, Chelsea (now Ebury Street). Here he wrote two symphonies, K.16 and K.19, and it is to be hoped that he took a little time off to walk round the corner to the famous Bun House and buy a Chelsea bun.

1775 was a year of feverish gaiety with storm clouds threatening across

---

[1] Thomas Arne, 1710-78, composer. Remembered chiefly for his Shakespeare songs, 'Rule Britannia' and *Love in a Village*.

the Atlantic. On July 23 there was a Regatta and Ball. This was something new, and was carefully worked out in advance. The Regatta started from the City—to the accompaniment of the bells of St. Margaret's, Westminster—and the barges of the Lord Mayor and City Companies were to move upstream to Westminster Bridge, followed by private pleasure boats, for the start of the Watermen's Race.

According to a contemporary account, the whole river from London Bridge to Millbank was covered with gaily painted boats: the river banks were like a fair, and the Thames a floating town. At 7.30 a cannon was fired to signal the start of the race. After the prizes—'First men to have ten guineas each, with Coats and Badges; Second Men, Seven Guineas each, with Coats and Badges of an inferior value: Third Men—Five Guineas each, with Coats and Badges of less value than the second'—the procession moved 'in a picturesque irregularity' towards Ranelagh.

The ticket for this gala night was designed by Cipriani and engraved by Bartolozzi and admitted revellers to the Temple of Neptune, a temporary octagon built in the grounds. A Mrs. Cornelys had been given 700 guineas to supply the supper, which unfortunately turned out to be 'indifferent, and the wine very scarce'. This was a pity, when everything else had been so successful, and there were so many distinguished visitors, including the Duke of Gloucester, Lord North, the Duchess of Devonshire, Sir Joshua Reynolds, and David Garrick; but perhaps the indifferent supper was forgotten by those who enjoyed listening to the band of 240, under Giardini, which performed while it was being eaten, in the Rotunda.

Marylebone Gardens closed in 1776, and now the competition between Vauxhall and Ranelagh became more acute.

> The Lords and the Ladies who Ranelagh fill
> And move round and round like a horse in a mill
> Come hither al fresco to take a cool walk
> When tir'd of small coffee, small tea, and small talk.

So sang Vauxhall's Mr. Vernon. And there seemed to be truth in it: Ranelagh's attendances dropped, and economies had to be practised. After the death of Dr. Arne in 1779 the quality of the music noticeably declined. Patrons complained that the management were not paying enough to the musicians, and consequently the music was not worth listening to. The management argued that nobody listened to the music anyway. It was a new management: Sir Thomas Robinson, Ranelagh's Maypole, was dead, and his good taste in entertainment was missed.

The money saved on music was spent on furbishing up the Rotunda. It was repainted inside: the domed ceiling, instead of sky blue, became olive green, with a rainbow round the base; the thousands of candles, which so constantly required snuffing, were covered by glass shades. In the centre was 'an elegant fire-place that cannot smoak or become offensive' and which warmed the whole place in cold weather. A great deal of trouble was taken about ventilating the boxes where the company took their refreshments, and in each box was hung 'a droll painting in the mimic masquerade or pantomime taste'.

The indifferent supper after the Regatta must have left its mark, for Mr. T. Scott of the Gentlemen's Hotel, Pall Mall, took the opportunity of opening an eating house nearby where patrons might retire for 'suppers and suitable refreshments, so necessary to give a relaxation to that fatigue which the constant walking in the Rotunda and Gardens must inevitably occasion'.

Fortunately, as Ranelagh opened in April 1789, the King recovered from a bout of insanity, and there was something to celebrate. A Grand Concert was arranged, with music by Handel, Bach and Haydn (a newcomer), and at both the interval and finale 'God Save the King' was sung 'with a full chorus on the joyful RESTORATION OF HIS MAJESTY'S HEALTH'.

Later in this season the Spanish Ambassador celebrated His Majesty's recovery by giving a Gala Entertainment. It was a very grand affair, and the Rotunda was festooned with scarlet and gold hangings and crammed with baskets of 'natural flowers', one of which, hanging too near a chandelier, caught fire—but was extinguished before serious damage was caused. The King was apparently not recovered enough to attend in person—but the Queen and the four Princesses with their attendants and an escort of Horse Guards drove in state to the Royal Hospital, where they were received by the Governor, and afterwards walked through the gardens into Ranelagh. In the Rotunda they were given a rather tame entertainment: the singing of a highly sentimental Ode composed by a Colonel Arabin on the King's recovery, some Spanish dances, and 'God Save the King', after which they watched fireworks through the windows at the back of the Royal Box. The dancing then began, and the Princesses took it in turns to dance with their cousin, Prince William of Gloucester, who was the only person of high enough rank to stand up with them. In the interval supper was served by two hundred footmen and valets de chambre, dressed respectively in scarlet and gold and sky blue and silver: it was an elaborate repast, accompanied by luscious fruits and wines brought specially from Spain. When it was over, 'God Save the King' was played once again, after which the band struck up for more dancing. The Queen and her party went home at three in the morning. The party was formal, expensive, and sadly dull for the Princesses, but they were used to dullness, and —unlike their brothers—had to put up with it.

The Prince of Wales and his brothers York and Clarence were also at this Gala, but kept well away from the Royal Box. For some reason, the Duke of York had arrived wearing boots, which precluded him from entering the Rotunda but was a splendid excuse for not joining the Queen's party, and for all three brothers seeking more amusing company outside in the gardens.

That season ended on July 17, with a firework display, and Handel's Music for the Royal Fireworks was performed. Three days earlier, the Paris mob had invaded the Bastille, and the French Revolution had begun.

In the 1790s, despite alarming news from France, Ranelagh's fortunes began to look up again. The quality of the music improved, and there were new entertainments. In 1793 a curious hermaphrodite, the Chevalier —later known as Chevalière—d'Eon, fenced in the Rotunda, successfully vanquished his or her opponent, M. Sainville, and received the congratulations of the Prince of Wales and Mrs. FitzHerbert. There was some doubt as to this person's sex: on the available evidence it seems likely that he was a man who enjoyed dressing as a woman. Henry Angelo tells us that visiting the Chevalier at his rooms in Brewer Street he was welcomed by 'a lusty dame dressed in black silk'. After dinner, however, when the ladies retired, the lusty dame remained to drink and smoke with the gentlemen.

In 1797 there was a particularly successful Masquerade, in which the costumes included Dutch Skippers, lunatics, coachmen, quack doctors and watercress girls. There was 'good nature and pleasant hilarity, without riot'.

There is a suggestion here that not every masquerade went through 'without riot'. And indeed, although Ranelagh never achieved the notoriety which Cremorne was to gain a hundred years later, although Dr. Johnson pronounced it to be 'a place of innocent recreation', and the highly respectable King and Queen graced it with their presence, there were scandals. It was inevitable that there should be, particularly at masquerades, in those shadowy lamp-lit gardens where hidden orchestras provided an accompaniment to love-making, and identities were half-concealed behind masks. Clerics thumped their pulpits, inveighing against the immorality of masked balls, and tracts were published demonstrating that Ranelagh was on the road to hell. We have no example to quote of a marriage having been wrecked at a Ranelagh masquerade, but there is the story, in the early days, of Lady Elizabeth Chudleigh, who was already notorious for improper behaviour. A famous beauty, and maid of honour to the Princess of Wales, Lady Elizabeth (whose father had been Lieutenant Governor of the Royal Hospital) appeared at a masquerade as Iphigenia, dressed in flimsy draperies which barely held together, causing shocked comment. We do not know what became of Lady Elizabeth that night, but she seems to have been a reckless girl, and in the end paid dearly for it. Some years before appearing as Iphigenia she had secretly married the Hon. Augustus John Hervey (brother of the Earl of Bristol)—secretly because she did not want to lose her income as Maid of Honour—and had given birth, also secretly, to a child, which was baptized in Chelsea Old Church and put out to nurse in the village. The baby died, to her great grief, and was buried in Chelsea. Lady Elizabeth continued to conceal her marriage, which was in any case a failure: she was by this time the Duke of Kingston's mistress, and her indiscretion at Ranelagh was only one of many shocking things reported of her. She complained to Lord Chesterfield that she had been accused of having twins, to which he replied that he made a point of only believing half of what he was told. At last, having waited in vain for her husband to become Earl of Bristol through the death of his brother, she lost patience and married the Duke of Kingston. Her trial for bigamy drew all fashionable London: it lasted five days, and when it was over, poor Lady Elizabeth, though she escaped being branded in the hand because she was a peeress, was obliged to go abroad, where she spent the rest of her life.

This was a major scandal, and a subject of conversation for many Ranelagh nights. No doubt there were others, for at one point the masquerades were suppressed:

'The foolish Justices of Middlesex so far carried their point that the managers of Ranelagh were obliged to consent that they would make no more masques' . . . but by 1769 we hear again of people appearing in 'fancied dress', so the ban must have been lifted.

A lesser scandal, which may be said to have been inspired by Ranelagh, concerned William Hickey, the eighteenth-century diarist who makes no attempt to disguise or soften his own profligacy. Over-indulged by his father, an Indian lawyer who retired to England, Hickey grew up a problem boy. He lied and stole, drank and kept bad company, fell in love with a fashionable prostitute, Charlotte Barry, and was finally, after cooking the books in the family law firm and keeping the proceeds, shipped out to the East Indies. He came home, committed further dishonesties, and was sent to Jamaica. By 1775 he was back in England again, but cast out by his father, who had given up trying to reform him. Through a family friend he was sent to board in 'a neat, new house in Chelsea', exactly opposite the avenue leading up to Ranelagh. His host, Mr. Malton, was to teach him perspective and geometry, until the reformed William could decide what line of life he would adopt.

Unfortunately the Maltons had—besides five other children—a daughter of sixteen called Ann, 'with a sweet and interesting countenance'. Hickey must have been helped in his deplorable career by considerable charm, for the whole family, he said, 'soon became wonderfully attached to me, the elegant Ann too much so for both our comforts! I was happier,' he adds disarmingly, 'than I had ever been before.'

The Ranelagh season opened at the end of April. The Maltons happened to know the caretaker, who lived in Ranelagh House, and this 'well-informed, gentlemanlike man' gave the charming William a silver ticket, which admitted him to the gardens at any time. 'Of this privilege,' he writes, 'I availed myself frequently, spending several hours of the morning roving about the gardens' (where was Mr. Malton, with his set-squares and protractors?) 'or rowing upon the canal, after which I entered the room [the Rotunda], and amused myself in playing the few tunes I knew upon a very fine harpsichord that stood in the orchestra. In these rambles Ann Malton often accompanied me . . .'

It was too easy. The delicious Miss Malton was no prude: after the first 'snatched kisses' she indicated that she was ready for more. 'The liberties she allowed me to take with her person increased; and I was more than once upon the point of accomplishing the grand object, when her terror lest we should be discovered . . . alone prevented it.' Miss Malton, who by this time saw herself as Juliet, threw caution to the winds, and 'proposed during the next moonlight night to admit me to her bed'.

But now parental suspicions were aroused, and Hickey was gently lectured. ' "I have too much confidence in your honour, Mr. Hickey, to suppose you could deliberately lay a plan of seduction . . ." '

Alas, this 'mild and sensible address' came too late. Nothing could keep the lovers apart, and an assignation was made in Miss Malton's bedroom. As the Ranelagh clock struck eleven Romeo left his bed 'and with palpitating heart crept downstairs . . . Slowly and cautiously I turned the handle of the lock. The door opened, but in doing so creaked. I paused, anxiously listening for some seconds; when, everything remaining quiet, I advanced, approached the bed and got into it, but had scarcely encircled the object I sought within my arms and our panting bosoms met, when, oh dreadful sound! I heard the door upon the middle floor open violently, and ere I had time to jump out of bed and reach the passage, the father stood before me.'

'Never,' said Hickey, 'can I forget the pang I endured at that moment.' The deceived father made a speech.

' "Base and unworthy young man, how can you face me after thus attempting to injure me . . . by depriving my unhappy child of her only inheritance, a good name, for ever?" ' And so on. Perhaps he really did talk like that. Anyway, it had its effect. 'Like a detected thief,' writes Hickey, 'I skulked upstairs.'

The temptation was quickly removed: Miss Ann was sent off to live with a relation of her mother's at Islington. Time, said William, now dragged heavily. His host and hostess eyed him coldly and seldom spoke to him: no doubt they hoped that he would go. He whiled away his time at the Red House, across the river from Ranelagh, where the innkeeper had a blonde daughter called Sally. Finally, to everyone's relief, William was sent to the West Indies. Ann, who had made one attempt to see him, which he nobly resisted, did her best to forget him and married a man of property.

The story has a tragic sequel, which concerns the Maltons' friend, who gave William his silver ticket of admission to Ranelagh. This man had been at school and college with Sir Thomas Robinson, who, hearing that he was down on his luck, installed him at Ranelagh House as house-keeper. Here he and his wife lived rent free, with coals and candles supplied, and a salary of £150 a year. All seemed to be well, but one night during Hickey's stay in Chelsea this unhappy man went out and flung himself, fully clothed, into the canal.

We do not know why: perhaps he was deeply in debt, perhaps for some other reason life had become unendurable. Possibly from a sense of the macabre he chose to end it in the shallow waters of the Ranelagh canal, between its flimsy Chinese Temple and the painted gondola which carried musicians in carnival dress on masquerade nights.

Ranelagh survived the turn of the century, and in 1801, although the war with France was causing shortages, it was reported that 'the supper and wines were of the best quality, and in profusion', which must have been encouraging. There had been many complaints about the catering. In 1802 the short-lived Peace of Amiens was an excuse for celebrations, and on June 28 the newly formed Pic Nic Club gave an afternoon break-fast. (This fashionable club had invented a new entertainment, the Pic Nic Supper, for which a numbered bill of fare was prepared in advance, and the members drew lots, each being obliged to bring the dish whose number he drew.) After they had breakfasted, an interesting event took place. M. Garnerin the French aeronaut, wearing a French hat with the tricolour cockade, and Captain Sowden of the Royal Artillery, dressed for some reason as a sailor, and carrying a Union Jack, climbed into the basket of a captive balloon, rose slowly to a height of about three thousand feet, and sailed away eastwards over London. (The flight, spectacular as it appeared to the watching crowds at Ranelagh, ended, owing to bad weather, in a violent forced landing in a field near Colchester.)

In the same year Ranelagh, which seems by now to have grown increasingly dependent upon novelty, engaged Mr. Thomas Todd, the diver, who undertook to descend into a tank of water twenty-five feet deep, and remain at the bottom for an hour. It can hardly have been an enlivening performance at the best of times, and unfortunately the diver's appearance in a garment of leather and metal drew laughter from the audience. Then Mr. Todd forgot to take his lamp with him when he descended. Worse still, something went wrong with his headgear: as the report put it, he was 'misfitted by his coppersmith', and after five minutes under water was obliged, ignominiously, to climb out.

This is a far cry from the Ranelagh of the 1740s, and indeed the sands were fast running out. Fashions in entertainment had changed, and the nineteenth century demanded something more lively than the unending promenade round and round the floor of the Rotunda, the music which served as a background to conversation, and the traditional tea and coffee. This century had its own pleasure gardens, as will be seen, but there is a world of difference between the full-blooded cockney flavour of Cremorne and the formal elegance of Ranelagh.

On July 8, 1803, Ranelagh opened for the last time. Two years later, in the year of Trafalgar, the great house and the Rotunda were pulled down. The organ upon which the child Mozart had performed was sent to Tetbury Church in Gloucestershire. The canal was filled in, the octagonal pool with its fountain was removed: the Temple of Pan and the Chinese Pavilion were torn down. The demolition men did their work well, for a year or so later not a trace remained. It was almost as if the eighteenth century had been swept away.

'When I first entered Ranelagh,' said Dr. Johnson, 'it gave an expansion and gay sensation to my mind, such as I never experienced anywhere else. But, as Xerxes wept when he viewed his immense army, and considered that not one of that great multitude would be alive a hundred years afterwards, so it went to my heart that there was not one in all that brilliant circle that was not afraid to go home and think . . .'

It is two hundred years since that was written, and Ranelagh is a garden still, but frequented chiefly by nurses and babies. The trees and lawns are beautiful: there are little hills and dark corners hidden by flowering shrubs. The place where the Rotunda stood is faithfully marked, but it needs a great effort of imagination to reconstruct that place of enchantment which was, in its way, unique.

CHAPTER SIX

WESTWARD FROM Walpole's House and also overlooking the river, was a small mansion built at the end of the seventeenth century in the Dutch style, by the Earl of Carberry, a President of the Royal Society. Charles II had made him Governor of Jamaica where he accumulated a fortune, partly, it was said, by the sale of Welshmen as slaves. The same account adds that he sold his chaplain to a blacksmith, but does not say what the blacksmith wanted him for. This nobleman died in his coach, on the way back to Chelsea after a visit to his banker. His unmarried daughter, Lady Ann Vaughan, inherited his wealth, and promptly bought six horses, after which she married the Duke of Bolton. But it is to be feared that the Duke was more attracted by the fortune than the lady, for he took fright and left her at the church door. Lady Ann, with her six horses, left Chelsea, and the house was sold to Sir Richard Gough, a city merchant and Member of Parliament. It became known as Gough House, and survived into the nineteenth century, when it became a school. In 1866 the building was enlarged and converted into the Victoria Hospital for Children, with the original house, as was the way with so many Chelsea mansions, still at its core. After a hundred years' service, the hospital was demolished in the 1960s. Nothing remains of Gough House and its formal terraced garden but a building site awaiting development.

Beyond, to the west, lies Swan Walk, where four beautiful eighteenth-century houses remain, giving the Walk an air of spaciousness and dignity, a glimpse of what Chelsea must have been before the industrial age. Number 1 was built in 1719 and remodelled later in the century when the house on the corner of Royal Hospital Road was added. This house has a charming window with a cornice and semi-circular head (there is a similar one in Upper Cheyne Row). Numbers 2 and 3 are fine examples of mid-Georgian architecture, standing a little back from the road; number 4 is of earlier date, and was lived in between 1736 and 1739 by Alexander and Elizabeth Blackwell, of whom more will be heard later.

It was down this lane that in 1666 Pepys and his ladies drove on their way to the Swan Tavern, which stood on the river bank. With its wooden balconies which hung over the water, the Swan must have been a pleasant place to spend a summer evening watching the pageantry of the Thames.

This old inn was the original goal of the famous race for Doggett's Coat and Badge. Thomas Doggett, comedian, became Manager of Drury Lane in Queen Anne's reign. He was an ardent Whig and anti-Jacobite, and celebrated the accession of George I by instituting an annual race for watermen's apprentices who had just completed their training. On his death in 1721 he left a sum of money to provide 'for all time' the waterman's coat and badge. Ever since the race has been rowed against the tide on a date near the first of August; Doggett's Coat was orange, the Whig colour, and the Badge bore the prancing white horse of Hanover. The coat is now scarlet and the arm-badge is inscribed 'The Gift of Thomas Doggett'. The course, from London Bridge to Chelsea, is four and a half miles, and the race now ends at the Cadogan Pier.

In 1780 the Swan was converted into a brewery, and another Swan, confusingly known as the Old Swan, was opened a little higher upstream, at the point where Royal Hospital Road and Chelsea Embankment now converge. It had arbours and gardens overlooking the river, and in the nineteenth century a landing stage for steamboats; but this Swan had its song too, and was swallowed up by that ruthless devourer of old Chelsea, the Embankment. A tall elaborate house designed by Norman Shaw stands on the site, and is named Old Swan House.

Between these two Swans was—and still is—the piece of land known as the Physic Garden, the oldest existing botanical garden in England.

In 1617 the London Apothecaries, backed enthusiastically by King James I, broke away from the Grocers, with whom they had hitherto been combined, and formed themselves into a separate City Company. In future, King James decreed, medicines were only to be concocted by Apothecaries. Many lives, it was considered, would be saved by this new arrangement.

The Apothecaries' Company established themselves at Cobham House, on the Thames at Blackfriars. They were short of funds, but had high ideals: they imposed a strict qualification for membership, and all medicines were analysed. Bad or dangerous drugs were seized and burnt. Although animal ingredients such as wood-lice, crabs' eyes, vipers' fat and millipedes were still used by reputable apothecaries, most of their remedies were made from plants or parts of plants, many of which could be found in and around London: on the banks of ditches near Piccadilly wild bugloss grew, and belladonna was found in Islington.

This renaissance in the study of medicinal plants prompted Thomas

Johnson, a bookseller of Snow Hill, to bring out, in 1633, an enlarged edition of Gerard's *Herball* with 800 descriptions of new plants and 700 woodcuts. (On the title page is Johnson's portrait, with a bunch of bananas beside it. The first of this fruit to reach London had been exhibited by Johnson in his shop window, a present from his 'much honoured friend, Dr. Argent, President of the College of Physicians'. They had come from Bermuda.)

After the loss of their Blackfriars home in the Great Fire, the Apothecaries decided to lease three and a half acres of land at Chelsea from Charles Cheyne for a yearly rent of £5. Here they planned to make a garden, and there was a good mooring for their new barge up a creek in the south-east corner. The site of their boathouse is still preserved. In moving further afield, they no doubt considered the advantage of getting out of London's smoke, which was bad for tender plants, and this Chelsea garden proved a good choice: there was plenty of sun and the soil was light but well watered (at times too well) by the Thames. By degrees it was dug and planted. There were the usual difficulties: Pigott, the first gardener, who was given £30 a year and a house, demanded higher pay and left. Workmen defaulted, valuable plants were stolen.

In 1680, John Watts, a learned botanist, was appointed Curator, and under his management the garden began to prosper. He built a high wall to shut out thieves and cold winds, and he planted trees, including several kinds of fruit trees: 'nectarines of all sortes, peaches, apricockes, cherries and plums.' About 1683 four Cedars of Lebanon arrived—the first ever seen in this country. They were about three feet high when planted, but they grew enormous, too big, perhaps, for the comfort of neighbouring plants, for in 1771 two were cut down and sold for £23 9s. 8d. as timber. The other two became celebrated as the Chelsea Cedars, standing for over two hundred years one on each side of the river entrance.

In 1685 John Evelyn visited the Apothecaries' Garden and admired the large collection of plants, and also the new invention introduced by Mr. Watts. 'What was very ingenious was the subterranean heat, conveyed by a stove under the conservatory, all vaulted with brick, so as he has the doores and windowes open in the hardest frosts, secluding only the snow.'

Another wonder was the Chinchona—'the tree bearing Jesuit's bark'. This tree had acquired an almost magical reputation since Robert Talbot had used the powdered bark to cure Charles II of the ague. The bark contained quinine—a drug rediscovered by Jane Carlyle and other Victorians nearly two hundred years later, and acclaimed as a cure for headaches,

influenza and numerous ills. In the seventeenth century quinine was pro-
hibitively expensive because of the extreme difficulty of importing plants
into countries where they would grow into trees. It was not till 1862 that
it was discovered that the trees could be grown in India, and quinine
became available to all.

By the end of Queen Anne's reign the Apothecaries ran into money
troubles and were obliged to lay up their barge to save the bargemaster's
wages. They sold some South Seas Stock, happily before the bubble burst.
But even that was not enough, and the fate of the Physic Garden hung in
the balance till in 1722 Sir Hans Sloane, who has appeared in earlier
chapters in less heroic guise, stepped into the breach. As a young man he
had spent hours there, studying botany: now, as Lord of the Manor of
Chelsea he conveyed the Physic Garden, for a yearly payment of £5, to
the Apothecaries' Society 'to hold the same for ever . . . for the manifes-
tation of the power, wisdom and glory of God in the works of creation'.

This sentence conveys something of the humility with which men of
science, in an age of exploration and eager research, regarded the materials
among which they worked. The discoveries they made were achieved in a
deliberate endeavour to benefit humanity 'to the glory of God'. The men
who later became associated with the Physic Garden—Miller, Banks,
Forsyth and others—display this inspired dedication, which was doubtless
what Sir Hans meant. In saving the Apothecaries' Garden for posterity,
Sir Hans showed particular generosity, for the Apothecaries' Society,
fearing the consequent loss to their members, had opposed a pet scheme of
his, to provide free dispensaries for the poor. His only stipulation in giving
them the garden was that every year for forty years fifty specimens, all
grown in the garden and no two alike, were to be dried, mounted, labelled
and sent to the Royal Society. This agreement was faithfully observed, and
the specimens—all two thousand of them—are now in the Natural History
Museum.

Sloane bestowed a further benefit upon the Apothecaries by introducing
Philip Miller as gardener in 1722. A highly skilled, self-educated man,
Miller was the author of *The Gardeners' Dictionary* published two years
after he came to Chelsea, which went into many editions and was translated into Dutch, German and French. He became known as 'the prince of
gardeners' and remained in charge of the Physic Garden till just before his
death, aged ninety, in 1771. During this time the garden became celebrated all over Europe, and he organized exchanges of plants with many
countries. It was Miller who unwittingly fathered the cotton industry in
the southern states of America by sending some seed to Georgia, a British

colony founded by the philanthropist James Edward Oglethorpe for poor debtors and 'foreign persecuted protestants'.

During Miller's reign Carl Linnaeus, Assistant Professor of Botany at Uppsala, paid a visit to the Physic Garden. This learned Swede had made a study of the sex life of plants, and classified them according to the presence or absence of reproductive organs. Those which had them he divided into twenty-four classes, and subdivided into orders, founded upon sexual peculiarities. This revolutionary idea became the accepted method of botanical classification. But now, in 1736, Linnaeus was engaged upon a more ambitious enterprise: he was, in fact, classifying the whole living world 'from buffaloes to buttercups'. Unfortunately, he was not a pre-possessing character, and his visit to Chelsea, though it may have been beneficial to Science, was socially a failure. Sir Hans found him a crashing bore, and Miller, surprisingly, considered him ignorant.

Joseph Banks lived with his mother in Turret House, Paradise Row, nearly opposite the east corner of the Physic Garden, and as a boy on holiday from Eton, when he was not fishing in the Thames, he was learning, under Miller, the names of plants. As he grew up he developed a longing to see far-off countries and study their trees, flowers and butterflies; and being a wealthy young man he was able to realize this dream. On August 26, 1768 he sailed with Captain Cook to the South Seas, in search of a new continent, 'Terra Australis Incognita'. Banks, aged twenty-five, provided the ship (*Endeavour*) and took as his personal entourage two Swedish naturalists, one a pupil of Linnaeus, two artists, two servants, two negroes and two dogs. The ship, a Whitby collier, had barely enough room to house these passengers as well as the crew, and Banks's collection of plants grew so large that after the new continent had been discovered he was obliged to dry his specimens ashore, spread out upon a sail. The shore he chose was given the name—later to acquire such a sinister significance—of Botany Bay.

Among the burials recorded at Chelsea Old Church is that of Elizabeth Blackwell, on October 27, 1758. She was sixty-nine, and had outlived her husband, Alexander, by eleven years. Dr. Blackwell, a Scot, went bankrupt in 1734, and brought his wife and two children to Chelsea, perhaps with the hope of setting up in practice there. Whatever his plan, it cannot have prospered, for his wife was obliged to think of a way in which to support the family. She was a gifted artist, and someone told her that a new *Herbal* was wanted, to record the many new plants now in use since the opening of the Physic Garden. So she went and made a few careful drawings, delicately coloured, of flowers and fruit, by permission of the

Curator, Isaac Rand, to whom later she acknowledged her indebtedness, 'for his READINESS to ASSIST and INSTRUCT' her. 'I had no skill in Botany,' she added modestly. Nevertheless, her drawings were approved by Sir Hans Sloane, Dr. Rand and Mr. Miller, and, installing herself and her family in Swan Walk (to be near her work), she embarked upon the long series of meticulously detailed drawings which were to become, after three years, *A Curious Herbal containing Five Hundred Cuts of the most Useful Plants which are now used in the Practice of Psysick: Engraved on folio copper Plates, after Drawings, taken from the LIFE by Elizabeth Blackwell.*

Each plate has one plant, engraved and hand-coloured, showing flower, fruit and seed—and sometimes root. Occasionally an insect is introduced —a Leopard moth, or a mole cricket eating a radish. She calls a tomato a love apple, and a crocus a saffron. The remedies make interesting reading. The root of Great Centory is good for 'stopping bleeding at Nose, Mouth, or any part. It is also esteemed good to heal wounds, taking its name, as Pliny says, from the centaur Chiron, who cured himself of a Wound he received by one of the Arrows of Hercules by the use of this Plant'. Pomegranates grew on the eastern wall of the garden, and these fruits, we are told, 'strengthen the Gums; fasten loose Teeth, help the falling down of the Uvula, and cancerous ulcers in Mouth and Throat'. And how much nicer than tablets with incomprehensible names, to be given cowslips for insomnia, speedwells for sore eyes, bay leaves for wind in the stomach, and motherwort for palpitations and swooning.

Mrs. Blackwell's long labour must have been rewarding, not only for the money it earned: the work itself must have given her great interest and pleasure, even if her eyes may sometimes have had to be anointed with speedwell. But apart from her achievement, life held little joy for the poor thing: in 1736, soon after she began her drawings, her children William and Ann both died, within six months of each other. A few years later her reckless and improvident husband (or was he just unlucky?) took himself off to Sweden, where he somehow became involved in politics, was suspected of treason, found guilty, and beheaded. Whatever her feeling for him, the suddenness and horror of her husband's death must have been unbearable; but Elizabeth survived, comforted, it is to be hoped, by her good friends in Chelsea, and perhaps a little gratified by the success of her *Herbal*.

In 1739, Samuel Dale, F.R.S., left a legacy to the Apothecaries' Society of a valuable collection of books, on condition that the Master and Wardens should 'make or erect proper conveniences for the reception thereof'. Book presses were accordingly made, and approved by Sir Hans Sloane: these cases still hold the books, a rare and fascinating collection of tomes, mostly leather-bound and of immense size and weight. Gerard's *Herball* is there, both the 1597 and 1633 editions, and Miller's *Gardeners' Dictionary* (1733); Elizabeth Blackwell's two folio volumes are dedicated to Richard Mead, M.D., Physician-in-Ordinary to his Majesty (Dr. Mead lived for a time in Cheyne Row and later in Paradise Row). There is also Forsyth's *Management of Fruit Trees*, presented by the Author in 1802, which reminds us of another famous name in horticultural history: William Forsyth succeeded Miller as head gardener in 1771, and every spring the shrub named after him shines like the sun in Chelsea gardens.

The Physic Garden is not open to the public, but it may be seen from Swan Walk and Chelsea Embankment: carefully tended and scientifically planned, with its numerous hothouses and nurseries, and a team of gardeners. Groups of students study and attend lectures in the building which houses the Superintendent; and there is a regular despatch of specimens to schools and colleges. The garden is continually changing: new plants still arrive from overseas. There is the Shui-sa (water spruce), a tree described from fossil records found in North America and Asia, and thought to be extinct. But a living species was found in China: in 1946 Professor Wan-Chun Cheng of the National Central University, Nanking, sent an expedition and found about twenty-five trees. The specimen at Chelsea is beautiful with golden leaves in spring which turn pink in the autumn.

At the heart of the garden stands the white marble statue of its founder, cleaned at intervals by an expert from Westminster Abbey. Although a little worn by age and weather, Sir Hans looks satisfied, as well he may, with the work that has gone on there uninterruptedly over two and a half centuries.

CHAPTER SEVEN

I N THE early eighteenth century what is now Cheyne Walk was a pleasant wide roadway running along the bank of the Thames. The low river wall was broken at intervals by flights of steps and mooring poles for private barges and pleasure boats. Opposite ran the high, buttressed brick wall of the Great Garden of Henry VIII's manor, and further westward were the entrance gates to the Tudor palace, lived in till 1712 by the Cheyne family. In that year, the manor, with all the estates pertaining to it, was bought by Sir Hans Sloane. He was the last occupant of the old house: after his death in 1753 it was torn down, and a row of houses built upon the site. These are numbers 19 to 26 Cheyne Walk, and pieces of Tudor wall are still be to found in their gardens.

The houses at the eastern end of Cheyne Walk, on the site of the Great Garden of Henry's palace, were built earlier. In 1717 Sir Hans decided to let this land off in building plots: he was a shrewd business man and must have seen how 'desirable' these properties facing the Thames would become. Accordingly, within a year or so, a line of handsome brick houses grew up along the southern end of the garden, obliterating Lord Cheyne's orchard and his 'ingenious waterworks' which had so pleased John Evelyn. These houses were the beginning of Cheyne Walk. Some were designed for specific owners, others put up as speculative property by Sir Hans and his builder, John Witt, but they all had—and those which remain still have—an air of distinction and a grace of individual design and fine workmanship, qualities even more appreciated today than at the time when they were built. Over the years they have housed many distinguished persons, but their tenants in the eighteenth century were for the most part respectable rather than spectacular.

Number 6 is the largest in the row, with fine entrance gates whose pillars are topped by stone balls. In 1765 this house was described as having four parlours, two dining rooms and thirteen bedchambers, and it was occupied by a Venetian of noble birth, Dr. Dominiceti. He claimed to have spent £37,000 on converting the house into a sanatorium where patients might be accommodated after receiving his medicated steam bath treatment, and advertised that 'the building which contains this apparatus

. . . is situated in my garden, 220 feet in length, 30 in breadth, and two stories high; it contains 36 Sweating and Fumigatory chambers'.

This steam bath treatment was something quite new, and for a time Dr. Dominiceti was all the rage. The Duke of York became his patient, and although unfortunately he died soon afterwards, a Mr. John Dove of Bush Lane, Cannon Street, was ready to testify to other almost miraculous cures he had witnessed: 'some leperous, some scrophulous . . . asthmatical, hectical, ulcerous, rheumatic . . .' there was no end to the diseases. He even claimed that he had seen the lame and blind restored to health and sight. Perhaps in his enthusiasm he went too far. But Sir John Fielding, whose word could not be doubted, vouched for the efficacy of the treatment, adding, 'Dr. Dominiceti has most happily situated himself at Chelsea, as the Thames and the gardeners' grounds are his great Apothecary's shop, the one furnishing him with water and the other with herbs.' Dominiceti had his enemies among the medical profession, however, and it was unkindly suggested that the noble Venetian had bribed Sir John to boost his treatment by offering him a shilling out of every guinea earned by the baths towards his scheme for training poor boys.

For seventeen years the doctor battled on, against increasing opposition from the Faculty and a decline of patients when the craze had faded. Fumigatory baths became a joke, and Dr. Johnson, faced with an enthusiast, told him, 'Well, Sir, go to Dominiceti and get thyself fumigated, but be sure that the steam be directed to thy head, for that is the peccant part.' At last poor Dominiceti, forsaken and hopelessly in debt, abandoned his thirty-six sweating chambers, and fled back to Italy.

Number 6 became a highly successful school, presided over for more than thirty years by the Rev. Weeden Butler.

Some of the other Cheyne Walk houses and their occupants will be described later on; in the meantime, remembering Chelsea's reputation for housing eccentrics, we should perhaps take note of number 5, which in the nineteenth century was lived in by a curious character who went by the name of 'Miser Neild'.

James Neild, the miser's father, was a fashionable jeweller of St. James's Street, and retired in 1792 to Cheyne Walk. A widower with two sons and plenty of money, he had become deeply concerned with the frightful conditions inside British gaols, and wrote and campaigned to bring about prison reform. After he came to Cheyne Walk, though old and in bad health, he forced himself to visit, in three months, every gaol in fifty-nine counties of England and Scotland, gathering material for a book. 'It has been a severe contest,' he wrote to his friend Dr. Lettsom, 'between a strong mind and a weak body, which at length became so enfeebled by constant fatigue that I could neither get in nor out of a carriage without assistance.'

In 1812 his book appeared: *The State of the Prisons*, the fruit of many years' painful experience. He lived for another two years, long enough to know that he had started the slow stirrings of public conscience. The way was paved for Elizabeth Fry.

In his home life this charitable man seems to have been less amiable. Dr. Butler, his friend and neighbour, trying to be fair, could only say of Neild in the bosom of his family that 'he regulates his expences with rigid economy', but the poor, he quickly adds, are the better for his prudence. Neild's two sons can hardly have been happy. He so disliked the elder that life became intolerable for the young man, and he took himself off to the West Indies and died at the age of thirty-two. The second son, James Camden Neild, inherited his father's frugality but not his charity. He also inherited his fortune, which included a number of properties in the Home Counties. He devoted the rest of his life to being a landlord and collecting his rents. He walked miles to save coach fares, carrying his luggage in a brown paper parcel, and expecting his tenants to give him bed and board for the night. At Cheyne Walk he lived alone in the tall empty house with its dirty windows festooned with cobwebs. A short, stocky man in his threadbare swallowtail which he never brushed for fear of spoiling the nap, 'Miser Neild' became a well-known figure on the waterside—a figure of mystery, half pitiful, half comical. It was said that all he had in his house was an old bed with a board down the middle, a few old sticks of furniture, a tallow candle and a cat.

He died in August 1852, having persistently refused to call in a doctor. When his will was opened it was found that he had left the bulk of his fortune, amounting to half a million pounds, to Queen Victoria.

The Queen graciously accepted her legacy and told her Uncle Leopold, who wrote rather enviously:

'That Mr. Neild should have left that great fortune to you delighted me. It gives the possibility of forming a private fortune for the Royal Family, the necessity for which no one can deny. Such things only still happen in England where there exists loyalty and strong affection for Royalty, a feeling unfortunately much diminished on the Continent . . .'

With the life and death of Mr. Neild we have moved ahead in time, and must now move back to the eighteenth century, and to number 18, Cheyne Walk, the last of the houses built on the site of the Great Garden. From 1718 the original number 18 (it was completely rebuilt in 1867) was occupied by Don Saltero's famous Coffee House, which moved there from Prospect Place near the church. It was run by an Irishman, James Salter, whose Spanish-sounding title was bestowed upon him by one of his customers, Admiral Munden, lately returned to Chelsea from the Spanish Main.

Salter had been Sir Hans Sloane's travelling valet, and had evidently picked up from his master a passion for collecting curiosities, but without the taste or knowledge to make his museum of any worth, except as a kind of fairground raree show. 'A starved Cat found between the Walls of Westminster Abbey when the east end was repaired' was one exhibit, 'A Frog, fifteen inches Long, found in the Isle of Dogs' another. Many of the items—'A Necklace made of Job's Tears', 'A Piece of Queen Catherine's Skin', 'Pontius Pilate's Wife's Chambermaid's Sister's Hat'—suggest the Irishman's love of the fantastic, an attempt to bamboozle the credulous, and then join in the laugh when it seems that the joke has gone too far.

But museums were still rarities, and the size and variety of the Don's collection, crammed into one or two rooms, must have been, as Steele said, astonishing. Some of the exhibits were throw-outs from Sir Hans Sloane's vast private collection, which gave an air of authenticity to the whole thing.

Salter (a poet too) advertised himself and his Knackatory in the *Weekly Journal*, June 22, 1725:

> Through various employs I've past
>   A scraper, Vertuos'-Projector
> Tooth Drawer, Trimmer, and at last
>   I'm now a Gimcrack Whim Collector.
>
> Monsters of all sorts here are seen,
>   Strange Things in Nature, as they grew so,
> Some relics of the Sheba Queen,
>   And Fragments of the Fam'd Bob Cruso.
>
> Knick-knacks, too, dangle round the Wall,
>   Some in glass cases, some on shelf,
> But what's the rarest sight of all,
>   Your humble Servant shows himself.

There is an almost Shavian touch about the last two lines. Certainly the irrepressible Don had power to attract customers. People came from far and wide to drink his coffee and his home-brewed punch, and to stare at his lizards in bottles and his literary customers. Of these, Addison was one in the early days, with Swift; and Steele who wrote his famous piece in *The Tatler*: 'When I came into the coffee-house I had not time to salute the company, before my eye was diverted by ten thousand gimcracks round the room and on the cieling. When my first astonishment was over, comes to me a Sage of a thin and meagre countenance . . .' It took Steele, a fellow Irishman, to unmask the old humbug and reveal him as the Jack-of-all-trades he was, but the article must have been excellent publicity.

James Salter prospered: he died in 1728, but the Tavern, run by his daughter Molly and her husband, was carried on for another thirty years, after which it changed hands. Then, on Monday, January 7, 1799, the lease was sold, together with the museum of curiosities, probably by this time rather the worse for wear. Sad to say, the entire collection, the 'ten thousand gimcracks', fetched only £50, the best price, thirty-six shillings, being given for 'a curious Model of Our Blessed Saviour's Sepulchre at Jerusalem very neatly inlaid with Mother-of-Pearl'. It was the end of an epoch. The coffee-house was a thing of the past, and the tavern became a smoking club where, on Sundays, you could get 'a rare good dinner for two and sixpence, including beer'. The nineteenth century had moved in.

Sloane is a familiar name to Londoners, and has a certain cachet about it: Sloane Square and Sloane Street are at the end of Chelsea which has always been exclusive and elegant. Hans Place and Hans Crescent, too, have a luxurious air. These places owe their names to a young man from Killyleagh in County Down who became a fashionable physician and a distinguished scientist, and whose descendants own a large part of Chelsea.

Although he did not live there till the end of his life, he had long been attached to the place, and as a young man studying medicine in London he used constantly to visit the Apothecaries' Garden in the pursuit of further knowledge. His thirst for learning in all branches of science shocked his first patron, the celebrated Dr. Thomas Sydenham. 'Anatomy! Botany!' he exclaimed on reading Sloane's credentials. 'Nonsense! Sir, I know an old woman in Covent Garden who understands botany better. As for anatomy, my butcher can dissect a joint full as well. No, young man; all this is stuff. You must go to the bedside; it is there alone you can learn disease.'

But the young man was determined to go to other places as well as the bedside for the learning he wanted. In September 1687, when he was twenty-seven years old, Hans Sloane was invited to go to Jamaica as private physician to the Duke of Albemarle, the newly-appointed Governor of the island. It meant leaving a promising London practice, but it was the sort of opportunity for which he longed, to explore new possibilities in medicine, and to find new plants and creatures.

The Duke paid him £600 a year, and he earned this princely salary conscientiously, investing his savings in quinine, which, as we have seen, was a rare and expensive commodity. He spent part of his spare time in writing a *Natural History of Jamaica*; and he was also collecting and drying plants, employing a local clergyman, the Rev. Garrett Moore, to make coloured drawings of fruits, birds and insects; and studying the eating habits of the natives. Turtles, he noted, were the main food of the poorer people; when Europeans ate them, the oil turned them yellow, which was a pity, for the meat was very tasty. Rats, he said, were eaten by the Jamaicans, 'and when they have been bred amongst the sugar canes, are thought by some discerning people, very delicious victuals'. Snakes and woodworms were also enjoyed by Indians and negroes, apparently with no ill effects.

As well as being personal physician to the Duke, Doctor Sloane was available to the islanders, upon whom he used the accepted remedies of the time, bleeding, applying leeches, inducing vomiting and, of course, taking medicine. His medicines were for the most part based on herbs, the samples whose ingredients he had studied in the Physic Garden; but he used some of the witch-brews still in fashion, such as vipers' fat, crabs' eyes, or 'fifty live millipedes in a glass of water twice a day', and the percentage of deaths was no higher than it had ever been. Indeed, he must have effected an unusual number of cures, for after he returned to England the Rev. Mr. Moore wrote, 'Never man's absence is soe univerally lamented as yrs is heare, everyone that is ill creys if Dr. Sloane were heare wee would be cured.'

There was an ex-Governor living on the island: no other than the notorious pirate and cut-throat, Henry Morgan, now knighted, respectable, yellow as a guinea, and a heavy drinker. Sloane, called in to advise on his failing health, could do little but offer medicines and urge his patient to cut down the drink. The case was beyond cure. Unfortunately, the Duke of Albemarle, though only thirty-four, was in much the same state, after a dissipated life at Court, and his Duchess, said to be 'of a wayward and peevish temper', probably drove him to further excesses. Jamaica was not the best place for a man with sclerosis of the liver, and in 1688, after less than a year there, he died. The following March Doctor Sloane returned to England with the Duchess and her servants, taking with him eight hundred specimens of plants, a large yellow snake, a guana and a crocodile. The snake escaped from its prison, caused a panic among the Duchess's servants and was shot dead; the crocodile also died, and the guana, frightened by a sailor, leapt overboard and was drowned. 'Thus,' wrote Sloane in his *Natural History*, 'I lost by this time of the voyage all my live creatures; and so it happens to most people, who lose their strange wild animals for want of proper air, food or shelter.'

Upon their arrival in England the company were surprised to find a new monarchy: King James II had fled to France and King William (and Queen Mary) reigned. Doctor Sloane now set himself to the task of building up a practice, and in a few years was established in Bloomsbury as a fashionable physician.

He was one of the many doctors who were consulted by poor Queen Anne, who must have been a godsend to the medical profession. In 1714 he was among the seven doctors in attendance during the Queen's last illness, another being Richard Mead, who had a way with the ladies and lived at the time in Cheyne Row. Sloane may be said to have played his part in history, for after Dr. Mead had pronounced that her Majesty had only a few minutes to live, Sloane insisted that she should be bled. This drastic measure enabled the all-but-dead Queen to make a last, momentous gesture: she placed the Lord Treasurer's staff in the hands of the Duke of Shrewsbury, a Whig, thus giving her blessing to the Protestant Succession.

Under George I, Sloane became a baronet, and the Princess of Wales—Walpole's Queen Caroline—thought highly of him. Sloane had made a study of inoculation against small-pox, which had been practised successfully abroad, particularly in Turkey: it was a far more drastic method than the vaccination from cow-pox discovered by Jenner, as it caused the patient to suffer from an attack of the disease, usually mild but occasionally fatal. The Princess of Wales, whose daughter Princess Anne had nearly died of small-pox, considered having her two other little girls inoculated. She consulted Sir Hans, who said that he 'would not persuade nor advise the making trials upon patients of such importance to the public'. But the Princess was determined: guinea pigs must be found. She arranged for six charity children, suitably rewarded, to be inoculated. Only one died, having already had the disease and concealed the fact, tempted by the reward, so it was considered safe for the royal children to undergo the operation, which was successfully performed by Sir Hans. It was a victory for the cause of inoculation, and another feather in Sloane's cap.

He was by now a rich and busy man. But he treated the poor for nothing, and made it known that he would see anyone who came before ten in the morning free of charge. There is a horrific story of a beggar woman bringing a child with sore eyes to him, 'the inside of whose eyelids he very charitably tore out with a beard of corn, under which cruel operation the girl fainted'. It is to be hoped, however, that this drastic remedy, in a day of drastic remedies on rich and poor alike, brought about a cure.

Sloane was interested in diet and digestion, and invented a health food which sounds more appetising than his concoctions of millipedes and crabs' eyes. It was advertised as Sir Hans Sloane's Milk Chocolate, made (only) by Nicholas Sanders of Greek Street. To avoid disappointment the public was earnestly begged to note that 'on each quarter of Chocolate is pasted "Sir Hans Sloane's Milk Chocolate" '. It was made into a drink, and sounds delicious:

'Take a pinte new milke in a pinte water, and when boyle putt in 2 ounces Chocolate & 3 ounces sugar, & mill it on ye fyer as aboue & when itt is readye to boyle upp take it of ye fyer & mix with itt two new layd eggs, but lett yor eggs be broke with ye mill in a spoonfull of cold water in a pinte pott, then mix it all togather & lett it be a little coole, as you may drinke it.'

It was recommended for 'its lightness on the stomach, and its great use in all consumptive cases'.

In 1712 Sloane felt the need to get away from London at week-ends, and decided to buy the Manor House at Chelsea from William, the second Lord Cheyne. He installed a steward and gardener, George Burr, to look after the place, and drove down with his wife on Saturdays. Little is known about Lady Sloane. The daughter of a London alderman, she had previously been married to Fulk Rose, a Jamaican planter, and it is presumed that Sloane first met her on his visit to the island. There were four little Roses, all daughters, and these in due course all married suitably, with handsome settlements arranged by their stepfather. Sloane had four children of his own, but two died in infancy. His elder daughter, Sarah, married George Stanley, of Paultons in Hampshire, and the younger, Elizabeth, became Mrs. Charles Cadogan, later Lady Cadogan of Oakley, names which are part of Chelsea today.

All through his life Sloane had a passion for collecting rare and interesting objects, and his tastes were wide and impeccable. At first his chief interest was in plants, fruits, birds and insects: then fossils and minerals, gold, silver and precious stones were added, as well as antiquities and curiosities. A busy doctor, President of the Royal Society, Governor of most of the London hospitals, with endless calls on his time, Sloane somehow managed to gather together, meticulously arrange, label and catalogue a collection of rarities from all over the world, which was to form the basis of the British Museum.

In 1741 he decided to move, with his collection, from Bloomsbury to Chelsea. He was over eighty, and planned to spend his retirement among his treasures; but his step-daughter, Mrs. Philippa Stanley, was concerned for his health: Henry's palace must have been draughty.

'I have heard by some people that you talk of removing your great treasures to Chelsea. I hope it is not with a thought of passing any of your time with them their, for I shall much dread the change of climate, I think one may call it, so near the watter, and so bleak and expos'd every way to the weather. Let me beseech you Sir to way well its being proper for your health before you set about so vast an undertaking. Excuse the freedom I take in speaking where I so sincerely wish a life prolonged to its utmost stretch and that you may long enjoy it surrounded by your children and best freinds is the prayer of, Sir, Your most dutyfull, P. Stanley.'

He disregarded his stepdaughter's affectionate warning and moved; but it is to be hoped that he was sometimes, in Chelsea, 'surrounded by his children and best freinds', although the picture we get from contemporary accounts is a lonely one.

Edmund Howard, the forthright Quaker who was employed by Sir Hans to look after—and pull down—Beaufort House, was in charge of the move. All the items in Sloane's vast collection passed, said Howard, through his hands, 'except a few which he used to bring himself in his chariot'. 'I doubt not', writes Howard with obvious disapproval, 'but he had many gods of gold and gods of silver, for I one day unpacked a large case full of gods of the ancient Egyptians, Greeks and Romans, &c.' The library of nearly 50,000 valuable books was apparently transported 'loose in carts', and the books, when Sir Hans had decided where they were to go, were 'tossed from the cart to a man on a ladder, who tossed them in at a window . . . to a man who caught them as men do bricks'—an operation which might cause a bibliophile to shudder, but which seems to have been successful.

Visitors from afar made their way to Chelsea in the hopes of seeing Sir Hans and his collection. Linnaeus's pupil, Pehr Kalm, wrote a starry-eyed account of the wonders he saw on two visits: 'all kinds of stones . . . all sorts of vessels, Tea-cups, saucers, snuff-boxes, caskets, spoons ladles, and other small instruments, all manufactured out of agates and Jaspis.' There were butterflies and humming birds, 'the head of a frightfully large whale', and 'a great collection of snakes, lizards, fishes, birds, cater-pillars, insects', preserved in bottles. 'To describe all this great collection in detail,' he declares, 'would fill several *Folios*;' but he continues his eulogy, equally impressed by the antiquity of the Egyptian Mummies and the ingenuity of 'Sir Hans's Chair with three wheels under it, and a little one behind, in which he was drawn about the garden'.

Sir Hans, by this time, was eighty-eight. In the same year he was honoured by a visit from Frederick, Prince of Wales and his Princess, and *The Gentleman's Magazine* for July 1748 reported that Sir Hans 'being antient and infirm' was obliged to receive them sitting. The Prince tactfully took a chair himself and sat beside the old man, informing him 'how much the learned world was obliged to him for having collected such a vast library of curious books, and such immense treasures of the valuable and instructive productions of nature and art'. The Prince and Princess were then taken through all the rooms where the collection was displayed, and on their return found the same tables covered with a different display, an impressive demonstration of the size and variety of Sloane's museum. The Prince, when he left, 'express'd the great pleasure it gave him to see so magnificent a collection in *England*', adding significantly 'how great an honour will redound to *Britain*, to have it established for publick use to the latest posterity'.

But Sir Hans had already made up his mind that the nation ought to have his collections, and he wanted them to remain in Chelsea Manor House, 'in which it is my desire the same shall be kept and preserved'. His stipulation in making this bequest was that the King or Parliament should pay his family the sum of £20,000, which, he said, was less than a quarter of the value of his treasures.

'Sir Hans Sloane is dead,' wrote Horace Walpole in February 1753, 'and has made me one of the trustees to his museum . . . He valued it at four score thousand: and so would anybody who loves hippopotamuses, sharks with one ear, and spiders as big as geese! It is a rent charge to keep the foetuses in spirits! You will think that those who think money the most valuable of all curiosities, will not be purchasers . . .' He was right, of course: it was quite impossible to put a value upon the collection, and the Nation, handing over its £20,000, can have had little idea of the bargain it was getting. Unfortunately for Chelsea, the Government decided that it did not want the Manor House, and the collection was moved back to Bloomsbury, where, in Montagu House, it became the British Museum.

Sir Hans died on January 11, 1753, and was buried with modest pomp in the churchyard of Chelsea Old Church, where his monument stands today, a marble urn entwined with serpents—emblems of his profession—under a canopy over which a vine has spread its branches.

He has been abused for his ruthless destruction of More's house, an action hard to forgive, particularly in a man who valued antiquity, and who held among his treasures Holbein's portrait of More. But it must be re-membered to his credit that he intended to save the Manor House for posterity by housing his museum in it, and that he did save the Physic Garden for the Apothecaries' Society. He also, in 1719, saved the King's Road after George I had closed it to the public, signing a successful pet-ition to the Lords of the Treasury. He may thus be said to have laid the foundation of modern Chelsea. In 1736 he presented to the parish the Burial Ground which remains a shady oasis on the north side of the King's Road; and he also gave the land adjoining it for a much-needed Work-house, proving in these ways a conscientious Lord of the Manor.

John Martyn, F.R.S., a fellow botanist, who lived in Old Church Street, had a son, Thomas, who wrote: 'I beg leave to consider Sir Hans Sloane as one of my patrons. The condescension of the venerable and amiable old gentleman to me, when a school-boy, will never be forgotten by me. His figure is, even now, presented to my eye, in the most lively manner; as he was sitting fixed by age and infirmity in his arm-chair. I usually carried a present from my father of some book that he had pub-lished, and the old gentleman in return always presented me with a broad piece of gold, treated me with some chocolate, and sent me with his librarian to see some of his curiosities.'

With this pleasing portrait we will leave Sir Hans, and his century, going forward to a Chelsea in which his descendants, the Cadogans, played an important part.

PART THREE

'THE LUNATIC, THE LOVER AND THE POET'

Sir Hans Sloane.
Painting by Slaughter

Philip Miller

MILLER.

De la société Royale de Londres
De l'Academie des Botanistes de florence
Et Directeur du Jardin de Botanique
Des Apothicaires de Chelsea

Cheyne Walk: water-colour showing
number 18, Don Saltero's Tavern

Number 6, Cheyne Walk (Dr. Dominiceti's house).
Water-colour by Elizabeth Gulston

Henry Holland

Jane Austen.
Pencil sketch by her sister Cassandra

Letitia Landon

Yours faithfully,
T. Carlyle

Thomas Carlyle.
Pencil drawing by Daniel Maclise, 1832

CHAPTER ONE

THE BEGINNING of the nineteenth century saw great changes in Chelsea. Its population was increasing rapidly, and rows of small houses sprang up to accommodate the newcomers, country people for the most part, who came to London in search of work. There was also a growing tendency among the prosperous middle class, merchants, bankers, lawyers and the like, to move their homes away from the City where they worked, and settle in the suburbs. In their quest for rural seclusion they went as far afield as Hampstead and Norwood; but Chelsea had the advantage of being within easy reach of London by boat or coach.

This growth in Chelsea's population had been anticipated as far back as 1770 by an enterprising young architect, Henry Holland. With the co-operation of his father, a master builder who lived in Fulham, Holland planned a new residential district on the north-eastern side of Chelsea, which, in honour of Sir Hans Sloane, was to be called Hans Town. He accordingly opened negotiations in 1771 with the second Lord Cadogan for the lease of eighty-nine acres of land, known as Blacklands, upon which he planned to build Sloane Street, a broad straight street running north from Sloane Square to Knightsbridge, with lesser streets on its western side, connecting it with Hans Place. This latter was designed in the shape of a long rectangle with the corners cut off; there was to be a large central garden surrounded by terraced houses, each with its own small garden. South of Hans Place Holland reserved twenty-one acres for his own house and grounds.

Holland's ambitious scheme was held up, first by the outbreak of war with America, and then by the death of Lord Cadogan. The final agree-ment with Charles, the third baron, was drawn up in 1777, and building began at once. Some of the first groups of houses in Sloane Street were designed by Holland himself; those which followed later fitted in with his general scheme. All had the simplicity and elegance of the Neo-classical style, with charming fanlights and varied door-heads. Only one remains—number 123.

Building on the east side of Sloane Street did not begin till 1790. Here Holland had planned to build a church of stuccoed brick with Portland stone dressings: it was to be a handsome edifice, with sixteen Gothic windows, a tower and a bell turret. The estimated cost was £4,750. The scheme met with the approval of the local residents, and a clergyman, the Rev. J. Duché, already living at number 63 Sloane Street and eager to minister to the spiritual needs of Hans Town, applied for the post of incumbent. Unfortunately his application was received by the Bishop of London with a disappointing lack of enthusiasm; and in 1791 it was decided that Chelsea did not need a new church, and the land was laid out, as it still is, in the form of two long strips of garden surrounded on three sides by houses. Upper Cadogan Place on the north side, where the fine Sonesta Towers Hotel now stands, originally consisted of a terrace of twelve houses. The garden facing it, which now covers an underground garage, was first laid out by the great Humphry Repton, while the larger, southern enclosure was, during the nineteenth century, occupied by Salisbury's Botanic Garden.

Henry Holland became a highly successful architect, and enjoyed the patronage of the Prince Regent. In 1784 he rebuilt Carlton House; and the first Pavilion at Brighton was designed by Holland—a simple, classical building: the domes and minarets came later. Many beautiful pieces of Regency furniture, at Carlton House and at Brighton, were made to his design, and he employed some of the finest craftsmen, French and English, several of whom rented houses in Hans Town. Holland's own house grew up under these devoted and expert hands, and must have been a building of some distinction. The architect showed originality in his choice of materials, for the house was largely built of timber, faced with weather tiles made in the New Forest. Even the Ionic Columns on the south front were of wood, 'sanded to imitate stone'. There was a long garden running south to the King's Road, and Holland's father-in-law, the famous Capability Brown, designed it as a miniature landscape, with lawns and walks, ornamental shrubs and fine trees, adding a small serpentine lake with an island, together with the fashionable Gothic Ruin, in the form of an ancient Priory, in which, says Faulkner, 'the appearance of age is strikingly faithful'. The ruin was given added authenticity by the introduction of fragments of stonework from Cardinal Wolsey's recently demolished palace at Esher, and was approached by a 'variety of fanciful intricate paths, profusely ornamented with shrubs'.

Holland called his house Sloane Place, but it became known as The Pavilion, from a persistent tradition that the south front with its colonnade was the model for Brighton. After Holland's death in 1806 the house was bought by Mr. Peter Denys, 'a performer on the violin who often gives expensive musical entertainments', and who, according to Faulkner, 'unites to a taste for the fine arts a particular esteem for that of architecture'.

In 1879, the house was pulled down. All that remains today is the name 'Pavilion' which has attached itself to the narrow road that runs parallel with Sloane Street. Perhaps in compliment to Holland, a very ornate Victorian-classical colonnade runs along the massive houses on the northern side of Cadogan Square—roughly the position of the back of Holland's house. The building itself, lawns, lake, shrubbery and Gothic ruin, are replaced by Cadogan Square and Cadogan Gardens. But Henry Holland, in his lifetime, saw the success of his imaginative planning of Hans Town, and the foundation of a new and fashionable quarter of Chelsea.

Miss Mitford, who went to school in Hans Place in 1798, tells us that 'the houses, bright, fresh, newly painted, looking into a garden full of shrubs and flowers, were in no slight request among persons of moderate incomes and gentle condition'.

The school which welcomed the plump, shy child of nine, Miss Mary Russell Mitford, was successfully established at number 22. It had already done its best to tame the untameable Lady Caroline Ponsonby who, after her marriage to William Lamb, came sailing back to present prizes, to please Miss Rowden who had once been her governess at home. The school was kept by a Monsieur St. Quentin, a handsome refugee from the French Revolution, who taught the young ladies French, history, geography, and 'as much science as he knew'; while Miss Rowden (who eventually became the second Madame St. Quentin) provided all that was needed to complete their education, assisted by visiting masters for Italian, music, dancing and drawing. The original Madame St. Quentin, alive, but somnolent, in Miss Mitford's day sat dozing in the drawing room with a piece of embroidery in her hand, and woke to receive visitors.

Monsieur, Miss Mitford tells us, was a lively, kind-hearted man, who delighted 'to assemble as many as he could of his poor countrymen and countrywomen around his supper table. Something admirable and wonderful it was,' she says, 'to see how these dukes and duchesses, marshals and marquises, chevaliers and bishops bore up under their unparalleled reverses! How they laughed, and talked, and squabbled, and flirted, constant to their high heels, their rouge and their furbelows, to their old liaisons, their polished sarcasms, and their cherished rivalries!'

One can imagine the strange spectacle of this troop of exiles in their bedraggled finery, issuing from number 22 into the prim respectability of

Hans Place, and seeming all the more incongruous by contrast with the orderly crocodile of young ladies who walked out from there daily under the watchful eye of Miss Rowden.

Some twenty years later, in 1807, a quiver ran through the ranks of the St. Quentin crocodile. Miss Letitia Landon, aged five, had just joined the school as a boarder: her parents lived close by, at number 25, and she resented being removed from her home, breaking loose whenever she saw her nurse or a servant in the street, and trying to go back with her. 'Nothing,' we are told, 'could make L.E.L. walk quietly in the ranks with other children.'

It was this non-conforming spirit which won her—a solitary young woman without influence or introduction—success and fame as a writer; but which, in a period mistrustful of female independence, ultimately brought about her downfall. This gifted and tragic figure, L.E.L., as she came to sign herself, spent the greater part of her life in Hans Place. After her father's death, she decided to part from her mother and took a room at number 22, where M. St. Quentin's successors, the Misses Lance, had decided to take paying guests after retiring from teaching.

Here, in her bedroom overlooking the street, with its narrow white bed and 'small, old, oblong-shaped sort of dressing table, quite covered with a common worn writing-desk heaped with papers', Letitia, seated on a little high-backed cane chair, composed the verses, the reviews and the romantic prose that flowed so freely from her pen on to the pages of *The Literary Gazette* and *The New Monthly Magazine*. Her theme-song, in prose as in verse, was 'a broken heart, an early grave'; her heroes were borrowed from Byron and all her heroines were consumptive. She was immensely popular. Her novels were best-sellers.

Disraeli, who saw her at a party given by the Bulwer Lyttons, was disappointed in her appearance: '. . . the very personification of Brompton— pink satin dress and white satin shoes, red cheeks, snub nose, and hair à la Sappho.' But he refers to her as a 'blue', showing the respect in which she was held in the literary world of 1832.

For ten years Letitia lived and wrote at 22 Hans Place, tended by the Misses Lance, growing older but not maturing; virtuous but provocative and indiscreet in her friendships with men. Then, in her early thirties, she announced her engagement to John Forster—only to break it off after a few weeks, in great agony of mind. She had enemies: libellous letters had been written: she was accused of making love to Daniel Maclise, the Chelsea artist who had painted her three times. Worse, she was accused of writing endearments to a married man, a fellow journalist, William

Maginn. Forster's friend, the actor Macready, noted regretfully in his diary, 'She is fallen.'

In her bedroom at Hans Place she wrote with a shaking hand the letter to Forster which cost her far more than the innumerable death scenes which had poured so freely from her pen.

'The more I think, the more I feel I ought not, I cannot, allow you to unite yourself with one accused of—I cannot write it. The mere suspicion is dreadful as death. Were it stated as a fact, that might be disproved . . . But what answer can I give, or what security have I against the assertion of a man's vanity, or the slander of a vulgar woman's tongue? I feel that to give up all idea of a near and dear connection is as much my duty to myself as to you . . .'

Three years later, she married Captain Maclean, the Governor of Cape Coast Castle, West Africa. Literary London paid a respectful farewell to L.E.L. in the summer of 1838, when, with her silent and apparently totally unsuitable husband, she left England for ever. Three months later she was found dead, with a bottle of prussic acid in her hand.

Did she commit suicide? Was she poisoned by the jealous African 'wife' of the Governor? Or was her death from natural causes, and had the bottle only contained the medicine she took for her 'spasms'? The riddle remains unanswered. There was no post-mortem; the papers containing the statements made at her inquest were 'temporarily mislaid' at the Colonial Office, and have never been seen again; and the bones of L.E.L. lie forgotten under the hot African soil. Here, in her own country, no urn, no weeping willow commemorates her, but perhaps among the shrubs and flowers of Hans Place her spirit wanders, in the garden over which she gazed as she composed the verses that she hoped were immortal.

> Will the young maiden, when her tears
> Alone in moonlight shine—
> Tears for the absent and the loved—
> Murmur some song of mine?
>
> Will the pale youth by his dim lamp,
> Himself a dying flame,
> From many an antique scroll beside,
> Choose that which bears my name?
>
> Let music make less terrible
> The silence of the dead;
> I care not, so my spirit last
> Long after life has fled.

Hans Place has changed. Only two of the houses designed by Henry Holland remain, number 30 and number 15, Hans House. The rest are tall, imposing edifices, some built in the 1870s when the original leases came to an end: elaborate houses of red brick and terracotta, built for large, well-to-do families with large staffs of servants—and now divided into expensive flats. Now, instead of M. St. Quentin's young ladies, the boys from Hill House in their tomato-coloured caps walk out two by two, on their way down Sloane Street to their sports ground. Hans Place is urban, sophisticated; but looking at the charming, simple outlines and the modest height of the original houses the passer-by may imagine how pleasant and how pretty this part of Chelsea was in the days of Jane Austen.

In April 1811, a few months before the publication of *Sense and Sensibility*, Miss Austen came to stay with her brother Henry and his wife in their new house, number 64, Sloane Street. Her sister-in-law, the elegant Frenchified Eliza, was an accomplished hostess, and during Jane's visit she sent out eighty invitations to a musical party. We do not know the names of all the guests; but perhaps one of them was the new owner of Holland's Pavilion, Mr. Peter Denys, who gave such expensive musical entertainments himself.

Jane described the party in a letter to her sister Cassandra. The rooms looked very pretty, she said, decked with flowers.

'At half past seven,' she wrote, 'arrived the musicians in two Hackney coaches, and by eight the lordly company began to appear . . . Including everybody we were 66 . . . quite enough to fill the back drawing room and leave a few to be scattered about in the other, and in the passage.'

The back drawing room of 64 Sloane Street was a large, octagonal room, connected with the front drawing room by a short, spacious passage or ante-room. Jane herself withdrew from the crowd and sat in this ante-room, where she was at a comfortable distance from the music, which, she said in her detached way, was 'extremely good . . . The harp player was Wiepart, whose name seems famous, tho' new to me. There was one female singer, a short Miss Davis all in blue . . . whose voice was said to be very fine indeed; and all the performers gave great satisfaction by doing what they were paid for, and giving themselves no airs. . . . The house was not clear till after 12'.

Two years later, in April 1813, Eliza Austen died, and Henry Austen moved into rooms over the bank in which he was a partner, in Henrietta Street, Strand.

He evidently missed the amenities of Hans Town, for in 1814 he moved again, into number 23 Hans Place, a corner house with a larger garden than its neighbours. James Tilson, junior partner in the banking firm, lived at number 29, and probably found this house for Henry. Jane seems to have been dubious about it till she saw it, when she wrote enthusiastically to Cassandra:

'It is a delightful place—more than answers my expectation. Having got rid of my unreasonable ideas, I find more space and comfort in the rooms than I had supposed, and the garden is quite a love.'

It was August, and hot weather, and Jane, having seen her brother mount his horse and ride off to Henrietta Street after an early breakfast, enjoyed sitting downstairs in a cool room that opened into the garden. She later paid several visits to Hans Place: Henry took pleasure in his sister's growing fame, and acted as her adviser and intermediary with her publishers. It was at Hans Place, in the autumn of 1815, that she learned from the Prince Regent's librarian that His Royal Highness was a great admirer of her books.

'Your late works, Madam, and in particular *Mansfield Park*,' wrote this rather pompous gentleman, 'reflect the highest honour upon your genius and your principles; in every new work your mind seems to increase its energy and powers of discrimination. The Regent has read and admired all your publications.'

This was gratifying. The authoress allowed herself to be conducted round Carlton House on a sightseeing tour, and decided to dedicate her latest book, *Emma*, to the Prince Regent.

During this same visit of Jane's, Henry Austen fell ill.

'Henry's illness is more serious than I expected . . . It is a fever—something bilious but chiefly inflammatory.'

She called in Mr. Haden, 'the apothecary from the corner of Sloane Street'.

Mr. Haden, a clever young man of twenty-eight, was in fact no common-or-garden apothecary, as Jane soon found out. He had studied medicine in Edinburgh and in London, and at the age of twenty was elected a member of the Royal College of Surgeons. After this, he went to Paris and studied French techniques of medicine, learning among other things the use of the stethoscope, which he introduced into this country. On his return, a year before his encounter with Jane Austen, he set up practice at number 62 Sloane Street.

Jane, who nursed her brother through this illness, wrote with growing enthusiasm about Mr. Haden. At first she merely refers to his efficiency—'he is certainly very attentive, and appears hitherto to have understood the complaint.' But when the patient begins to recover, venturing 'first on the balcony, and then as far as the greenhouse', Jane, who has been joined by her niece, Fanny Knight, announces:

'To-morrow Mr. Haden is to dine with us. There's happiness! We really grow so fond of Mr. Haden that I do not know what to expect.'

After dinner, in the drawing room, Mr. Haden sat so close to Fanny that her Aunt Jane wondered if they were on two chairs or one. 'And what is to be fancied next? Why, that Mr. Haden dines here again to-morrow.'

Sometimes it is hard to decide whether it is the niece or the aunt who is attracted by Mr. Haden. Jane is pleased by his interest in her books. 'He is reading *Mansfield Park* for the first time, and prefers it to *Pride and Prejudice*.' And to her sister, Cassandra, who has evidently expressed surprise at such eulogies of a mere apothecary, she defends him almost too enthusiastically.

'You seem to be under a mistake as to Mr. H.—you call him an Apothecary; he is no Apothecary, he has never been an Apothecary . . . he is a Haden, nothing but a Haden, a sort of wonderful nondescript creature on two legs, something between a Man and an Angel—but without the least spice of an Apothecary.'

Early in December, wearing what Jane calls 'a strengthening plaister', which he had some difficulty in keeping on, Henry Austen set off for his bank in Henrietta Street by the Chelsea coach, which obligingly picked him up at his own door. With the recovery of his patient, Mr. Haden's visits came to an end, and Jane prepared to return home to Chawton. Just before leaving Hans Place she wrote to him, returning two books which he had lent her. She added:

'As we were out ourselves yesterday evening we were glad to find you had not called—but shall depend upon your giving us some part of this evening. I leave Town early on Saturday, and must say "good-bye" to you.'

It was good-bye. Two years later Charles Haden married a Miss Emma Harrison; their son, born at 62 Sloane Street, became a well-known surgeon, Sir Francis Seymour Haden, who was a brilliant etcher, and brother-in-law of Whistler.

Jane Austen did not visit Chelsea again. We do not know how much of the district she saw: did she, for instance, drive with Fanny to the Old Church on Sundays? It is possible. We know that she walked in Kensington Gardens; but there is no written evidence that she ever made her way southwards past the toll-gate at the bottom of Sloane Street. It would be nice to think of her, upright, neat, and bright-eyed, walking arm in arm with her brother past the Royal Hospital, or along Paradise Row into Cheyne Walk, whose fine houses with their pleasing prospect of trees and river would surely have charmed her.

But perhaps old Chelsea, in spite of its historic associations, would have disappointed the fastidious Jane. For the great days were over; the aristocracy had begun to move eastwards to Mayfair; the riverside village was falling out of fashion. The Tudor palaces were deserted or gone: Gorges House and Monmouth House were turned into schools; Shrewsbury House, after being used as a wall-paper factory, was pulled down in 1813. The elegant seventeenth- and eighteenth-century terraces which had been inhabited by persons of quality were let to middle-class tenants, or fell into disrepair and became lodging houses; for although the population had enormously increased, the number of well-to-do residents had dwindled. Socially, Hans Town and old Chelsea belonged to different worlds.

A good deal of trading, in a small way, went on in the old village, particularly near the river, where fresh fish were caught and sold; and the village boys laid night-lines for eels near the Old Swan Brewery to the east of the Physic Garden. The rich refuse from the brewery made excellent ground bait, and the eels were fat and plentiful.

In the summer, the grass boat came twice a week to the draw-dock. This ramshackle vessel had a roughly built half-deck cabin which housed an old man and his wife and daughter. They sold bundles of coarse rush grass, cut in the marshes further up-stream, for three halfpence a bundle. It was bought by local tradesmen, who fed their horses on it, and what was left went cheap to anyone who had a cow.

On the river bank there were breweries and wharves where the sailing barges tied up to load or unload. Just beyond the church was Alldin's Coal Wharf, where the coal merchants' drays picked up supplies. A large quantity of coal was used in the tall narrow houses with their basement kitchens, where the day's work could not begin until the range was cleaned and re-lit, and where each floor had its two or even three fireplaces. Smoke poured from the chimneys, filling the air with smuts, and over to the east the City of London was always seen dimly through the haze of its sooty breath.

On the river bank too were innumerable small taverns, some ancient, some new, and open at all hours for the accommodation of a passing trade of sailors and bargees as well as the local regulars. It is hard to imagine how such a number managed to make a living, but there they all were—the Green Man and the Adam and Eve, near Battersea Bridge, the Waterman's Arms and the Rising Sun in Lombard Street, the Cricketers, the Dog, the Bell, the Magpie, the Old Swan and many more along the waterfront, while others flourished further inland up Church Street and Lawrence Street.

Chelsea in the 1830s was a curious mixture of town and country, of squalor and beauty. 'A singularly heterogeneous kind of spot, very dirty and confused in some places, quite beautiful in others,' wrote Thomas Carlyle when he first saw it, after paying a visit to Leigh Hunt.

In 1833 the Hunt family moved into number 4 (now 28) Upper Cheyne Row, a pleasant cul-de-sac of eight houses facing south, of which the first five were built about 1716, the other three rather later. The most easterly is dated 1767; and to the east of this there stood till the 1930s a small mansion 'of ancient gravity and beauty', Cheyne House. Originally standing in its own grounds, with its own right of way to the river, it had been built in 1715 for the widowed Duchess of Hamilton. It was altered and added to later in the century, and eventually became a school. On Thompson's map of Chelsea (1836) it is marked as the Cheyne House Academy; but despite its convenient proximity, it has not been recorded that any of the young Hunts attended this place of learning.

Leigh Hunt was pleased with his new home, which, he wrote, 'was of that old-fashioned sort which I have always loved best . . . It had seats in the windows, a small third room on the first floor, of which I made a *sanctum* into which no perturbation was to enter, except to calm itself with religion and quiet thoughts (a room thus appropriated in a house appears to me an excellent thing).' When one remembers something of the Hunt ménage this parenthesis is understandable.

Cheerfulness in affliction was Leigh Hunt's besetting virtue, which never failed him throughout his numerous trials. He was a devoted father and husband, though his wife, Marianne—a gifted sculptress and cutter of silhouettes—was lazy and feckless, took to drink and sponged upon her husband's friends. His children—there were seven of them—were wild and undisciplined, 'dirtier and more mischievous than Yahoos', said Byron when they were in Italy.

By the time they reached Chelsea the family had been through many vicissitudes: even in London—generally, alas, for financial reasons—they had never settled for long in one district. 'We had found that the clay soil of St. John's Wood did not agree with us,' wrote Leigh Hunt. 'Or perhaps it was the melancholy state of our fortunes, for the New Road . . . agreed with us as little. From the noise and dirt of the New Road, my family removed to a corner in Chelsea, where the air of the neighbouring river was so refreshing, and the quiet of the "no thoroughfare" so full of repose, that although my fortunes were at their worst, and my health almost at a piece with them, I felt for some weeks as if I could sit still for ever, embalmed in the silence.'

The back of the house looked on to a small garden, and beyond it lay the meadows known as Cook's Ground (now Glebe Place). There was a row of lime trees in front of the house, but the street, and Cheyne Row which ran at right angles to it, were busy with hawkers. Leigh Hunt, in his optimistic way, was interested, not distracted by their cries.

'I fancied they were unlike the cries in other quarters of the suburbs, and that they retained something of the old quaintness and melodiousness which procured them the reputation of having been composed by Purcell and others . . . The primitive cries of cowslips, primroses, and hot cross buns seemed never to have quitted this sequestered region. They were like daisies in a bit of surviving field.

'There was an old seller of fish, in particular, whose cry of "Shrimps as large as prawns" was such a regular, long-drawn and truly pleasing melody, that in spite of its hoarse and, I am afraid, drunken voice, I used to wish for it of an evening, and hail it when it came. It lasted for some years; then faded and went out; I suppose, with the poor old weather-beaten fellow's existence.'

The street noises of Cheyne Row were to meet with a very different reception, a year or two later, from Thomas Carlyle. In 1834 he came to London from Craigenputtock, a remote farmhouse in Dumfriesshire, and tramped the streets for days looking for a house where he and his wife might live cheaply while he tried to make his name as a writer. After searching in Bayswater, Brompton and Hampstead, he arrived one day in Chelsea and called upon Leigh Hunt. He found the household disconcerting.

'Mrs. Hunt asleep on cushions; four or five beautiful, strange, gipsy-looking children running about in undress, whom the lady ordered to get us tea. The eldest boy . . . a sallow, black-haired youth of sixteen, with a kind of dark cotton nightgown on, went whirling about like a familiar, providing everything: an indescribable, dreamlike household. Am to go again tomorrow to see if there be any houses.'

There was a house—just round the corner, as it turned out—number 5 Cheyne Row. Built in Queen Anne's reign, it was a solid brown and red brick house, panelled inside 'to the very ceiling', and in a good state of repair. 'On the whole a most massive, roomy, sufficient old house,' he told his wife, with numerous cupboards and closets which he thought would delight her. The rent was low, only £35, but the district was unfashionable.

'It was once the resort of the Court and great, however; hence numerous old houses in it, at once cheap and excellent.'

Carlyle, a stone-mason's son, had an eye for good workmanship: he admired the staircase with its hand-turned balustrade, he stamped on the floors and found them firm as rocks, he paced the rooms to give Jane an idea of their size. 'I confess I am strongly tempted,' he wrote.

Jane, in Scotland packing, was doubtful about all that panelling: would it not harbour bugs? And the neighbourhood—'Is it not too near the river? I should fear it would be a very foggy situation in the winter, and always damp and unwholesome.'

She begged him to make no decision till she came; and indeed, after her first visit to the Chelsea house she was still doubtful. Then, after looking at others, she made up her mind. The Carlyles would live, not in Brompton, not in Kensington, not in Hampstead, but in Chelsea. They became tenants of 5 Cheyne Row 'for one year certain'.

It was to be their home for the rest of their lives. And through its connection with these two brilliant, turbulent, nerve-ridden characters this old Chelsea house has become invested with its own unique fascination for posterity.

CHEYNE ROW, or Great Cheyne Row, was built in 1708 on the site of a bowling green belonging to an inn called the Three Tuns, which stood round the corner in Cheyne Walk. The land belonged to William, Lord Cheyne, and was bounded by the Tudor wall of Shrewsbury House: this wall still runs along the gardens of Cheyne Row. There were originally eleven houses in the Row: number eleven, slightly larger than the others, was called Orange House, and between 1876 and 1882 it was used by William de Morgan as a warehouse and showroom for his pottery. Its site is now filled by the Roman Catholic Church of the Holy Redeemer, built in 1894.

The ten houses which remain, a dignified, solidly built terrace, are all designed on the same plan: on each floor (there were originally three and a basement) are two well-proportioned panelled rooms, with a small closet opening out of the back room. Since they were built, most of the houses have had attic rooms added: only three still have their original cornices; one has a Victorian portico, and two have nineteenth-century balconies.

On his first visit to number 5, Carlyle noticed the charming staircase with its hand-turned spiral banisters. There is a pretty curled-leaf design carved on the outside base of each stair.

Above the second floor, the stairs ran up a short way, leading to a mysterious cupboard with a window in it, which existed in all ten houses, but was altered or removed when attics were built on. This was probably designed in Queen Anne's reign as sleeping accommodation for a page boy. Our ancestors did not pay much attention to where servants slept: two partitioned-off recesses with primitive wooden ventilators were found in the basement kitchen of number 9, where maids evidently bedded down. The Carlyles' maid had her bed in the front kitchen and kept her clothes in the washhouse; and even as late as the 1880s, Oscar Wilde's manservant, Arthur, is described as sleeping in an alcove somewhere between the second and third floors of number 16 Tite Street.

The Cheyne Row houses had an uninterrupted view at the back, over a tangle of gardens (once the grounds of Shrewsbury House and Winchester House) and the roof-tops of Cheyne Walk, to Westminster Abbey and St. Paul's. In the front they faced a wall, containing a garden of sorts where washing hung to dry, but no other house; so the inhabitants of Cheyne Row, by twisting their necks a little, could see the river, and had a good view of the Church tower and the old tiled roofs below it.

Carlyle lived for so long in Cheyne Row that the house has become identified with him; but before he arrived on the scene number 5 (now 24) had had in its 126 years a surprising number of tenants: no one seemed to stay longer than a year or two. The only arresting name in the ratebooks is 'Ellers' (who actually remained for three years): this may be one of the brothers Elers, who came to this country from Germany in 1715 and were connected with the Chelsea Porcelain Works in Lawrence Street.

Only one previous occupant left his mark on the house. In 1794, during the tenancy of Mr. Tobias Knowles, a young man (his son, perhaps?) decided to clean the windows. So pleased was he with the result that he left a message for posterity scratched on a pane in the back bedroom. 'John Tarbit (Tobit?) Knowles cleaned all the windows in this house and painted part in the 18 year of age, March 7, 1794.'

Number 4 next door had been more distinguished in its inhabitants. In 1713 the tenant was the eminent doctor, Richard Mead, who was called into consultation during Queen Anne's last illness; and though, as we know only too well, Queen Anne died, Doctor Mead became physician to her successors, George I and George II. In 1716, after the doctor's removal, the house was lived in for a short time by Henry, Duke of Kent, who became Lord Privy Seal: 'a good natured man,' according to Swift, 'but of very little consequence.' At his death in 1740, the dukedom became extinct till George III bestowed it upon his son Edward, Queen Victoria's father.

When the Carlyles arrived in Chelsea, Thomas was thirty-eight, Jane nearly thirty-three, and they had been married for close on eight years. They were poor. Coming to London was a courageous gamble on the abilities of Thomas to make a living as a writer. They brought with them just under £300 and the manuscript of *Sartor Resartus*, which the publisher Fraser reluctantly agreed to print, though he gave little encouragement as to its chances. 'Bookselling,' wrote Carlyle to his brother John, 'is still at its lowest ebb: literature seems done, or nearly so . . . Nothing seems to thrive but penny journals.'

Nevertheless, he was determined that his work must be 'to *write truth*'. Jane Carlyle was equally determined that he should do so in comfort. Her first consideration, after Pickfords had delivered their furniture, was to lay a carpet in the front room upstairs and convert it into a study, where her husband might start as soon as he pleased on his new book, a history of the French Revolution.

But he was not ready for work yet: he was too taken up with the novelty of being a Londoner. The contrast with Craigenputtick was dramatic. There, the silence was so intense that you could hear the sheep cropping the grass. Here, as Jane told her cousin Bess Stodart, there was 'an everlasting sound . . . of men, women, children, omnibuses, carriages'—the very air seemed to vibrate with activity. 'And where is the stillness, the eternal sameness, of the last six years? Echo answers, at Craigenputtock!' 'This stirring life,' she added, 'is more to my mind, and has besides a beneficial affect on my bowels.'

Carlyle the historian enjoyed himself pottering round the old village.

'I know not,' he wrote to his brother, 'if you were ever at Chelsea, especially at Old Chelsea, of which this is a portion. It stretches from Battersea Bridge (a queer old wooden structure, where they charge you a halfpenny) along the bank of the River, westward a little way; and eastward (which is our side) some quarter of a mile, forming a Cheyne Walk (pronounced Chainie Walk) of really grand old brick mansions, dating perhaps from Charles II's time (Don Saltero's Coffee House of "The Tatler" is still fresh and brisk among them) with flagged pavement; carriage-way between two rows of stubborn-looking high old pollarded trees; and then the River with its varied small craft, fast moving or safe moored, and the wholesome smell (among the breezes) of sea *tar*.'

By July, Carlyle was able to tell his family in Scotland that he was getting 'rather stiffly' to work on the new book. As yet, they saw few people: of the few that they knew in London, the greater part were still away.

Leigh Hunt was most attentive, sending little notes offering rather unpractical help, and paying evening visits, when, said Carlyle, 'he would give us an hour of the prettiest melodious discourse'. Jane played the piano for him and they both sang: he gave a spirited rendering of the highwaymen's chorus, 'Let us take the Road', from *The Beggar's Opera*, and finished the evening with a basin of porridge, which he ate 'with a teaspoon, to sugar, and many praises of the excellent, frugal and noble article'.

According to Nathaniel Hawthorne, Leigh Hunt desired sympathy as a flower needs sunshine, and Jane, in those early days, had plenty to bestow. No doubt, after the hugger-mugger of his own household, and the haphazard meals (his supper often consisted of dried fruit, bread and water), the orderly comfort of the Carlyles' house seemed very pleasant.

But although Jane enjoyed Hunt's gallantries and wit, although Carlyle sympathized with the many problems that continually beset him, the friendship flagged. Between the two writers there was too great disparity of thought. 'He talks forever about happiness,' said Carlyle, 'and seems to me the very miserablest man I ever sat and talked with.'

Moreover, Mrs. Hunt, it soon became clear, was quite impossible.

'She torments my life out with borrowing,' wrote Jane to her mother. 'She is every day reduced to borrow my tumblers, my teacups; even a cupful of porridge, a few spoonsful of tea, are begged of me because "Missus has got company and happens to be out of the article"; in plain unadorned English, because "missus" is the most wretched of managers, and is often at the point of not having a copper in her purse.'

Jane Carlyle, in eight years of marriage to a poor man whom she believed to be a genius, had trained herself in economy: she had no patience with the Hunt muddle. 'She actually borrowed one of the brass fenders the other day, and I had difficulty in getting it out of her hands . . . Is it not a shame to manage so, with eight guineas a week to keep house on!'

In the autumn of 1835, when Carlyle was in Scotland, Jane wrote describing an unfortunate evening at the Hunts' when both husband and wife won her displeasure. She took with her a tall thin Miss Susan Hunter from Edinburgh, who was what we should now call one of Leigh Hunt's fans. While their host, half hidden on the window seat, chattered to his admirer, 'who drank it all in like nectar', or ran to the piano and dashed off a song, Mrs. Hunt sat beside Jane, pouring whispered confidences into an ear that grew less and less sympathetic.

'She behaved smoothly,' said Jane, 'and looked devilish and *was* drunkish.' The devilish looks may have been aimed at her husband, who was, as he put it, 'uplifted to the third heaven' by the admiration of Miss Hunter. 'God bless you, Miss Hunter,' he was heard to murmur, not once but several times, 'in tones of ever increasing pathos and tenderness', and when at last Jane rose to go, as she led the way downstairs she caught the sound of amorous farewells followed by two smacking kisses. 'If he had kissed me,' said Jane unkindly, 'it would have been intelligible, but Susan Hunter of all people!'

In the spring of 1840 the Hunts—for the usual reasons—removed from Chelsea to Kensington. Carlyle, who, in spite of their differences, had been a good friend to Hunt, viewed his departure with mixed feelings.

'Leigh Hunt has left this quarter for Edwardes Square, Kensington; we are decidedly rather sad of it. Our intercourse lately had reduced itself altogether to the lending of sovereigns. Poor Hunt had great difficulty to get away at last; had to prowl about borrowing, etc., etc. He is a born fool . . . They are a generation of fools. They are better in Edwardes Square.'

One of the Carlyles' first visitors in the early days at Cheyne Row was Edward Irving, the great Scottish preacher. He had been Carlyle's boon companion when they were young men in Annandale, and it was Irving who introduced his friend to Jane Welsh, his brilliant pupil. Dismissed from the Church of Scotland for his unorthodox beliefs, but refusing to give up the work which he believed to have been given him by God, Irving continued to preach, fighting poverty and ill-health. He was dying of tuberculosis when, in 1834, he called at Cheyne Row. 'You are an Eve,' he said to Jane, as he looked round the parlour, 'and make every place you live in a Paradise.'

When he said good-bye, he was setting out on the first stage of a journey to Scotland, where it was hoped he might regain his health. The Carlyles watched him mount his horse and ride up the street, turning to wave to them as he rounded the corner and disappeared from sight. A few weeks later—after preaching in the open air in pours of rain—Irving died. It is interesting to note that one of the seven London churches of the Catholic Apostolic (or Irvingite) persuasion was opened at this time in Elystan Street near Chelsea Common, where large congregations worshipped till the building was destroyed by bombs in the 1939 war.

In the summer evenings, that first year in Chelsea, Thomas and Jane strolled out together. They turned eastwards along the river bank, watching the white-shirted Cockneys skimming along in their narrow green-painted boats; they walked along the river terrace below the grounds of the Royal Hospital, where the Pensioners in their red coats sat smoking. It was peaceful, picturesque, but after Scotland it seemed a little tame, looking across the river to the Battersea windmills and the distant gentle slopes of Clapham and Sydenham.

'I long much for a *hill*,' wrote Carlyle, 'but unhappily there is no such thing . . .'

For both Thomas and Jane, a feeling of airlessness, of being shut in, was to recur again and again in the summer. In August 1860, twenty-six years after their arrival in Chelsea, Jane wrote, 'I feel choking here . . . I want to be away on the top of a hill!'

Carlyle, at least, could go for long walks. But even this did not satisfy him. 'Our worst fault,' he said, 'is the want of a good free *rustic* walk.' He had to make do with open carriage ways and lanes, and 'really a very

pretty route to Piccadilly' through the newly built Eaton Square and Belgravia. He was half fascinated, half appalled, by the 'great Babylon' into
whose heart he could stride in half an hour.

South, over Battersea Bridge, there was country, of a kind; but the
paths were rough, and so were some of the inhabitants. Carlyle left watch
and purse at home.

'I had a good stick in my hand,' he wrote of one of these walks, which
led him eastwards along the river to the Red House, a fine old inn which,
in the eighteenth century, had provided Canaletto and other painters with
a background from which to depict Chelsea across the river. Now it was
largely given up to bargees and prostitutes. But it is a peaceful scene
which Carlyle describes.

'Boat people sat drinking about the Red House; steamers snorting about
the river, each with a lantern at its nose. Old women sate in strange cottages trimming their evening fire . . . Windmills stood silent. Blackguards,
improper females, and miscellanies sauntered harmless all. Chelsea lights
burned many-hued, bright over the water in the distance—under the
great sky of silver, under the great still twilight.'

In 1838 he acquired a horse, the first of several. Riding was better than
walking—'green lanes, swift riding and solitude.' His mare, Citoyenne, a
present from an admirer of *The French Revolution*, carried him away over
the river through Clapham and Wandsworth to Wimbledon, where he
heard the cuckoo 'almost with tears', or to the slopes of Sydenham, where
he turned to survey the Metropolis—'infinite potter's furnace, sea of
smoke, with steeples, domes, gilt crosses, high black architecture swimming in it, really beautiful to look at . . . while the sun shines on it. I fly
away, away, some half dozen miles out. The monster is then quite buried,
its smoke rising like a great dusky-coloured mountain melting into the
infinite clear sky.'

After the publication of *The French Revolution* Carlyle became a
celebrity, and Jane began to entertain upstairs, in the handsome room
which they called the library, and which gradually became transformed
into a drawing room. Now, in the mornings, carriages drew up at the door,
and Jane's country-bred Scots maid came hurrying up from the basement
to admit Mr. and Mrs. Dickens—Miss Harriet Martineau—Mr. and Mrs.
Macready—General Cavaignac—Monsieur Chopin (what did she make
of these names?)—and bid them step upstairs.

We have accounts from both Carlyles of the arrival of one caller, the
Count d'Orsay.

'The sound of a whirlwind rushed through the street,' wrote Jane, 'and there stopt with a prancing of steeds and footman thunder at this door, an equipage all resplendent with skye-blue and silver, discoverable thro' the blinds like a piece of the Coronation Procession.'

From this chariot, which 'struck all Chelsea into mute amazement with splendour', stepped the Count, immaculate in light drab greatcoat and azure satin cravat, with yards of gold watch-chain looped over his broad chest. He was a stunning sight: immensely tall and of godlike beauty, with fine hazel eyes, clear skin and long, curling, dark auburn hair. Unfortunately, he had one flaw: his teeth, though even and of dazzling whiteness, were set too far apart, which spoiled the picture when he smiled.

Confronted by this vision, Carlyle remained calm, finding his guest 'rather a substantial fellow at bottom, by no means without insight, without fun, and a sort of rough sarcasm rather striking in such a porcelain figure'.

Count Alfred d'Orsay was thirty-eight years old, and famous in London as a dandy and wit. He was an athlete, an amateur painter and interior decorator, and for some years had maintained a dubious relationship with that full-blown Irish rose, the Countess of Blessington, his wife's stepmother. In his book *Blessington-d'Orsay, a Masquerade* the late Michael Sadleir claimed that this relationship was platonic—that d'Orsay was in fact homosexual. The shrewd Jane Carlyle did indeed find that 'at first sight his beauty is of that rather disgusting sort which seems to be, like genius, "of no sex" '. But listening to him talking to Carlyle she decided that his manners were manly and unaffected, and in spite of the fantastic finery of his dress, he was 'a devilish clever fellow'.

D'Orsay was no stranger to Chelsea, having lived for a time at number 10 Cheyne Walk, which was known as Gothic House. The Georgian front had been romantically embellished by elaborate bow windows with Gothic ornamentation and a castellated, ivy-entwined balcony, to please a previous tenant, a Mr. Harrington Moore. This gentleman was evidently a bulky person, for, according to Sir Seymour Haden, 'when he died, [he] could not be got out of either door or window—a rather curious instance of the undesirability of being your own architect'. (The architect, in fact, was Pugin.)

Carlyle returned the Count's call, but merely left his card. Nevertheless, he admitted to a curiosity to see—once—the notorious d'Orsay-Blessington ménage, adding rather surprisingly, 'and then oftener, if agreeable'. But it was not agreeable. He went, with Walter Savage Landor, to dine at Gore House: the Count made a rather amateurish pencil sketch of his profile as he sat and talked after dinner; but he did not take to Lady

Blessington—'an *Elderly* "wild Irish girl!" '—and the acquaintance did not flower into friendship.

Though nothing could compare in magnificence with d'Orsay's arrival, many interesting comings and goings at number 5 must from time to time have been 'discernible thro' the blinds' of Cheyne Row neighbours, and many rewarding moments spent peering out of windows, back and front, at the Carlyles.

On hot summer days Mr. Carlyle might sometimes be seen by those immodest enough to look, pacing the garden in his nightshirt, smoking and pondering on the mysteries of the universe (or of his own ill-digestion and inability to sleep); and one morning in July 1843 the neighbourhood were startled to see Mrs. Carlyle on hands and knees, making herself a tent 'from clothes-lines, long poles and an old brown floor-cloth'. 'Many heads peer out on me,' she wrote, 'from all the windows of the Row, eager to penetrate my meaning!'

Her meaning, she could have told them, was that, Carlyle being away, the house was being re-decorated, and she chose to sit out of doors to escape the smell of paint. Even though the tent fell down about her ears from time to time, it was better than being in the house among the 'carpenters, painters, whitewashers and nondescript apprentice lads' who had taken possession of it.

At night, being obliged, on account of the paint, to sleep with windows wide, it occurred to her that 'with several ladders lying quite handy', thieves might, with the greatest ease, 'drop in'. But Jane was undeterred, even when her next-door neighbour, Mr. Lambert, who slept on the ground floor at the back, armed with a loaded gun, came in and offered her 'his protection (in the virtuous sense of the word of course)'. 'From all that he said,' added Jane dryly, 'he left me with the idea that *he* stood much more in need of *my* protection than I did of his.' And, laying a policeman's rattle and a dagger on her spare pillow, she went to sleep, feeling 'quite secure'.

There was some reason for Mr. Lambert's vigilance. During the 'hungry forties', crime, in Chelsea as in the rest of London, was on the increase. The streets were badly lit, and Peel's uniformed Police, instituted in 1829, were still far too few. An old inhabitant, writing in 1901, remembers the first policeman coming on duty in Chelsea in 1830 or thereabouts.

'He was a tall, ungainly-looking countryman, dressed in a blue bob-tailed coat with white metal buttons, white duck trousers, heavy Blucher boots, and a top hat and white gloves. For several days an admiring crowd persistently followed him up and down his beat, a little way behind him like the tail of a comet.'

These strange phenomena, the Peelers, many of whom appear in *Punch* cartoons, soon became familiar objects in the London streets; but in the 'forties they were not yet in great supply in Chelsea. Perhaps this was because they were only paid a guinea a week, which, even then, was not a tempting wage.

Carlyle was in Germany, and Jane in lodgings in Hemus Terrace on the other side of the King's Road, as once again the house was being altered and re-painted. Her maid of the moment, Fanny, was left in charge. On this particular morning, Jane woke with a headache, and 'dragged home' through pours of rain, 'thinking resolutely of the hot coffee that Fanny would have all ready for me, to be taken at the kitchen fire, and the kind sympathy that she would accompany it with'.

But alas, it was not Fanny who appeared at the door of number 5 but the charwoman, Mrs. Heywood, 'a decent, disagreeable young woman'.

' "Oh," she said, the first thing, "we are so glad you are come! Fanny is in such a way! The house has been broken into during the night! The police are now in the kitchen!" '

'Here,' said Jane, 'was a cure for a sick headache!'

In the kitchen were no coffee, no fire, no kind sympathy, only two police sergeants slowly and laboriously writing down what had been stolen, at the dictation of a white and frightened Fanny. The thieves, it seemed, had got in through the larder window: the larder led into the back kitchen, whose door—fortunately!—had been bolted on the outside, saving the rest of the house from being robbed. The burglars had to make do with the contents of the back kitchen, which included Fanny's trunk, and anything they could find in the larder, such as a silver spoon, 'which had unluckily been left, after creaming the milk for my tea'. They drank the milk, said Jane, and ate the cake she had just made, and made off with two shawls and two new dresses belonging to Fanny (who must have been a smart and careful girl); but fortunately they missed her savings—'three sovereigns, which she had wrapped in a bit of brown paper at the bottom of her box', and also a number of things lying about in the back kitchen, which Jane considered would have been useful to them.

Fanny, sound asleep in the front kitchen, never heard a thing; but something awoke her, and she stretched out her hand for a handkerchief, knocking over a brass candlestick, which made, she said, a devil of a row. It was rather, said Jane, 'an angel of a row', for it disturbed the thieves, who made off through the larder window, leaving prints of dirty naked feet on the new shelves, and a lighted candle which burnt a hole in the wood. 'A mercy,' Jane declared, 'that the fine new house was not set on fire!'

During the next few days, policemen in plain clothes and in uniform were constantly turning up, 'talking the most confounded nonsense'. But though suspicious incidents were reported in the Row, ladders moved and a pair of 'bad worsted stockings' found in the conservatory at number 4, the thieves were never caught.

Jane, brave as a lioness now, and reckless of paint smells and headaches, came home to sleep, armed with a pair of pistols. She had bars put in the larder window, and 'I took care,' she wrote, 'to let all the workmen and extraneous people about know of my loaded pistols. The painter . . . came and examined them one day when I was out, and said to Fanny: "I shouldn't like to be a thief within twenty feet of your mistress, with one of these pistols in her hand. I shouldn't give much for my life; she has such a devil of a straight eye!" '

A week or two later, she was disturbed in the night by a loud crash. She rushed downstairs, brandishing one of the pistols. ' "What do you want?" I asked; "who are you?" "It's the policeman, if you please; do you not know that your parlour windows are both open?" ' The noise she had heard was the policeman beating on the door with his truncheon. 'I could not help laughing at what the man's feelings would have been,' she wrote, 'had he known of the cocked pistol within a few inches of him.'

D URING the period of Carlyle's residence in Chelsea, the old village was spreading out in all directions: new streets and squares were being built at a great rate on both sides of the King's Road, from the modest countrified Jubilee Place leading up to Chelsea Common (the Jubilee was George III's) to the urban Walpole Street and Oakley Street which grew up in the 'forties and 'fifties.

On October 18, 1824, ten years before Carlyle arrived, Chelsea's handsome new Parish Church had been consecrated: St. Luke's, Sydney Street (then Robert Street). This was one of the first parish churches of any size to be built in London since the Middle Ages, and its architect, James Savage, chose an ambitious design, in the perpendicular style with flying buttresses, high-pitched nave, and a tower 142 feet high. The first rector was the Hon. and Rev. Gerald Valerian Wellesley, brother of the Iron Duke, and one of his successors was the Rev. Charles Kingsley, father of the two novelists. But when, on May 12, 1836, young Mr. Charles Huffham Dickens was married in St. Luke's to Miss Catherine Hogarth, the ceremony, which was a very quiet affair, was performed by the curate.

St. Luke's has a large burial ground. Here Signor Carlo Rovedino, a bass singer of some reputation, and a native of Milan, was interred; and also two actors, William Blanchard, a 'useful comedian' who played Bob Acres at Covent Garden; and 'Kingly Egerton' who played all the royal personages who made entrances with great pomp and dignity—but who had very little to say.

The Old Church was now All Saints and served by an incumbent. But the old village of Chelsea was still there by the river, in the narrow streets which surrounded the little church. It was losing its countrified air; it was crowded and dirty, but it remained a village. It was noisy: it is true, there were some country noises—cocks crowed, and at the top of Cheyne Row there was a farm where pigs squealed and cows mooed—but most of the noises were human. People shouted. On the river-front there were shouts from the coal-heavers loading up at the wharves; shouts from aboard the barges called billy-boys which tied up at the draw-dock opposite Cheyne

Walk to unload their heavy cargoes of bricks, granite blocks, massive tree-trunks and paving-stones, all of which had to be dragged ashore up a ramp by four or five goaded cart-horses above their hocks in water. From time to time a horse slipped, fell back into the water, and was drowned before it could be rescued, though a special apparatus was on hand to recover— no doubt with shouts of advice and encouragement from bystanders— the heavy corpse.

Other bodies as well as horses' fell, by accident or design, into those muddy waters. Drowning was the easiest way to dispose of unwanted dogs and cats: even Jane Carlyle, usually tender-hearted in advance of her time, alludes without emotion to one of her cats having been drowned for 'un-exampled dishonesty'. Attempts were made to recover, alive or dead, human bodies, and a notice displayed by the Thames Coffee House on Cheyne Walk proclaimed significantly, 'Royal Humane Society's Drags in Constant Readiness'.

The streets leading off Cheyne Walk were full of activity and noise: carts and hand barrows of all kinds rattled over the cobblestones, accom-panied by cries from their drivers, encouraging their beasts or advertising their wares. Leigh Hunt, as we have seen, found these cockney cries inter-esting and pleasant. Carlyle was not so tolerant, and when, in 1836, a Punch and Judy show joined in the din, he lost his temper.

'An accursed *Punch*,' he wrote, 'is shrieking under my windows! The curtains keep out squalid sights; but how exclude distractive sounds?'

How indeed? Carlyle spent the next thirty years trying to find the answer; years during which Mrs. Carlyle was frequently obliged to write diplomatic letters to keepers of cocks, parrots and macaws, parents of piano-playing young ladies, owners of barking dogs and other nuisances, begging, bribing, cajoling, even offering her services as instructor to a backward child, to obtain a few hours of silence for Mr. Carlyle.

The noises—or their power to drive him frantic—changed with the years. After the so-called silent room had been built at the top of the house, the crowing of cocks in the next-door garden passed unremarked, 'his whole attentions,' according to Jane, 'having been morbidly devoted to— *Railway Whistles*.' At this time Italian organ grinders and the fireworks at Cremorne drove him to fury; yet in 1857 when Jane was away ill he con-fessed to her that he was learning to endure these nuisances. 'Yellow scoundrels', as he called the organ boys, were really not troublesome, he said. 'A young lady, very tempestuous on the piano at one of those open back windows, really does me no ill almost; nor does your friend with the accordion. He rather tickles me, like a nigger song; such an enthusiasm is in him about nothing at all; and when he plays "Ye banks and braes", I almost like him.' Jane must have been astonished when she read this. Here was a change! Could it be that Carlyle was deliberately feigning tolerance for her sake? Or had he at last begun to accept the 'distractive sounds' which were part of life in Cheyne Row?

There were many small shops in the village. Piecing together descriptions in a fascinating anonymous account of Chelsea in the 'sixties, and comparing them with the drawings and water colours of the Greaves brothers, it is possible to visualize where some of the old shops were, and how they looked; and so, from chance references in the Carlyles' letters, to guess with some degree of accuracy where and how they did their shopping.

Jane Carlyle was particular about tea and coffee, and went by omnibus to Fortnum and Mason for these commodities. Both Carlyles were particular about their porridge: oatmeal was sent from his family in Scotland, as, from time to time, were delicious home-cured 'bacon hams', and, in the winter, barrels of butter. Otherwise, keeping a careful eye on prices, Jane did her shopping locally.

Carlyle, who disliked even going into a shop, and was overcome with embarrassment when sent to inquire for blue pills for his wife, did, when they first came, allow himself to be led into 'some dim ironmonger's' (there was one in Cheyne Walk), where Jane bought kettles and saucepans and he a tinder box, and a set of garden tools for six shillings. After that, he left all shopping to his wife, but agreed to pay for wines and spirits from the coopers. He also patronized a chemist called Allsop in Cheyne Walk, who made up his blue pills and supplied the castor oil with which he dosed himself.

Several tobacconists competed for his custom: there was a little old shop in the King's Road (it is still there, though no longer a tobacconist) which stocked his particular brand of coarse-cut shag; there was also a shop in Church Street where he bought his cigars. The house, number 34, until quite lately went by the name 'Carlyle's Retreat', and bore over its door the traditional tobacconist's sign, a small kilted Scotsman. Also in Church Street was a Hosier and Haberdasher's, with (in the 'sixties) a leash of crinolines hanging up high over the entrance. This shop was probably more patronized by maids than mistresses; but in May 1836 Jane did 'run out and buy a cotton gown', or rather the material for it, from a similar local establishment. Later, she was more adventurous: she was fastidious and had a natural elegance, and by 1858 was going to Howell and James, a smart firm in Pall Mall, to have a new dress made.

The butcher called daily for orders (there was one on Cheyne Walk called Carless); and the Carlyles ate about one and a half pounds of meat each day, including bones for the dog and for making 'Mr. C's clear essence of beef' which was an important part of his diet. There was a fish shop in Lombard Street, past the old Church, and a greengrocer in Cheyne Walk, where Jane went, after an illness, to have herself weighed on the potato scales. The Carlyles' order for greengrocery can never have been large: too much fruit, in Jane's view, caused colic and was, in any case, an extravagance; while Carlyle did not care for vegetables, only potatoes, of which he ate a great many.

The baker's boy came to the door with his basket of loaves, and on Sundays in winter the muffin man walked down the street ringing his bell, with a baize-covered tray balanced on his head. There were several dairymen: the Carlyles dealt with Mr. Brimlicombe, and later with Mr. Shakespeare, who both kept their own cows, which were stable-fed and milked on the premises. The milkman wore a smock, clean on Sundays and growing grimy during the week; on his shoulders he carried a yoke from which hung two brass milk-cans. Despite this rural appearance, and the milk being so obviously 'straight from the cow', it was not always very nice, and there were complaints at the Carlyle breakfast table that the milk was blue, which meant that it had been watered.

Eggs, too, were a problem. Shop eggs were unreliable, and a bad egg at breakfast could ruin Mr. C's day. Jane sent for eggs from Scotland, but they were apt to arrive 'all in a state of *mush*': the only hope was to find somebody local who kept hens and had eggs to spare, and this was evidently difficult. From time to time there was nothing for it but to buy shop eggs: they came from the Egg and Butter Merchant, who made up for the unreliable quality of his hen eggs by selling unreliable turkey, duck, and even plovers' eggs as well.

Shopping had its ups and downs; but householders could be supplied locally with everything they needed, and shopkeepers took a friendly interest in their customers: everyone knew one another by sight if not by name, and the cobbler, the baker, the milkman, the greengrocer and all were seen in church every Sunday, dressed in their best clothes, with their wives and families.

On July 21, 1845, an important event in Chelsea's history took place: an Act of Parliament was passed for 'Better Paving, Lighting, Cleansing, Regulating and Improving' the Parish of Saint Luke: that is to say, the whole of Chelsea except Hans Town, which did not need improvement. Streets were to be lighted 'with Gas, Oil, or otherwise'; sewers and drains were to be laid, and the streets paved. Moreover, 'it shall and may be lawful for the Commissioners to put up and erect in such places as they may think most convenient Public Urinals'.

The details of this Act are interesting, if only to show how necessary the changes must have been. Owners or occupiers of every house were ordered to fix 'troughs or gutters connected with drain-pipes running from roof to ground, to carry off the water from the roof . . . in such Manner that the Water . . . shall not fall upon the Persons passing near the same'. Finally, the streets were to be kept clean and when necessary watered by persons to be known as Scavengers, who were also appointed to 'collect together all Dirt, Ashes and Rubbish from householders, and carry it away'. The Act did not say where they would put it.

In 1847 the Improvement Act became law, and the Carlyles, and all rate-payers, received an impassioned appeal from a body calling itself The Chelsea Improvement Society.

'The Improvement Bill is now Law,' it announced. 'The means of placing Chelsea in its proper position amongst the Metropolitan Parishes and of turning its great natural and local advantages to account, have been obtained!' In a few days, ratepayers were reminded, they would be called upon to elect Commissioners under the new Act. 'If you choose WISELY, the foundation of Improvement will be securely laid, and the future progress of Chelsea will be inevitable.'

Chelsea's population had enormously increased, and so had the traffic on the streets, there being now as many as 72 omnibuses making 694 journeys into town and back each day; 'and when we further direct your attention to the Splendid Neighbourhoods springing up all around us, we think you will agree with us that something besides mere paving the Footways and reforming the Roads is required; and that New Roads . . . are absolutely necessary to our future Prosperity as a Parish.'

Among the new roads contemplated was one to run across the grounds of the Royal Hospital, giving a direct route to Pimlico, Millbank and Westminster. It must be remembered that at this time there was no Chelsea Embankment, and that Queen's Road, now Royal Hospital Road, ran only from Cheyne Walk as far as the Hospital grounds. It was also suggested that Beaufort Street should be continued northwards from the King's Road, to give a direct route from Battersea Bridge to Kensington.

All this would clearly be a great advantage to Chelsea, which with its dirty, dark, ill-paved streets had fallen behind its smart neighbours, Belgravia, Knightsbridge and Kensington. The new Commissioners (if WISELY chosen) would change all that. 'We warn you,' added the notice, 'against being deluded by the address of the Rate Payers' Association, into a belief that the rates under the new Act can be high. This is impossible!'

In due course the improvements were carried out. But no amount of improving could lessen the problem of poverty, which at this time was becoming a growing disgrace and menace. Hideous slums were to be found in the back streets of London, and Chelsea was not without her share. Paradise Walk, nowadays a row of pretty, elegant cottages, leading from Royal Hospital Road towards the river, was one of the worst areas. In Jane Carlyle's time it was a notorious slum; by the 1870s it was the poorest and dirtiest street in the parish of Christ Church, and a few years later Oscar Wilde, whose smoking room windows overlooked the back of Paradise Walk, felt obliged to hide the sordid view with a Persian screen. Ladies were cautioned not to walk alone down this street, where grimy ragged children swarmed, and several families were crammed into each of the four-roomed hovels.

Even more sinister was Jew's Row, a labyrinth of narrow courts and passages between Burtons Court and Lower Sloane Street. Here were filthy lodging houses and thieves' kitchens, and at one point where the roadway ran at some depth below the path, prostitutes crouched together on the curb to hurl insults at passers-by or set upon some unwary traveller and pick his pockets.

It was many years before these districts were 'improved'; though even in the 1840s and '50s the Victorian conscience, stirred by the writings of Charles Dickens and Charles Kingsley, was becoming alive to the misery of the London slums. Charitable ladies, of whom Jane Carlyle was one, helped the (deserving) poor with gifts of clothing and food: it was thought unwise to offer money, for fear it should be spent on gin. But Jane, giving a shilling to a 'decent looking woman' who came to the door with a baby in her arms and a plausible story, excused herself with the thought, 'if a poor wretch have no fire, no warm breakfast, and for three farthings can get gin enough to both warm and strengthen her, who shall say that her taking it is a fatal sign—not I!' Unfortunately the woman's story was found to be false and the baby borrowed, but Jane went on with her imaginative and generous attempts at charity.

But these isolated efforts were of little avail to stem the terrible advance of poverty and disease which were the product of the new town life.

It was not only the poor who suffered. In the 1850s, in spite of the national prosperity brought about by the railways and the triumphant Great Exhibition, food prices began to go up; so did rates in Chelsea; and the cost of the Crimean War caused Income Tax to be increased from eightpence in the pound to one and fourpence.

Jane Carlyle, reluctantly obliged in 1855 to ask for an increased allowance, decided to compose a financial report in the form of a Parliamentary Budget—'the Budget of a *Femme Incomprise*'—in the hopes of avoiding what she called a money row. Carlyle had been making her an allowance of £50 a quarter, from which, most unusually for a Victorian wife, she settled all bills, including Income Tax Demands, Insurance and Rates, as well as household expenses.

'I will show the Noble Lord,' she wrote, 'with his permission, what the new current expenses are, and to what they amount per annum ("Hear, hear!" and cries of "Be brief!").'

She began by reminding her husband that they now had a more expensive servant than ever before, who received £16 a year and who expected (unheard-of luxury) a regular meat dinner every day—'the others *scrambled* for their living out of ours.' Her food, Jane judged, would add quite £3 a year to the bills.

They now, she continued, had water laid on, and a tap in the kitchen instead of a pump. This luxury cost one pound sixteen shillings a year, with a shilling to the turncock. As well as this new water rate, with all the improvements the other rates had gone up, as had been feared.

'Within the last eighteen months,' wrote Jane, 'there has been added to the Lighting, Pavement and Improvement Rate ten shillings yearly, to the Poor Rate one pound, to the Sewer Rate ten shillings; and now the doubled Income Tax makes a difference of £5 16s. 8d. yearly.'

And, as if this were not bad enough, food had gone up. Bread cost four shillings a week, she said, instead of two and sixpence; butter was now a shilling a pound. Meat, coal (twenty-nine shillings a ton, 'bought judiciously'), even candles, were dearer; bacon had gone up twopence a pound, and even the humble potato was now a penny a pound instead of three pounds for twopence. 'Who could imagine,' said Jane, 'that at the year's end that makes a difference of fifteen and twopence on one's mere potatoes?'

There only remained, she concluded, 'to disclose the actual state of the Exchequer. It is as empty as a drum. (Sensation).' She is at her wits' end. 'If I was a man,' she declared, 'I might fling a gauntlet to society, join with a few brave fellows, and rob a diligence. But my sex kind o' debars from that.'

Signing herself 'Your obedient humble servant', she placed her document on Carlyle's desk overnight, and nervously (though surely with some degree of confidence in her own cleverness) awaited his reply. It was all she could have hoped for. Carlyle, who loathed 'money rows' as much as Jane, was quick to appreciate her tact and humour.

'Excellent, my dear clever Goody,' he wrote at the foot of her last page, 'thriftiest, wittiest and cleverest of women. I will set thee up again to a certainty, and thy £30 more shall be granted, thy bits of debts paid, and thy will be done. T.C.'

Almost to the end of his life, Carlyle walked, alone or in company, through Chelsea and the neighbouring districts. In the early days he walked and talked with Leigh Hunt or John Stuart Mill. Later, he walked out at night with Jane's dog, Nero—long walks for a London dog, through Kensington Gardens and Hyde Park, the master cogitating on Cromwell or Frederick the Great, the dog running uncurbed through the dark empty streets. One night, 'the vermin' got lost on the way home, and Carlyle, who wanted his supper, was obliged to retrace his steps—'no whistle would bring him'—all the way from Cadogan Place to Wilton Crescent where 'the miserable quadruped appeared, and I nearly bullied the life out of him'. A curious love-hate relationship existed between Carlyle and Nero. When the dog jumped out of the drawing room window and fell stunned upon the pavement, 'Mr. C. came down from his bedroom with his chin all over soap' and asked what had happened. Jane and the servant, incoherent with shock and emotion, informed him. 'God bless me!' said Carlyle, and returned to his shaving. Nero recovered; but ten years later, after being run over by a butcher's cart, developed asthma and died. Carlyle was in tears, his heart 'unexpectedly and distractedly torn to pieces' by the loss.

Jane only outlived her dog by six years. After her sudden death while out driving, in April 1866, we find the lonely old man walking indefatigably, along the Fulham Road, the Cromwell Road, in Kensington Gardens and in Hyde Park (where he always doffed his hat at the spot where he believed his wife to have died). William Allingham the Irish poet joined him on many of these walks, and the two of them were joined by others: Lecky, Martineau, Froude, 'too many,' said Allingham jealously, 'for hearing well what Carlyle said.'

Walking with Carlyle was not without its dangers. Caught up in the exposition of a theory, he was oblivious of traffic, and Allingham, 'dodging the carriages' with him at Hyde Park Corner, was on tenterhooks. 'He may catch his death thus, for he usually insists on crossing when he has made up his mind to it, carrying his stick so as to poke it into a horse's nose at need.' In Chelsea, his disregard of passing vehicles was well known, and hansom cab drivers pulled up, calling out, 'All right, Mr. Carlyle!' while he crossed. The tall bent figure in long great-coat and wide-brimmed hat taking his constitutional along the riverside became a feature of local life; and a parrot which lived at the corner of Manor Street and Cheyne Walk used to make noises like a stick thumping the pavement and cry, 'There goes old Carlyle!'

In 1874 the beautiful Chelsea river front with its low wall and double row of pollarded elms was gradually blotted out by the building of an embankment with a new wide road which ran beside and above the curbed river to Millbank. The water which at high tide had spread across Cheyne Walk and sometimes flooded the cellars of the old houses, was imprisoned behind high grey granite walls. Below the river bed sewers were laid: the smells which had issued from the water in hot weather grew less pungent. Handsome new gas lamps ornamented the Embankment wall. By the side of the old Cadogan Pier, where Carlyle, on his way to Scotland, caught a boat to St Katherine's Docks, arose a new suspension bridge, the Albert Bridge.

With the building of the Embankment many historic landmarks disappeared. The ancient river wall and the flights of stairs that led from Cheyne Walk to the water were demolished; the secret passage leading from Shrewsbury House to the river was blocked; as were other secret passages, from other houses, including the Magpie and Stump, made for hurried escapes, of Huguenots, of Jacobites, of enemies to King or Parliament. Old water-gates, old inn signs, like the rusty iron Magpye, were swept away or buried under the new Embankment Gardens. Walpole's octagonal summer house, on the river wall near the Royal Hospital, was pulled down when the new road was built alongside the Embankment. Slowly, relentlessly, the nineteenth century imposed its practical plans for the enrichment and enlargement of a district that was beginning to attract the more opulent professional classes, as well as the artists and writers for whom the Carlyles had led the way.

EVEN IN the mid-nineteenth century, Chelsea's most down-at-heel period, the fine houses in Cheyne Walk maintained their dignity, and continued to attract distinguished and discriminating tenants. Number 4 bears a plaque which states that in 1880 George Eliot died there: but it should first be recorded that twenty years earlier Daniel Maclise, the Irish artist beloved of Dickens, lived there.

This house bears the date 1718 upon the leaden head to a rain-water pipe, and shows signs of having been designed for a particular owner. It has a beautiful hooded doorway with Corinthian pilasters, and a delicately designed wrought-iron gate. The classical paintings on the walls and ceiling of the staircase are of the same date as the house; but the forest scenes on the walls and the plump goddesses with their attendant cupids overhead were almost certainly touched up by Maclise.

Born in Cork in 1811, Daniel Maclise came to London when he was sixteen to enter the Royal Academy Schools, where he won a gold medal. During the 1830s, under the pseudonym of Alfred Croquis, he made sketches of famous literary personages for *Fraser's Magazine*, and through these encounters, with the aid of an attractive personality and handsome looks, he stepped into that small brilliant world which Jane Carlyle found such good company—that 'little knot of blackguard literary people who felt ourselves above all rules, and independent of the universe!'

Maclise evidently felt himself above all rules when, in 1837, he rashly embarked upon a love affair with the notorious Lady Sykes, who had been Disraeli's mistress. Unfortunately her husband surprised them in bed together, and sued Maclise. The scandal even reached the ears of the young Queen, who seems to have taken it calmly, blaming the lady. In her journal for February 2, 1839, she wrote, 'Talked of Maclise having run away with Lady Sykes; Lord M. said "They're a bad set; they're granddaughters of Elmore, the horse-dealer . . . Old Elmore trafficked with his daughters as much as he did with his horses." '

In 1839 Maclise painted a portrait of Dickens—the 'Nickleby Portrait' —which is probably his best known work today. It hangs in the National Portrait Gallery. In its lighting and composition, and in the pose adopted

'A Chelsea Interior': Thomas and Jane
Carlyle. After a painting by Robert Tait, 1857

Cheyne Row *c.* 1870.
Photograph by James Hedderley

Cheyne Walk. Water-colour by Henry and Walter Greaves

The Chelsea shore from Battersea Bridge, *c.* 1870.
Photograph by James Hedderley

J. M. W. Turner, R.A.
Drawing by Charles Martin

Turner's house. Water-colour by Thomas Hosmer Shepherd

Dante Gabriel Rossetti in his back garden.
Cartoon by Max Beerbohm

by the young author, it emphasizes Dickens's love of the theatre. Thackeray when he saw it exclaimed, 'Here we have the real identical man, Dickens!'

Maclise refused to be paid for this picture.

'My dear Dickens,' he wrote, 'how could you think of sending me a cheque for what was to me a matter of gratification? I am almost inclined to be offended with you. May I not be permitted to give some proof of the value I attach to your friendship?'

The friendship was an affectionate one on both sides. 'Mac' was evidently an enchanting companion, with 'a quaint oddity that in him gave to shrewdness itself an air of Irish simplicity'. We catch glimpses of him in Dickens's letters: on a trip through Cornwall with Dickens, Forster and Stanfield, Maclise 'singing songs' as the Pickwickian party drive through the night in an open carriage, its pockets bulging with bottles—'I never laughed in my life as I did on this journey,' said Dickens.

Elsewhere we hear of Maclise describing himself as 'a discursive devil' and 'I wish you could form an idea of his genius,' Dickens wrote to Professor Felton. 'He is in great favour with the Queen, and paints secret pictures for her to put upon her husband's table on the morning of his birthday, and the like. But if he has a care,' added Dickens prophetically, 'he will leave his mark on more enduring things than palace walls.'

Maclise, who never married, was one of the rare people (Hans Christian Andersen was another) who appreciated Mrs. Dickens. Though poor Kate fell so short of her husband's expectations, she had in Maclise a true admirer. He painted two portraits of her, which display with loving care the beauty of her large, heavy-lidded eyes, and the pink and white plumpness which time and child-bearing so cruelly coarsened.

When, in 1842, Kate accompanied her husband to America and was obliged to leave her four small children behind, Maclise made a drawing of them for her. Kate's note of gratitude is one of the very few of her letters which survived the bonfire at Gadshill.

'My beautiful sketch of our darlings is more admired than I can possibly describe. It is in great demand wherever we go, and Willis, the author, asked me to give it to him. Imagine such impudence and audacity!'

It is sad that Chelsea only knew Maclise at the end of his life, when the wit that had endeared him to Dickens had grown a little sour. He was slowly wearing himself out in eight years of patient labour on his enormous, carefully detailed frescoes in the House of Lords—'Wellington and Blucher', and 'The Death of Nelson'. During those eight years, he left Cheyne Walk every morning at ten, and worked all day in what he called 'that gloomy hall', enduring, we are told, 'the alternations of oppressive heat in summer, and the fogs and damps of winter'.

When at last both works were finished, and the scaffolding removed, Maclise was dismayed to find that the new stained glass windows in the Royal Gallery completely obliterated Wellington and Blucher when the afternoon sun streamed through. 'I am mortified in the last degree,' he wrote to F. G. Stephens of the *Athenaeum* . . . 'Although we have reverent ideas connected with the "storied pane", still it ought to be a matter of telling its own story, and not, as in my case, be allowed to make commentaries and annotations and illustrations on mine.'

He spent the last months of his life at Cheyne Walk sitting upstairs making sketches of the river from his windows, which overlooked the draw-dock, where the cruel treatment of the carthorses drawing immense loads ashore, together with other disturbing sights and sounds, stirred him to write a letter to *The Times*.

'I write,' he said, 'on behalf of many of my neighbours who are devoted to quiet pursuits in Cheyne Walk, Chelsea. We like the place, and foreigners like it, for I see them meandering . . . opposite to my gateway and thinking with sighs how badly it represents the Cours de la Reine and the Lung d'Arno. Yet they come here as the best reminder of what they have left, and they find elm trees bordering the water, and a really grand expanse over Chelsea Reach to Battersea Park, crowned by the heights of Clapham, and the Crystal Palace gleaming on the nearest Surrey Hill. Yet what drawbacks are there to our otherwise pleasant situation.'

Cheyne Walk, in short, had gone to the dogs: he was oppressed not only by the offensive sights, but by even more horrible sounds, from the loud-mouthed bargees, and by open-air preachers and singers on Sunday evenings, 'who bray their sermons and howl their hymns to an auditory of mocking and smoking bargemen'.

He goes on to complain about washing lines—presumably, since he faced the river, attached to trees and walls belonging to the huddle of cottages adjoining the Old Swan, to his left—which offend the artist's eye by displaying garments 'inflated by the river breeze' into travesties of the human form.

His final grievance is his neighbours' cocks and hens—a grievance he shared with Carlyle.

'Everybody here, of course, keeps poultry, and a bantam on my right hand . . . is sufficient in his small treble to wake up and irritate all the hoarser cadences of full-size cocks who defy him, while, at the same time . . . we have to endure the cackling proclamation of some hen, varied by an interjectional scream celebrating some event which no-one cares to understand but themselves.

'Mr. Carlyle,' he continues '. . . is said to have remarked with regard to this last peculiar nuisance, "I have no objection to their hatching, if they would only do it in peace and let me do the same." '

After Maclise's death in 1870, number 4 was occupied by William Vaux, President of the Society of Antiquaries and Keeper of Coins and Medals at the British Museum. When he moved away in 1880, the house was taken by Mr. and Mrs. Cross, that is to say, by George Eliot and her newly-married husband. They moved in on December 3: she wrote that she looked forward to recovered health in the mild air of Chelsea. Nineteen days later she died, from a chill caught in an overheated concert hall, leaving no impression on the house except another famous name to add to Chelsea's list.

At the far end of Chelsea Reach, past Lindsey House, the buildings thinned out and had a humble, cottagey appearance. It was here that in 1846 a Margate landlady called Mrs. Booth bought a twenty-one year lease of a small house, number 6 Davis Place, which stood between Alexander, Boatbuilder and a tavern called The Aquatic Stores. Her gentleman lodger came with her, and wished for some reason to be known as Mr. Booth. He was an old man, seventy-one, with short thick legs, a red, weather-beaten face, and piercing grey eyes under heavy brows. He was J. M. W. Turner, R.A., John Ruskin's idol, in search now of a few years of peace and anonymity before he died.

He soon became a well-known figure on the Chelsea waterside: 'Puggy Booth' the boys called him; and because he sometimes carried a telescope, the boatmen dubbed him 'the Admiral'. There evidently was something nautical in his appearance: G. D. Leslie wrote of him, 'He always had the indescribable charm of the sailor both in appearance and manners; his large grey eyes were those of a man accustomed to looking straight at the face of nature through fair weather and foul alike.'

On visits to Margate Turner had lodged with the twice-widowed Sophia Booth for nearly twenty years; and for at least ten, since the death of Mr. Booth in 1834, their relationship had given rise to gossip, which followed them to Chelsea. Although Turner had been amorous in his youth, it is likely that the gossip was unfounded, and the arrangement an unromantic one which happened to suit both parties. Mrs. Booth was a dark, handsome, motherly woman and was evidently used to the ways of her taciturn and often parsimonious companion, while, though illiterate herself, she guessed at his greatness. Chelsea was not his official home: he owned a large house in Queen Anne Street, Marylebone, where he had a gallery at the back to display his paintings, and an ancient, hag-like house-keeper called Hannah Danby. But while Turner the painter was thought by the world to reside in the dusty mansion in Queen Anne Street, Admiral Booth (noticeably spruced up in appearance by his fond land-lady) succeeded in keeping his Chelsea address a secret. There is a story that after a dinner party given by David Roberts, R.A., Turner was helped into his cab by his host, who asked what address he should give the driver. 'Tell the fellow to drive to Oxford Street,' was the cunning reply, 'and then I'll direct him.'

There are many Turner stories. The son of a barber in Maiden Lane, he was rough in speech and clumsy in address. He was silent in company, even inarticulate, but enjoyed his private jokes, most of which were in-comprehensible to everybody but himself. Sometimes, however, he was ready with a quick riposte, as when a prospective buyer, staring at one of his paintings, complained, 'After all, Mr. Turner, cliffs are only chalk and stone and grass. I can't see these wonderful blues and reds and yellows in the combination.' 'Hm,' said Turner, 'but don't you wish you could?'

Yet in Society he was not without charm. There is a sketch of him by D'Orsay, quietly stirring a cup of tea at a party, with an air of gentle amusement at the scene before him. And on another occasion: 'He quite won the hearts of my two sisters,' wrote George Leslie, 'pretty girls of 22 and 20 at the time, flirting with them in his queer way, and drinking with great enjoyment the glass of hot grog which one of them mixed for him.'

On Varnishing Day at the Academy, Turner was in his element. In baggy tail-coat and tall hat, he worked all day, altering and improving his own pictures—and sometimes other people's as well. In Henry Howard's painting, 'The Trimmer Children', he went so far as to add, with the artist's permission, a cat wrapped in a red handkerchief, to give the picture light and life. In 1847, he found one of his works hung next to Maclise's 'The Sacrifice of Noah after the Deluge', and we are told by Solomon Hart:

'Turner, always a friend to talent, suggested to Maclise an alteration in his picture with the following colloquy—"I wish Maclise that you would alter that lamb in the foreground, but you won't." "Well, what shall I do?" "Make it darker behind to bring the lamb out, but you won't." "Yes, I will." "No, you won't." "But I will." "No, you won't." Maclise did as Turner proposed and asked his neighbour if that would do. Turner (stepping back to look at it): "It is better, but not right." He then went up to the picture, took Maclise's brush, accomplished his wish and improved the effect. He also introduced a portion of a rainbow, or reflected rainbow, much to the satisfaction of Maclise, and his work remains untouched.'

In Chelsea, he spent much of his time watching the river, from his first-floor window, or from the flat roof, where he put up a wrought-iron balustrade to prevent himself from falling into the street, and which is still there. He had a hole cut through which he could climb up on to the roof in the small hours to watch the dawn and sunrise, and drink in the changing splendours of cloud and sun, to the interpretation of which he had given his life. Sometimes, later in the day, he would hire a skiff and have himself rowed about the river. The boatman was, often as not, Charles Greaves, whose sons, Henry and Walter, became Whistler's disciples. Turner, generally accompanied on these expeditions by Mrs. Booth, would ask what the weather was going to do. If the report were discouraging, Turner would say, 'Well, Mrs. Booth, we won't go far.' If Greaves gave a good forecast, 'Mr. Booth', accompanied by his lady, would be rowed across the river and landed, a little downstream, at Battersea Fields, and from there they would walk to old Battersea Church, along the river bank. Here, Turner liked to sit in the vestry above the west door, and watch the sunset over the water. The armchair in which he used to sit is still preserved in the charming eighteenth-century church.

During the years at Chelsea he was still painting: he had a dread of idleness; but most of the work he did was touching up and altering earlier pictures. His legs ached and he suffered from indigestion caused by loss of teeth. Nevertheless he managed to exhibit four paintings at the 1850 Royal Academy: 'Mercury Sent to Admonish Aeneas', 'Aeneas Relating the Story of his Life to Dido', 'The Visit to the Tomb' and 'The Departure of the Fleet'.

That autumn his health broke. Sometimes he was too weak to work, and at night his sleep was disturbed by visions of paintings yet to be done. He had a horror of death and oblivion, and—in the hope that his name would live—he had long refused to sell his paintings, hoarding them in the big studio at Queen Anne Street and bequeathing the collection to the Nation.

'Old Time has made sad work with me,' he wrote on December 27, 1850, to Mr. Hawkesworth Fawkes,[1] thanking him for a Christmas pie. Of his failing health he adds, 'I always dreaded it with horror now I feel it acutely now [sic] whatever—Gout or nervousness—it having fallen into my Pedestals . . .' But he was still alert enough to watch the building of the Crystal Palace in Hyde Park, and to observe 'the vast Conservatory all looks confusion worse confounded'.

[1] Son of Turner's patron, Walter Ramsden Hawkes of Farnley Hall.

A few months later we hear of him 'looking better tho' not well', but he was too ill to attend the soirée at the close of the Royal Academy Exhibition in July.

Mr. W. Bartlett, 'surgeon Dentist and Cupper' of Park Walk, Chelsea, was now attending him. He supplied him with a set of teeth, but it seems doubtful if they were ever used. He never knew Turner, he afterwards told Ruskin, by any name but 'Booth'. 'There was nothing about the house at all,' he wrote, 'to indicate the abode of an artist . . . He was very fond of smoking and yet had a great objection to anyone knowing of it. His diet was principally at that time rum and milk. He would take some two quarts of milk per day and rum in proportion, very frequently in excess . . . He offered should he recover to take me on the continent and show me all the places he had visited.'

But this brave dream never materialized. At ten o'clock on the morning of December 19, 1851, Joseph Mallord William Turner died in his small bedroom overlooking the Thames. It was a foggy morning, but just before his death the pale winter sun broke through the fog and shone straight on to his face. 'He died without a groan,' said Bartlett, who was there, with Mrs. Booth.

CHAPTER FIVE

THE MOST impressive house at the eastern end of Cheyne Walk is number 16. It is not quite as large as number 6, where Weedon Butler kept his school, or as immaculately eighteenth-century in appearance: the middle of its brick front has been violated by the addition of a curious wooden bay, plastered over and painted brick-colour, which gives extra windows to the first and second floors.[1] But this house is distinguished by its fine wrought ironwork: there are charming balconies at the back and a tall and beautiful gateway in front, which has the air of an entrance to a noble estate, and is crowned by a monogram surrounded by curlicues.

This monogram led to interesting rumours about the house's origin: it is rather difficult to decipher, and we can hardly blame those nineteenth-century romantics who decided that the letters were C.R. and stood for Catherine Regina. Some wished to go a step further and identify this with Henry VIII's final and surviving queen, who did occupy the Manor; and here they became confused and tried to prove that the house was built on the site of the Manor: the back looked rather Tudor in design, so they called it Tudor House. But the gates, with the monogram, were not Tudor: they belonged to a later period. Whose, then, were the initials? Someone thought of Charles II's wife, poor neglected Catherine of Braganza. In this house, it was now decided, she must have spent long lonely summer days while King Charles disported himself on (and in) the Thames, and visited Mistress Gwynne at Sandford House. In support of this theory the road from the Royal Hospital to Cheyne Walk was named the Queen's Road, and finally, in 1882, when the Reverend and Mrs. Haweis became tenants of number 16, they changed its name from Tudor House to Queen's House. They were indefatigable in their efforts to prove the house's romantic and royal origin.

In 1900 the Rev. R. Haweis wrote:

'The extraordinary masonry of the cellarage and foundations of Queen's House is quite of the Hampton Court period, and bears out the tradition

---

[1] The latest owner, Mr. Paul Getty, has had this bay painted white, a great improvement.

that the house was built in Charles II's time—probably by Wren—on the foundations of part of Henry VIII's palace.'

He was impressed by the thickness and solidity of the cellar walls, and believed that the basement of the house was actually part of the old palace. 'In excavations for drainage,' he writes, 'Mr. Haweis unearthed the old water-gate, through which its occupants passed to the steps in the stone forecourt, by which they could reach their barges.

'Mr. Haweis,' he reiterates firmly, 'thinks that the present house was certainly built by Wren, the Royal architect, for Queen Catherine.'

But alas, when Mr. Randall Davies, F.S.A., began to make his accurate and valuable researches into Chelsea's history, this charming tradition fell to pieces. The house, like its neighbours, was built on one of the plots divided off by Sir Hans Sloane, on the site of the Great Garden. It could therefore have had no structural connection with the Tudor building. Further, it was built in 1717, and the widowed Queen Catherine went back to Portugal in 1692. The first lease-holder, for whom the house was designed, was Richard Chapman, described as an apothecary of St. Clement Danes, and whose initials R.C. form the monogram. The basement, according to Walter Godfrey's *Survey of London*, 'presents nothing more remarkable than the usual sturdy buildings of the [eighteenth-century] period.' The only remaining mystery is how an apothecary was able to afford such an imposing and beautifully designed house.

In the autumn of 1862, Dante Gabriel Rossetti, painter and poet, moved in. He occupied Tudor House for twenty years, till his death in 1882, and his finest work was done there.

When he came he was thirty-four years old, and had reached a crisis in his life, and in his career. The first exuberant, idealistic years of the Pre-Raphaelite Brotherhood were ended; the original Brothers, Millais, Holman Hunt and Rossetti, were embarked on disparate courses. Hunt was obsessed with the Holy Land, Millais married to Ruskin's ex-wife and beginning to degenerate into a fashionable painter; and Rossetti, accepting Ruskin's friendship, was inevitably and regrettably estranged from Millais. A new phase in the Pre-Raphaelite movement was about to come into being: new names—William Morris and Edward Burne-Jones—were in the air; and though Rossetti was eventually to disclaim the very name— 'Why should we go on talking about the visionary vanities of half a dozen boys?'—the name attached itself firmly to the new movement and to much that had nothing to do with it at all.

A few months before he came to Chelsea, Rossetti's short-lived marriage to Elizabeth Siddal had ended tragically with her death from an overdose of laudanum. The lovely, ethereal milliner's apprentice with her aureole of red-gold hair was seventeen when she was first persuaded to sit for the young Pre-Raphaelites. Rossetti, as was his lordly way, grabbed the 'stunner' for himself, and for ten years she was his model—and his pupil, having a fondness for drawing which Rossetti's Svengali-like magnetism transformed into talent. He was a poet: she, too, began to write—sad poems, harping on disappointed love and fulfilment in death.

She is an enigmatic character: a melancholy girl, jerked out of her own environment into a world of clever, joking young men; posing patiently for Millais's floating Ophelia in a bath of warm water which was allowed to grow cold (and her lungs were weak); holding herself aloof from other models, respectable at all costs. She grew more and more dependent upon Rossetti; but although he poured out drawings of Guggums (his oddly inappropriate name for her) he did not marry her. Her health declined; she grew difficult and demanding; and she was bitterly jealous of Fanny Cornforth, a strapping blonde from Wapping, who was Rossetti's mistress for many years.

In 1857, even Lizzie's position as Rossetti's spiritual love was threatened. At Oxford that summer he first saw Jane Burden. This tall gipsy beauty with her long neck and load of dark waving hair became the inspiration for much of Rossetti's later work—and married his friend William Morris.

Soon after this event, and perhaps because of it, Rossetti rushed down to Hastings where Lizzie was recovering from one of her many illnesses, married her and took her to Paris. For a time, her health improved, and perhaps Rossetti felt that his impulsive action had been justified. Then she gave birth to a stillborn daughter; and after this, slowly, relentlessly, the tuberculosis latent in her manifested itself, and she began to waste away before his eyes. There was talk of moving away from Chatham Place, Blackfriars, where the damp river air had a disastrous effect upon her weak lungs, but she had not the energy to move. It was a sad, muddled, uncomfortable ménage. Lizzie had never been domesticated; now she lay on a sofa, too languid even to write poetry. Rossetti was, after his fashion, kind, but not the man to cope patiently and efficiently with a permanent invalid. It was natural to him to seek more lively company. Blonde, buxom Fanny Cornforth with her radiant health must have been a comfort. Moreover, she was a good cook.

On February 10, 1862, the Rossettis dined with the poet Swinburne at the Sablonière Restaurant in Leicester Square. Lizzie had been suffering for some time from acute neuralgia, and trying to stifle the pain with laudanum. But she was fond of Swinburne, who was her devoted admirer, and during the meal she became unnaturally animated. After taking her home, Rossetti went off to teach a class at Ruskin's Working Men's Club. He did not return till nearly midnight: Lizzie was unconscious, with an empty laudanum bottle beside her. She never regained consciousness.

At the inquest a verdict of accidental death was returned; but was it accidental? In a moment of agonized grief and remorse, Rossetti placed his unpublished poems in her coffin; they were buried with her, wrapped in her hair, a desperate, belated peace offering. But in death, as in life, Lizzie remains an enigma.

When Rossetti came to Cheyne Walk this tragedy was eight months behind him. From the first, Tudor House cast a spell over him: the spacious beautiful house with its romantic garden offered peace, and—what he most needed—a hiding place. His large drawing room on the first floor had seven windows overlooking the river; his studio was at the back, on the ground floor, a panelled room which faced northwards over the garden. Here he set to work upon his memorial to Lizzie, the painting called 'Beata Beatrix', which hangs in the National Gallery. It is a portrait of Elizabeth Siddal, but it is also an idealized woman. John Piper (in *The English Face*) considers that 'the face is already nearer to Jane Morris'. Rossetti did not begin his series of paintings of Mrs. Morris till 1868; but perhaps already the lines of her face were printed on his mind and beginning slowly to obliterate those of his dead wife.

This is how Georgiana Burne-Jones described his two loves.

'They were as unlike as possible and quite perfect as a contrast to each other . . . The difference between the two women may be typified broadly as that between sculpture and painting, Mrs. Morris being the statue and Mrs. Rossetti the picture. The grave nobility and colourless perfection of feature in the one [Jane Morris] was made human by kindness that looked from "her great eyes standing far apart", while a wistfulness that often accompanied the brilliant loveliness and grace of the other gave an unearthly character to her beauty.'

Tudor House was spacious and expensive (the rent was £110 a year). Rossetti's plan in taking it was to share it with two other men. Swinburne, on an impulse of sympathy and comradeship after Lizzie's death, was the first candidate. Ruskin then offered himself, but had to be tactfully discouraged: living in the same house with the Don Quixote of Denmark Hill, who rose with the lark, lived frugally and went to bed early, was more than either Rossetti or Swinburne could face. In the end, it was George Meredith who joined the household; but his stay was brief. Rumour had it that the sight of Dante Gabriel at breakfast consuming a plateful of ham surrounded by six bleeding eggs was too much for his sensibilities; however, there may have been other reasons.

Swinburne remained; but he proved an erratic and undependable companion. He was always going away on visits; and when he was in residence he was frequently intoxicated (he had a weak head for drink), and apt to behave wildly and unpredictably. Between Rossetti and Swinburne there was a genuine affection and appreciation of each other's gifts; but both were governed by their emotions, and tormented by the problems of their art and of their lives. Rossetti, eight years older, was concerned at Swinburne's abnormal sex life: floggings at Eton had left their effect upon a poet already conscious of his puny size and lack (in an age of muscular heroes) of manliness. At twenty-five, during the summer before his arrival at Cheyne Walk, he had been disillusioned by the failure of his one attempt at a normal love affair: the lady, Miss Jane Faulkner, had received his proposal of marriage with a pause of embarrassed incredulity, followed by uncontrollable laughter. He was bitterly wounded:

> I shall go my ways, tread out my measure,
> Fill the days of my daily breath
> With fugitive things not good to treasure . . .

Thereafter he succumbed to the clandestine delights of flagellation, in St. John's Wood.

Swinburne, according to Edmund Gosse, possessed a very unusual appearance: 'a slight girlish figure, below the middle height, with a great shock of red hair, which seemed almost to touch his narrow, sloping shoulders.'

His eyes were light bright green, his chin, like Shelley's, receded, and his teeth were rabbity. He had tiny feet and hands, which were constantly in action—his hands, when he was excited, fluttering like wing-tips from arms held stiffly to his sides. He has been compared by Henry Adams to a bird—'a tropical bird, high-crested, long-beaked, quick-moving, with rapid utterance and screams of humour, quite unlike any English lark or nightingale.'

Amid Rossetti's collection of exotics, Swinburne was not out of place. Among his other peculiarities he had a highly sensitive skin, and in hot weather was apt to fling off his clothes and walk about the house stark naked, which was disconcerting for servants and guests. But in company he could be wildly amusing and, till overcome by drink, an asset to Rossetti's dinner parties.

While in residence at Tudor House Swinburne worked in his sitting room on the right of the front door, completing here his drama 'Chastelard', and composing part of his 'Poems and Ballads'. In 1863, at Rossetti's suggestion, he began a study of William Blake; and it was in the course of this labour that he formulated the theory of 'Art for Art's sake' which has been attributed to many people, and which later became the war-cry of the Aesthetic movement. To the artist, he wrote, 'all faith, all virtue, all moral duty or religious necessity, was . . . summed up . . . by the one matter of art'.

In the early days of Rossetti's partnership with Swinburne at Tudor House, the former arrived home one day with several copies of a poem which had been remaindered by the publisher, Quaritch, and sold on a stall outside his shop at a penny a copy. This sad failure was entitled 'The Rubaiyat of Omar Khayyam', by Edward FitzGerald.[1] On reading it, Swinburne became wildly excited, rushed off to Fulham to fetch Burne-Jones, and the three enthusiasts made their way to Quaritch, where they each bought a number of copies of the poem. The following day they found that the price had gone up to twopence.

'But we were extravagant enough to invest in a few more copies even at that scandalous price,' wrote Swinburne. The word went round among their friends that he and Rossetti had found a treasure. 'I think it was within the month,' he added, 'that Quaritch was selling copies at a guinea.'

But Swinburne never settled long at Cheyne Walk: a bird of passage, he was forever on the wing, to the sea, to a country house, to Paris. By 1864 Rossetti was bored: neither Swinburne nor his rent had been forthcoming for months, and at last he wrote an 'affectionate and cordial' letter, stating that he wished to have the house at Chelsea to himself. It was an amicable parting, and the friendship went on, unbroken.

Tudor House was always Rossetti's house, dominated by his strong personality. Believing in its Royal origin—that it was, in fact, the remaining wing of Henry VIII's palace—he furnished it lavishly but haphazardly with antiques: Venetian mirrors and chandeliers, Chippendale cabinets, pieces of Chinese lacquer, curious musical instruments, most of which he found in the junk shops of Lambeth and Hammersmith. His friendship with William Morris and Edward Burne-Jones and their shared delight in mediaeval craftsmanship must to some extent have influenced the furnishing of Tudor House; but Rossetti's taste was for more elaborate and luxurious pieces than the oak settles and rush-bottomed chairs designed

[1] The Iran Government have offered (1970) the Royal Borough of Kensington and Chelsea a statue of Omar Khayyam, which is to be placed in the Embankment Gardens near Tudor House, as a tribute to Rossetti and Swinburne.

in the Morris workshops—the Art Furniture now associated with the typical 'Pre-Raphaelite Room'.

Success came to Rossetti at Cheyne Walk; although he never held an exhibition, his paintings sold for high prices, or rather were commissioned at high prices and the work finished in his own, often prolonged, time. Although his income sometimes reached £4,000 a year, there were numerous financial crises. Treffry Dunn, the young Cornish painter who became his assistant in 1867, was surprised to find that Rossetti had no bank account: large sums of money were thrust into a bureau drawer, where members of the household helped themselves.

During the first ten years at Tudor House Rossetti entertained constantly and lavishly; but there is an impression, in letters and descriptions, that the house was badly run, untidy, and not over-clean. Servants came and went; we hear of rats and mice in the studio, and William Allingham found a mouse eating a kipper in the basement. But the rooms had a dignity which could not be spoiled. The room on the right of the front door—known variously as Swinburne's room, the dining room, and the parlour—struck Treffry Dunn on his arrival as 'one of the prettiest, and one of the most curiously furnished and old-fashioned sitting-rooms that it has ever been my lot to see'. The panelled walls, painted green, were hung with antique mirrors of all shapes and sizes which reflected the river view seen through the climbing jasmine outside, and the room itself from every angle. The chimney-piece was supported by panels of black Chinese lacquer with designs of animals, birds and flowers in gold; below it the fireplace was lined with old blue and white Dutch tiles (which are still there). There was an eighteenth-century brass grate, with fire irons and fender to match.

From Dunn also we have a description of the Master's bedroom. It was at the back, and you entered it through another, smaller, room, where in later years he breakfasted. The bedroom was very dark. 'I thought it a most unhealthy room to sleep in,' wrote Dunn. 'Thick curtains, heavy in crewel-work in 17th century designs of fruit and flowers (which he had bought out of an old furnishing shop somewhere in the slums of Lambeth) hung closely drawn round an antiquated four-poster bedstead.' This was, in fact, a family bed. Rossetti, like Jane Carlyle, slept in the bed in which he had been born.

'A massive panelled oak mantelpiece,' Dunn continues, 'reached from floor to ceiling, fitted up with numerous shelves and cupboard-like recesses, all filled with a medley of brass repoussé dishes, blue china vases filled with peacock feathers, oddly fashioned early English and foreign candlesticks, Chinese monstrosities in bronze, and various other curiosities, the whole surmounted by an ebony and ivory crucifix. The only modern thing I could see anywhere in the room was a Bryant & May's matchbox!'

The windows looked over the garden, but 'on this fine summer's day,' wrote Dunn, 'light was almost excluded from the room' by curtains of heavy Genoese velvet. 'The gloom of the place,' he commented, 'made one feel quite depressed and sad.'

It is to be hoped that those curtains were sometimes taken down and cleaned. When Rossetti slept inside the four-poster, behind those hangings 'heavy with crewel-work', what sort of air can he have breathed? These same curtains were there when, in 1880, Hall Caine was shown the room by his host. So were the 'black oak chimney-piece of curious design' and the black and white crucifix. So were the velvet window curtains. In thirteen years nothing had changed. How should it? There was no one, except Rossetti himself, to institute changes, and Hall Caine's description, read immediately after Dunn's, gives one an overwhelming sense of the gradual decline of Rossetti's interest in his surroundings.

Since Lizzie's death Rossetti had been tormented by insomnia, and he encouraged his friends to sit up talking and smoking into the small hours: they needed no inducement; Rossetti's charm was hypnotic. He rose late: 'I lie as long, or say, as late, as Dr. Johnson used to,' he told Hall Caine. After a huge breakfast he worked all day without another meal till he dined at night. Any exercise he took was after dusk, when he could no longer see to paint; then, with his curious rolling walk, he strolled along the river bank watching the hay boats with their red sails reflected in the darkening water.

The parson's children in *A Book with Seven Seals*[1] were hurried away by their nurse if Rossetti were seen approaching in his wide hat and flapping cloak, 'In Nurse's opinion,' wrote the authoress, 'he was only fit to be a bat and come out in the dusk, flitting up the Walk and in again to hide away from the sun in his great big house, where he painted pictures and kept a lot of poets and other wild beasts, so she had been told.'

Evidently local gossip had invested the artist-poet with the qualities of a bogeyman. ' "She wasn't going to have the children frightened by the likes of him," ' Nurse declared, and when she saw him coming she would turn up a side street.

The collecting of 'wild beasts' was a craze which began soon after Rossetti arrived in Cheyne Walk. He had always been fascinated by odd creatures, a taste shared by his sister Christina, whose goblins in 'Goblin

[1] An anonymous account of the life of a Chelsea family in the 1860's and '70's.

Market' with their 'demure grimaces' have faces 'cat-like and rat-like, Ratel and wombat-like'. Wombats had for Gabriel an irresistible charm, and he installed one at Tudor House. There is a pencil drawing at the Tate Gallery by William Bell Scott entitled 'Rossetti's Wombat Seated on his Lap'. Only the hand of the master appears, but the fat chuckling creature is faithfully depicted, drinking out of a cup—an endearing beast with a figure not unlike Rossetti's in middle life. This animal is said to have devoured the new straw hat of a patroness called Mrs. Virtue Tebbs while she sat for her portrait. When it was discovered, 'Oh, poor wombat!' cried Rossetti, 'it is so indigestible!'

In the garden Rossetti kept peacocks, and built wooden sheds to house armadilloes and kangaroos. There were squirrels, mice and dormice, and two owls called Jessie and Bobbie. There was a racoon.

Treffry Dunn describes his introduction to this beast, which was imprisoned in a packing case under a heavy slab of marble. When the lid was heaved up, Rossetti 'put his hand in quickly, seized the "coon" by the scruff of its neck, hauled it out, and held it up, in a plunging, kicking, teeth-showing state for me to look at, remarking—"Does it not look like a devil?" to which,' said Dunn, 'I agreed.'

This creature (and who can blame it?) was constantly gnawing its way out of captivity, paying nocturnal visits to a neighbour's chicken-house and eating the eggs, for which outlawry Rossetti eventually received a bill. The racoon was sent back to the man he bought it from.

Rossetti had a curious attitude to animals, treating them either as specimens to admire or as comical toys; but never apparently bestowing much thought upon their comfort in captivity. They were displayed enthusiastically for the entertainment of guests, one of whom, Miss Ellen Terry, gives several accounts of the Cheyne Walk menagerie.

'He bought a white bull,' she wrote, 'because it had "eyes like Janey Morris", and tethered it on the lawn . . . Soon there was no lawn left— only the bull. He invited people to meet it, and heaped favours on it, until it kicked everything to pieces, when he reluctantly got rid of it.'

His zoo must have been a sad disappointment to him: there were so many casualties. The young kangaroo murdered his mother and was in turn slaughtered—it was thought, by the racoon. A white peacock, released on arrival in the drawing room, dived under a sofa, where it remained, refusing to move, for several days.

' "The lovely creature won't respond to me," said Rossetti pathetically to a friend.

'The friend dragged out the bird.

' "No wonder! It's dead!"

'He tried to repair the failure,' continued Miss Terry, 'by buying some white dormice. He sat them up on tiny bamboo chairs, and they looked sweet.'

Winter came, and the dormice hibernated in a nest of cotton wool. As soon as the weather grew warm again, Rossetti gave a party to celebrate their awakening. He opened the door of their cage and looked in.

' "They are awake now," he said, "but how quiet they are! How full of repose!"

'One of the guests,' said Miss Terry, 'went to inspect the dormice more closely, and a peculiar expression came over his face. It might almost have been thought he was holding his nose.

' "Wake up, little dormice," said Rossetti, prodding them gently with a quill pen.

' "They'll never do that," said the guest. "They're dead. I believe they have been dead some days!" '

If the animals didn't die they annoyed the neighbours. The armadilloes disappeared, burrowing their way into other people's gardens, where they threw up heaps of earth and ruined the flower beds. One, more adventurous, burrowed under a neighbour's house and came up through the kitchen floor, sending the cook into screaming hysterics. The beautiful fallow deer pursued the peacock, trampling on its tail till all the feathers came out: the peacock flew up into the trees, calling its mate with piercing shrieks. Neighbours complained, and the Cadogan Estate inserted a clause in the leases of Cheyne Walk houses, which remains to this day, forbidding the keeping of peacocks.

Little by little, the disastrous zoo petered out, as Rossetti's energy and enthusiasm waned. At last, there was just a clutter of empty cages, which were left to rot. No doubt, the neighbours in Cheyne Walk heaved a joint sigh of relief.

CHAPTER SIX

VICTORIANS, in the 1860s, had a passion for being photographed. This new, almost magical process was still in its infancy, but clever photographers succeeded in producing some interesting results, the long exposure sometimes revealing depths of thought and character, as a painting might. Rossetti was intrigued by the new machine, and almost lost Ruskin's friendship through circulating a picture taken in the garden of Tudor House, of Bell Scott, Ruskin and himself. Owing to the necessity to stand completely motionless for some minutes, the figures of Rossetti and Ruskin look like cardboard characters in a toy theatre, arm in arm and propping each other up. Ruskin's expression is far from friendly (was he asked by the photographer to 'smile please!'?) and he is grasping his stick convulsively, while stout William Bell Scott, bowler-hatted in the foreground, seems about to hurl a chair at his host.

'Scandalous,' wrote Ruskin angrily, after seeing the result, and he proceeded to call the photographer, W. Downey, a blackguard who 'has been the cause of such a visible libel upon me going about England as I hold worse than all the scandals and lies ever uttered about me'.

But Rossetti went on inviting photographers to use his garden as a background, and some of the results were happier. On September 30, 1863, the Rev. C. L. Dodgson wrote in his diary:

'Called . . . at Mr. Rossetti's, he was most hospitable in the offers of the use of house and garden for picture-taking, and I arranged to take my camera there on Monday.'

And accordingly, on Monday, he wrote:

'Went over to Mr. Rossetti's, and began unpacking the camera, etc. While I was doing so, Miss Christina Rossetti arrived and Mr. Rossetti introduced me to her. She seemed a little shy at first, and I had very little time for conversation with her, but I much liked the little I saw of her. She sat for two pictures . . .'

It is a pity that the author of *Alice* did not obtain a photograph for posterity of Rossetti's wombat, which he evidently met, for it is said to have been the inspiration for the dormouse in the mad tea party. However, he was successful, more successful than Mr. Downey, in posing a charming and comparatively natural group of the Rossetti family—Dante Gabriel, Christina, Mrs. Rossetti and William Michael. There was also a rather odd-looking group, apparently taken on another occasion, with an enormous lolling Fanny Cornforth in the middle, flanked by the Rossetti brothers, and Swinburne beside her on a chair so low that he looks truncated like a glove puppet.

Fanny Cornforth, who had kept away from Rossetti during his brief marriage to Elizabeth Siddal, came back soon after his arrival in Chelsea. The large house certainly needed a woman to run it—a woman of taste and tact. Fanny had neither, but Rossetti was fond of her and he agreed to install her as his nominal house-keeper. For appearances' sake he rented a house for her nearby, at 36 Royal Avenue; but she spent nearly all her time at Cheyne Walk, where she upset the servants and sometimes embarrassed the guests.

In her youth Fanny must have been lovely. 'A pre-eminently fine woman,' wrote William Rossetti, 'with regular and sweet features, and a mass of the most lovely blonde hair.' She was the model for the country girl turned prostitute in 'Found'. Now, in her late thirties, she was corpulent but still decorative, and she liked to be accepted by Rossetti's friends as part of the household. William Allingham writes in June 1864:

'Down to Chelsea and find D.G.R. painting . . . Enter Fanny, who says something of W. Bell Scott which amuses us. Scott was a dark hairy man, but after an illness he reappeared quite bald. Fanny exclaimed, "O my, Mr. Scott is changed! He ain't got a hye-brow or a hye-lash—not a 'air on his 'ead!" Rossetti laughed immoderately at this, so that poor Fanny, good-humoured as she is, pouted at last—"Well, I know I don't say it right," and I hushed him up. Rows with Fanny could be very unpleasant indeed.'

In his kindness and good-nature—and for the sake of peace—Rossetti put up with 'the Elephant' as he called her; and still occasionally used her as a model. Fanny was acquisitive: she knew the value of 'Rissetti's' work, and clung to pictures which she said were hers. As she grew older, increasingly large sums had to be paid to her, ostensibly for her help as housekeeper. But in all his letters to Fanny, Rossetti shows remarkable forbearance and kindness, writing always as if to a too-demanding child. 'You must never think that I forget or neglect you,' he wrote from Kelmscott in 1873 (it was her forty-ninth birthday); and sent her £20 and a bunch of snowdrops. But, 'Just you find that pot!' he wrote a week later when one of his precious pieces of blue china had unaccountably disappeared. 'Do you think I don't know that you've wrapped your trunk round it and dug a hole for it in the garden? Just you find it . . . You know . . . you have no business with it, as I never gave it to you, and now I want it badly for my picture.'

'How much have you put away in the Elephant's hole now?' he asks a few months later, after numerous outpourings of 'tin'. He promises more 'as soon as I can'; but a day or two later, having heard from Treffry Dunn that Fanny wants to join him at Kelmscott, he is very firm in his refusal.

'I am very sorry indeed to disappoint you,' he writes '. . . but the thing is quite impossible. Please don't ever press the matter again, as it is very distressing to me to refuse, but as long as I remain here it is out of the question.'

Rossetti shared Kelmscott Manor, on the Thames near Lechlade, with the Morrises, and, between 1872 and 1874, spent nearly all his time there, while Treffry Dunn held the fort in Chelsea. He was by now deeply in love with Jane Morris, who, he knew, would hardly welcome Fanny with open arms. Fanny, no doubt, had an inkling of what was going on, and was jealous. She also resented the fact that he had sent for another younger model, Alexa Wilding (a beautiful red-head spotted by Rossetti in the Strand), and Miss Wilding on her return to Chelsea had made mischief, probably suggesting that Rossetti had finished with Fanny.

'I cannot understand,' he wrote, 'how Miss W. could be so stupid as to repeat such a pack of nonsense to you, wherever she may have heard it . . . You know very well that I am quite certain not to neglect or forget so good and dear an old friend as yourself at any time. It is painful to me not to see you oftener, but this cannot be helped at present . . .

'I find I can spare another little cheque, so I send it to you, as well as a new and beautiful picture for your gallery, which represents an Elephant putting black beadles in a hole . . . Take care of yourself, dear Fan . . .'

Fanny certainly did take care of herself. She was tenacious, and remained in the background of Rossetti's life till nearly the end, when she married her lodger Mr. Schott and left Chelsea to run a hotel in Jermyn Street.

It is impossible to explore the artistic world of Chelsea at this time without running into an extraordinary character who hovered on its fringe, Charles Augustus Howell. This plausible mountebank, who had been for a short time Ruskin's secretary, turned up in Chelsea in the '60s, a flamboyantly handsome man who claimed to be half Portuguese and descended from Boabdil el Chico. Rossetti, enjoying this, called him 'the cheeky'. Howell alleged that he had been involved in the Orsini conspiracy; and when dressed for dinner he wore a broad red ribbon of a fictitious order and numerous decorations.

He was a compulsive and talented liar, a fact which Rossetti was quick to recognize, firing off one of the spontaneous limericks at which he was adept, and which, often quoted, took various forms:

> There's a Portuguese person named Howell,
> Who lays on his lies with a trowel:
> When I goggle my eyes
> And start with surprise,
> It's at monstrous big lies told by Howell.

Among his accomplishments, Howell possessed a flair for art forgery, and made skilful copies of Rossetti drawings, which, with the artist's forged signature—or cleverly altered to look like the work of an old master, fetched high prices. He also, from time to time, filched the originals. Treffry Dunn describes coming in with Rossetti one evening to find Howell in the studio. 'He immediately launched into a dramatic account, as was his way, of the most astounding experiences and adventures he had gone through.' But as Rossetti very well knew, Howell had designs on a picture, and was determined to get it. 'I infer,' said Dunn, 'some bargaining had been going on between them, and that the drawing formed part of the bargain, but as Rossetti prized it highly, to gain possession of it was not a very easy matter and required much diplomacy.'

The drawing, Dunn explained, was one of many 'contained in a large, thick book, lying on a little cabinet in a distant corner. It was a great and unexpected treat to see this collection . . . amongst which were . . . pencil sketches of John Ruskin, Robert Browning, Algernon Charles Swinburne, William Morris, and other well-known men.

'At last we came to the page at which the drawing Howell had come to secure was affixed. It was a beautiful face, delicately drawn, and shaded in pencil, with a background of pale gold.' Rossetti's reluctance to part with it suggests that it was a drawing of Jane Morris. But the Portuguese was ruthless and uncannily skilful.

'Howell,' said Dunn, 'with an adroitness which was remarkable, shifted it from the book into his own pocket, and neither I nor Rossetti ever saw it again.'

It speaks much for Howell's charm that in spite of his outrageous and even criminal behaviour he continued to be received at Tudor House and accepted by Rossetti's circle. Of course, he had his uses. He possessed great gifts as a salesman, and Rossetti employed him as an agent, even taking his advice over the handling of difficult patrons, and benefiting by it. He was also a shrewd judge of antiques, and was encouraged by both Rossetti and Whistler to search out rare pieces of the blue chinese porcelain about which they both were crazy—and which, by fair means or foul, Howell obtained.

But although Rossetti was tolerant of Howell's roguery and amused by the enormity of his inventions, the time came when he began to find himself involved by the association in serious trouble. 'Here is a bloody writ!' he exclaimed in a letter to the solicitor Theodore Watts: it was served on him for having in his possession a dress bought for him by Howell for one of his pictures. 'The devil Howell has not been paid by me yet for the dress in question'—and to Howell himself: 'I hear you rather coolly propose that I should pay the £40 due from you to Mr. Levy! Why?? You know perfectly well that such a debt as there is from me to you was contracted on the clear understanding that the draperies &c. which it represents should be paid for in *work only*, and you know perfectly that otherwise I should not have dreamed of contracting so large a debt for such a purpose . . .'

Although—astonishingly—Howell continued still to be employed by Rossetti as agent, Theodore Watts (that same worthy Watts-Dunton who was to convert Swinburne to sobriety and respectability at The Pines, Putney) became his man of business and self-appointed bulwark. Slowly and with great firmness, Watts took over as Rossetti's agent. Howell was ousted.

In 1869, after seven years of silence since Lizzie's death, Gabriel began again to write poetry; to complete the cycle of verse he had begun before she died. It is typical that of all Rossetti's friends it was Howell who volunteered to organize the exhumation of Lizzie, and recover the volume of verses that Rossetti had thrust so impulsively into her coffin. The lost and half-remembered poems haunted him: he began to imagine that Lizzie herself was rejecting his needless sacrifice, urging him to take back the poems and publish them. Eventually the persuasions of his friends and his own obsessive belief in the need to recover the volume overcame his scruples. He decided to obtain permission for Lizzie to be exhumed, and the manuscript recovered.

Rossetti was not present when, late on an October evening, the flames of a blazing bonfire lit up the open grave in Highgate Cemetery. The coffin was prised open in the presence of a Dr. Llewellyn Williams, and the manuscript, bound in rough grey calf, extracted from its resting-place by Charles Augustus Howell.

Before the book could be given to its author it had to be disinfected, page by page: it was found to be in a bad state, discoloured, barely legible and partly eaten away. But the body of Lizzie, according to Howell, was scarcely touched by death: the laudanum which poisoned her may have acted as a preservative. Her red-gold hair, Howell asserted, must have continued to grow after death, for it flowed round her like a shining cloak. Howell's macabre romanticism made the most of the scene; but his description reassured Rossetti. At last he was able to persuade himself that Lizzie was at peace, and to ease his tormented conscience.

To Swinburne, who had been devoted to Lizzie, Gabriel wrote defending the exhumation:

'The truth is that no one so much as herself would have approved of my doing this. Art was the only thing for which she felt very seriously. Had it been possible to her, I should have found the book on my pillow the night she was buried; and could she have opened the grave, no other hand would have been needed.'

The period that followed saw Rossetti at the height of his powers as writer and as painter. He spent long periods at Kelmscott with Jane Morris and her children. Janey was his dream, his obsession: her face haunted his painting, even if the model were another woman; his idyllic love informed the poetry which he now wrote. Then suddenly in 1874 the Kelmscott idyll came to an end; the mysterious Janey disappeared to Italy with her family. Gabriel's health began to decline, and after five years of success and fame his career was threatened by a savage attack on his work in an article, later published as a pamphlet, by a Scottish poet, Robert Buchanan, called 'The Fleshly School of Painting'! This led to a breakdown and an attempt at suicide, from which he was saved by his brother William. He was sleepless, desperate; moreover he was under the influence of chloral, a new drug recommended to him by the American artist, William James Stillman. Taken in small doses, this drug was harmless, and produced sound sleep; but Rossetti became more and more dependent upon it, and in his desperate need of oblivion, dosed himself recklessly. For a time, it seemed that he could take large quantities without doing himself harm; but the effect was slow and insidious.

Gradually Rossetti, the warm, the friendly extrovert, who loved to fill his table with congenial spirits, became obsessed by suspicions and fears. One by one, he cast off his friends, and the walls of Tudor House closed round him like the walls of a prison. The house which had once bewitched him now held him in a powerful grasp, dragging him back whenever he broke away. He was compelled to go on painting: works which had been commissioned and long ago paid for demanded his presence. Solitary in the lonely, dark, echoing house he pondered upon the lives of former occupants.

> May not this ancient room thou sit'st in dwell
>   In separate living souls for joy or pain?
> Nay, all its corners may be painted plain
> Where Heaven shows pictures of some life spent well,
>   And may be stamped, a memory all in vain,
> Upon the sight of lidless eyes in Hell.

The house, like its master, had lost its gracious air and wore a forbidding, unkempt aspect. In Hall Caine's sad description written in 1880, the exterior betrayed years of neglect. 'Brickwork falling into decay, the paint in need of renewal, the windows dull with the dust of months, the sills bearing more than the suspicion of cobwebs, the angles of the steps to the porch and the untrodden flags of the little court leading up to them overgrown with moss and weed . . .'

The jasmine which had welcomed Treffry Dunn was choked by 'the tangled branches of the wildest ivy that ever grew untouched by shears'.

'The hall,' said Caine, 'had a puzzling look of equal nobility and shabbiness for the floor was paved with white marble, which was partly covered by a strip of worn out coconut matting.'

This emphasizes only too clearly the condition into which the household had fallen.

'I should say it looked like a house that no woman had ever dwelt in—a house inhabited by a man who had once felt a vivid interest in life, but was now living from day to day.'

Hall Caine was appalled when he learnt from his host the large quantities of chloral he was in the habit of taking.

' "I judge I've taken more chloral than any man whatever. Marshall" ' (his medical man) ' "says if I were put into a Turkish bath I should sweat it out at every pore."

'As he said this,' adds Caine '. . . there was something in his tone and laugh suggesting that he was even proud of the accomplishment. To me it was a frightful revelation.'

In spite of this, however, the young Manxman wrote after his first visit to Cheyne Walk, 'Rossetti was to me the most fascinating, the most inspiring, the most affectionate and the most magnetic of men.'

By now, Rossetti had quarrelled with his assistant, Treffry Dunn, who —lacking arrears of salary—had gone off to Cornwall to paint. The Master sent him £50 and sacked him: 'he proposes to remove his goods (or d——d bads) next week,' wrote Rossetti angrily to Watts Dunton. The Cornishman's room at Cheyne Walk was offered to the Manxman.

'You may have heard,' Rossetti wrote to his mother in August 1881, 'of a young man named Hall Caine who has shown himself very well disposed towards me. I am going to try the experiment of having him to live in the house . . . Caine has tastes similar to my own, and is a reading man . . . He is likely to be coming here next Saturday.'

Young Hall Caine found himself the companion of an exhausted, disillusioned man, still wearily working to fulfil commissions; but convinced that there was a conspiracy against him, that his painting and his poetry were reviled by a modern school of thought rapidly gaining in influence. Even W. S. Gilbert, ridiculing the Aesthetic Movement in *Patience*, was believed by Rossetti to be attacking him in the character of Bunthorne:

> Such a judge of blue-and-white, and other kinds of pottery—
> From early Oriental, down to modern terra-cottar-y.

This might equally have applied to Whistler—and indeed, Gilbert's poets were composites of various figures in the Aesthetic Movement, and had little bearing on Rossetti or what he stood for; but he refused to be convinced.

Other less fanciful worries crowded in upon him. With the building of the Embankment, and the new under-river sewers, he was called upon to make alterations to the drainage system of Tudor House; and this at a time when his lease was about to expire. If he renewed it, he would have to agree to give up a large slice of his long garden, upon which Cadogan Estate proposed to build a row of flats. This was an appalling thought; the flats would overlook his ground, the precious privacy of his wild garden would be gone.

'They are really setting about building at the back,' he told Caine. 'I do not know what my plans may be . . .'

There is a last picture of Rossetti in Chelsea. Increasingly lethargic, increasingly afraid of the world outside his own walls, he never went out, except into his garden. One night Hall Caine succeeded in persuading him to come for a walk on the Embankment.

'Every night for a week afterwards,' he wrote, 'I induced him to repeat the unfamiliar experiment . . . The Embankment was almost dark, with gas lamps far apart . . . the black river flowing noiselessly behind the low wall . . . and Rossetti in his slouch hat, with its broad brim pulled down low on his forehead . . . lurching along with a heavy, uncertain step, breathing audibly, looking at nothing, and hardly speaking at all . . .

'I seem to remember that on one of our walks along the Embankment late at night we passed in the half-darkness two figures which bore a certain resemblance to our own—an old man in a Scotch plaid, accompanied by a slight young woman in a sort of dolman. The old man was forging along sturdily with the help of a stick, and the young woman appeared to be making some effort to keep pace with him. It was Carlyle with his niece, and I caught but one glimpse of them as, out on the same errand as ourselves, they went off in the other direction.'

But for both Carlyle and Rossetti the journey was nearly ended. On February 4, 1881, Carlyle died aged eighty-six. Rossetti, worn out, surrendered to death on April 9, 1882. He was fifty-four. In the gardens before his house a memorial was erected to him—a drinking fountain designed by John Seddon, an early disciple of the first Pre-Raphaelites; at the head of the fountain was a bronze bas-relief bust of Rossetti, designed by his old friend Ford Madox Brown. This was unveiled in July 1887 by Holman Hunt. One night in January 1970, thieves ripped the bronze portrait from the stone, to sell it, presumably, as scrap. How Rossetti would have laughed!

CHAPTER SEVEN

'BALLOONING! BALLOONING! BALLOONING!

'CREMORNE GARDENS, CHELSEA. Can be reached from all parts of Town, by Omnibus 6d. Boat 4d. The First and Only Benefit taken by MR. GREEN, the Aeronaut, will take place on MONDAY NEXT, September 1st., 1845. Mr. Green will ascend at ½ past 5 o'clock in the Great Nassau Balloon! Taking up with him a Dozen Ladies and Gentlemen. The Admission is only One Shilling—Children, Half Price!'

SO RAN one of many advertisements proclaiming the delights of Cremorne Gardens, which were opened to the public in the summer of 1845, were patronized during the '60s and '70s by Rossetti and Whistler and their friends, were cursed by Carlyle, and finally closed down by public request in 1877.

At the westernmost extremity of Chelsea Reach, running from the River to the World's End Tavern, in the King's Road, the gardens occupied the site of the last remaining riverside estate, Cremorne House—or Chelsea Farm, as it was originally called, a modest Georgian house set among trees, with grounds running down to the Thames. The house was built in 1740 by Theophilus, Earl of Huntingdon, who died six years later. His widow, an ardent and practical supporter of the great religious revival inaugurated by John Wesley, became known as Queen of the Methodists, and founded some sixty chapels. In 1748 she invited George Whitfield to preach at Chelsea Farm.

'Blessed be God,' he wrote, accepting, 'that the rich and great have hearing ears.' Lady Huntingdon saw to it that a considerable number of the rich and great attended Whitfield's sermons at her house, and Horace Walpole wrote:

'Whitfield preaches constantly at my Lady Huntingdon's at Chelsea; my Lord Chesterfield, my Lord Bath, my Lady Townshend, my Lady Thanet, and others, have been to hear him. What lay you that next winter he is not run after instead of Garrick?'

Lady Huntingdon moved away, to devote herself more completely to the promotion of Methodism; and after several changes of ownership

Chelsea Farm was bought by Thomas Dawson, Baron Dartrey, who in 1785 became Viscount Cremorne. The estate took his name.

Lady Cremorne, who had been christened Philadelphia in compliment to her great-grandfather, William Penn, was another remarkable woman, of whom her friend, Mrs. Carter wrote:

> Friend of my soul! with fond delight each hour
>> From earth to heaven I see thee urge thy race,
> From ev'ry virtue crop the fairest flower,
>> And add to Nature ev'ry waning grace.

The virtues of Philadelphia Hannah Cremorne won her the esteem of Queen Charlotte, who paid several informal visits to Cremorne House, accompanied by her six daughters. On these occasions all the children in the Sunday and Charity Schools were marched to Cremorne and lined up to give three cheers for Her Majesty. Lady Cremorne was popular in Chelsea Parish, and, childless herself, distributed liberally to the children of the poor. She also did her household shopping locally, which was unusual, and appreciated.

After the deaths of Lord and Lady Cremorne the estate went to her cousin, Granville Penn, who sold it to Charles Random de Berenger, Baron de Beaufain, who, in spite of his name, claimed noble Prussian descent. The Baron had plans for a sporting club for the cultivation of 'various skilful and manly exercises': that is to say, shooting, sailing, rowing, swimming, fishing. There would also be opportunities, he announced (in *The New Sporting Magazine* for 1831) for fencing, archery, riding, driving, skating, coursing, hunting, and racing. The club, named the Stadium, flourished for over ten years; but after the death of the energetic Baron in 1845, the estate was taken over by Thomas Bartlett Simpson, who had very different ideas for its use. He had once been head waiter at the Albion Tavern, opposite Drury Lane Theatre, and knew something of the entertainment world. He was an enterprising man, and raised the then substantial sum of £6,000 to spend on preparations for the Grand Opening of Cremorne Pleasure Gardens. This was going to be something new: a Ranelagh for the masses. A noble estate, where the beauties of nature would act as background to 'attractions'—and Simpson stressed the artistic and respectable nature of these, which were planned to appeal to all the family.

From the first, ballooning was one of the biggest attractions, holding always a spice of danger. The intrepid Mr. Green, the Aeronaut, made countless ascents, usually taking a party of ladies and gentlemen up with him. But after a time, Mr. Simpson and Mr. Green decided to introduce comedy and drama. In 1846, a contemporary account described how 'after the ascension [sic] of the balloon, which rose very majestically, a parachute was seen descending, which caused great curiosity, the car of which contained a large monkey, who reached terra firma in safety, to the great gratification of many thousands'.

The monkey's debut was a success. Advertisements appeared in the newspapers: 'Do, Papa, take me to see Mr. Green go up in his Balloon and let the Monkey down in the Parachute, tomorrow from Cremorne Gardens? It's only 6d. for children.'

One night, Thomas Matthews, the celebrated Drury Lane Clown, joined the party in the basket, in full costume and make-up, and 'immediately before the ascent favoured his companions, and the thousands of persons who surrounded the balloon, with the favourite ballad of "Hot Codlins" '.

As the shouts of applause died away the balloon went up, and sailed in a light south-westerly wind over Chelsea Hospital and away to the north-east. After two hours and twenty minutes the shivering aeronauts (it was now nearly half past nine and very cold) made a safe landing 'in a large marsh at Tottenham'. 'When at the height of 3,000 feet,' the account continues, 'Mr. T. Matthews sang a new comic song called "Pigs' Pettitoes", which was rapturously encored'—presumably by the inhabitants of the marsh.

There was always a delicious uncertainty as to where these Cremorne balloons would land; they generally, carried by the prevailing wind, sailed across London and came down in the eastern suburbs. But one, navigated by a Lieutenant Gale, 'unceremoniously carried the gallant aeronaut across the Channel to Dieppe', which must have been, to say the least, inconvenient.

In 1852 the Proprietor of Cremorne was served with three summonses brought by the R.S.P.C.A. He had that season introduced a 'sensational novelty' invented by a French couple, M. and Mme. Poitevin. From *The Observer* of September 5, 1852, we learn that 'the Balloon being fully inflated, a Knight in gilt armour dashed into the arena, driving a profusely ornamented . . . chariot'. The knight, presumably, was Monsieur Poitevin, and by his side was Madame. 'She wore,' said *The Observer*, 'a wreath of roses and a scarlet tunic, and looked decidedly classical', as was fitting for the part of Europa. Her lover, Zeus in the shape of a bull, now made his appearance. 'The poor beast, who was not of gigantic proportions, was muffled in a scarlet robe, and a pair of gilt horns completed his decoration.' The scarlet robe, alas, was worn to conceal an elaborate arrangement of canvas strappings by which he was to be supported in the air, attached to the balloon by 'sundry stout cords, disguised as garlands'.

The bull was blindfolded, M. Poitevin stepped into the basket, and Madame vaulted gracefully on to the side-saddle placed upon the bull's back, kissing her hands in acknowledgment of the plaudits of the crowd.

As the balloon ascended it was noticed that at first the bull stretched his legs out stiffly as if trying to reach the ground; but 'when his diminishing size had made him resemble one of the inmates of a Noah's Ark,' said the reporter, 'he began to kick violently.'

Some five hours later, Madame Poitevin reappeared—a heroine, perhaps: for who would choose to sail across London, side-saddle on a kicking bull, dressed only in a scarlet tunic and a wreath of roses? She had landed in Ilford, where, we are told, 'ox and lady were most kindly received, and the bull hospitably taken by the horns to a comfortable stable'.

This ingenious and daring act was sometimes performed with a horse. A veterinary surgeon gave evidence that the animals were subjected to appalling discomfort, pain and fear; a letter appeared in *The Times* purporting to have been written by 'The Bull in the Balloon', which described the suffering and humiliation the creature may well have endured; and after some legal deliberation the act was stopped, and the proprietor and perpetrators fined.

But ballooning was only one of countless attractions. There was, of course, a band; sometimes several, perambulating. There was a maze, and a Gipsy fortune-teller. There were performing dogs and monkeys, nigger minstrels, marionettes. There was Signor Cristofero Buono Core, the Italian Salamander, who walked, unharmed, through a sheet of flame. There were dwarfs, a giant, and 'Two Human Beings with Dogs' Heads, whose Discovery in the Interior of Russia, and Exhibition in all the Principal Cities of Europe, has caused the Greatest Sensation ever known'.

There was also the Invisible Poet, who sat inside a tent, and composed doggerel to order.

> Those who would stir the bright poetic flame
> Must drop into the letter box a name,
> And from the opening, in language terse,
> Will issue rapidly four lines of verse.

And all for twopence. *Punch*, musing upon the prowess of this hidden genius, wondered what he would make of the name Buggins.

During the whole of Mr. Simpson's reign as proprietor, Cremorne continued to stress the innocence—the high-class nature—of its amusements. 'A Varied, Pleasing, and Chaste Programme of Entertainments is offered to the Visitor, including a Favourite Ballet entitled The SYLPH of the GOSSAMER GLADE.'

'TOURNAYS OF THE OLDEN TIME!' he announced proudly. 'Splendid Pictorial View of the Tilt Yard and Tented Grounds. Knights, armed Cap-a-Pie, on Richly Caparisoned Steeds. Grand Cortege of the QUEEN OF BEAUTY!'

A visit to Cremorne could be improving to the mind: you could watch Marriott's Working Bees in their Glass Hives, and see Maypole and Morris Dancing, Such as Delighted our Ancestors.

At 11.30 there were fireworks: rockets, set-pieces, catherine wheels; comical objects devised by Mr. Mortram, the Pyrotechnic Artiste, which fell from balloons emitting whizzes and bangs and bursts of light—a glorious gallimaufry of noise and colour which entranced the spectators, whose 'oohs' and 'aahs', together with the din created by the fireworks, brought complaints from citizens who wanted to go to sleep.

There was also dancing. In 1857, a magnificent pagoda was built at the south-west end of the gardens, which at night was lit by hundreds of coloured lamps. This housed an orchestra of fifty, and round it was built a dance floor known as the Chinese Platform. Chinese lanterns hung from the trees, and round the platform tall lampholders supported arches from which hung 'devices in emerald and garnet glass drops, and semicircles of lustres and gas-jets'.

Within the circle the dancers—the ladies in bonnets, the gentlemen in top-hats—revolved, glided and hopped; without, the older and more sedate paraded, or took refreshments.

Noisy, flashily beautiful, boisterous, Cremorne in its early days served out just the entertainment its customers sought. As yet, the Victorian Public House had not come into being: Cremorne at night offered the jollity, the loud music, the drinks—and in surroundings which provided space and fresh air as well. For the most part, it was the middle classes who gave it their support.

But in 1855 an attempt was made to raise its social status. On August 13 of that year, when the Crimean War was in everyone's minds, a Grand Military Fête was advertised, 'for the Benefit of Wellington College for the Education of Orphan Sons of Officers in the Army'.

The entertainments included 'A Collossal Panorama of Sebastopol'. 'The Storming of the Mamelon Vert and the Rifle Pits,' it was announced, 'will be effectively pourtrayed by 500 Soldiers and Three Battering Trains.'

This splendid spectacle was presented 'Under the Immediate Patronage of Her Majesty the Queen and His Royal Highness the Prince Albert'.

This was a feather in Cremorne's cap. Charming folding programmes of the Gardens were issued after this, printed in colour and announcing 'Patron, H.M. the Queen'.

Nevertheless, according to George Augustus Sala, it was 'not a place that ladies were in the habit of visiting, unless in disguise or on the sly'. It was, in his opinion, a place for the man about town.

Indeed, as far back as 1857, Chelsea Vestry had presented the first of its annual petitions that Cremorne should not be allowed to renew its licence. The late hours were complained of—and the immoral character of the female frequenters. The place, it was declared, was having a bad influence upon local morals.

In the early '60s, M. Hippolyte Taine, a Frenchman interested in social conditions, recorded his impressions of Cremorne. It was, he said, 'a sort of *bal Mabille* where the day's madness was carried on late into the night. A crush and much shoving at the entrance . . . Inside . . . the press of people was dreadful, but it was possible to get a breath of air in the darker corners.

'All the men,' he noticed, were 'well or at least neatly dressed: the women were prostitutes (*lorettes*), but of a higher rank than those in the Strand, light coloured shawls over white gauze or tulle dresses, red mantelets, new hats. Some of their dresses,' he estimated, 'must have cost as much as £12. But the faces are rather faded, and sometimes, in the crowd, they utter shocking screams, shrill as a screech-owl.'

The Frenchman may have been misled by the appearance and behaviour of some of the girls—boisterous Cockney types, servant maids and shopgirls out for an evening's pleasure—into believing that all were prostitutes. All at least, he was sure, were on the downward path.

'We sat down near three young women at a secluded table and offered them sherry and beer. They drank moderately . . . One of them was very gay and wild. I have never seen such overflowing animal spirits. Another, modest, quite pretty, rather subdued, was a milliner by trade, entirely dependent on herself. She has a friend (lover) who spends his Sundays with her. I looked at her carefully: it was clear that she had the makings of an amiable and respectable girl. What had been the turning point?'

According to William Acton, writing in 1870, there were two aspects of Cremorne. In the afternoons, the family parties filled the gardens, and all was innocent enjoyment.

But at sunset, wrote Acton, 'calico and merry respectability tailed off eastward by penny steamers', and at the Grand Entrance in the King's Road hansom cabs drew up, 'freighted with demure immorality in silk and fine linen'. At the pay box under its great illuminated star the top-hatted toffs streamed in, ogling and appraising. 'By about ten o'clock,' said Action, 'age and innocence had seemingly all retired', and now the grottoes and arbours shaded from the gaslight filled up with couples and quartets, and waiters ran to and fro, serving drinks.

The orchestra settled into its programme of popular music, and 'I suppose,' said William Acton, 'that a hundred couples . . . were engaged in dancing and other amusements, and the rest of society, myself included, circulated listlessly about the garden, and enjoyed in a grim sort of way the "Selection" from some favourite opera and the cool night breeze from the river.'

Watching the dancers, Mr. Acton evidently felt his age, and there is a hint of envy as his appraising eye follows the revolving couples, who, he said, 'enjoyed themselves after the manner of youth, but I may fairly say, without offence to the most fastidious eye or ear . . .'

The scene was also observed by the eye of the Law. A policeman, whose presence was now insisted upon by the Authorities, 'had taken up an amiably discreet position, where his presence could in no way appear symptomatic of pressure, and the chances seemed to be that had he stood so posed until his interference was necessary on behalf of public order, he might have been here to this day'.

Acton could find nothing to complain of except boredom. He could not even cite an instance of excessive drinking. 'Lemonade and sherry,' he observed, 'seemed to please the dancers, and the loungers indulged the waiters' importunity with a rare order for bitter-beer. A strongish party of undergraduates in a corner were deepening their native dullness with bottled stout, and more seasoned vessels struggled against depression with hot grog. In front of the liquor bar . . . two rosy capitalists (their wives at Brighton or elsewhere) were pouring, for mere distraction's sake, libations of fictitious Moet, to the memory of auld lang syne with some fat old dames de maison, possibly extinct planets of the Georgian era. There was no drunkenness.'

It was disappointingly dull. Perhaps Mr. Acton had struck a bad night.

'As I have recorded,' he concludes, 'there was among the general company barely vivacity, much less boisterous disorder.'

In 1861, Simpson retired, and the new manager of Cremorne was E. T. Smith, who had been Lessee of Astley's. He began his career at Cremorne with a daring novelty—a female Blondin who undertook to cross the

Rossetti. Self-portrait, 1847

Proserpina: Jane Morris.
Painting by Rossetti

The female Blondin crossing the Thames.
Water-colour by H. and W. Greaves

The bandstand at
Cremorne Gardens.
Engraving by Walter Greaves

Whistler. Painting by
Bernard Partridge

Oscar Wilde.
Water-colour by C. Pellegrini
('Ape'), 1884

The White House, Tite Street, designed for
Whistler by E. W. Godwin

Ellen Terry. Painting by G. F. Watts

Thames from Battersea to Chelsea on a tight-rope. This thrilling event, watched by thousands from the banks and in boats, nearly ended in tragedy. By some mischance—or deliberate sabotage—one of the guy ropes supporting the tight-rope broke, and Mademoiselle Genvieve, after an agonizing forty-five minutes when she stood, mid-stream, unable to advance or retreat on the loosened rope, suddenly dropped her spangled pole into the river, saved herself from plunging after it by grabbing a rope, and was hauled to safety in a nearby boat.

A week later the attempt was made again—and this time the rope remained taut, the perilous journey was accomplished, and Mlle. Genvieve, calmly triumphant, stepped towards the Chelsea bank to the strains of 'See the Conquering Hero Comes', which seems to have been the most appropriate tune the Cremorne orchestra could find in the flurry of the moment.

In July 1874 a sensational new act was advertised: Monsieur de Groof, the Flying Man.

This audacious performer had invented a flying machine, which was suspended from the car of a balloon, and looked like an enormous exotic bird. It was made of waterproof silk stretched over a framework of cane, and the batlike wings—thirty-seven feet from tip to tip—flapped realistically at the jerk of a lever by the aeronaut. The tail, which was eighteen feet long, was shaped and coloured to look like the tail of a peacock, and this also moved at the touch of a lever. In the centre of the bird was an upright wooden frame, inside which stood de Groof. Presumably, as the balloon ascended the 'bird' rose gracefully from the ground, and, once airborne, gave a realistic impression of free flight. Possibly, in open country, it could be cut adrift and make a successful landing.

But the bird was flimsy and vulnerable: the balloon rose quickly over the roof-tops of Cheyne Walk and the King's Road, but before it had gained enough height the wind carried it towards the high spire of St. Luke's Church. 'Shall I cut you adrift?' shouted the balloonist. 'Yes, yes,' cried de Groof, 'I will fall into the graveyard.'

The graveyard was, indeed, the end of his flight. He fell, poor man, into the middle of Sydney Street, entangled in the shattered body of his bird. The balloon, freed of its burden, sailed away over the city.

Chelsea was stunned by the tragedy, and a local ballad-monger quickly cashed in with his version:

> On Thursday in health and bloom
> To Cremorne Gardens he bent his way,
> Not thinking that the silent tomb

So soon would behold his lifeless clay.
Amid the cheers of thousands he ascended,
And like lightning he was borne
But when he to the earth descended,
The life from him alas was gone.

As near St. Luke's Church he did hover,
The balloonist he was heard to say
That he danger did discover,
So called on him to cut away;
His answer was, in the churchyard drop me
And in a moment cut the rope.
And then was seen a scene of misery,
For they were the last words that he spoke.

Perhaps this tragedy hastened the end of Cremorne, which—despite yearly protests from Chelsea Vestry at the increasing rowdyism and immorality—lingered defiantly for another three years. During Derby week it was a Mecca for returning racegoers, who celebrated their wins or drowned their losses within its welcoming shades.

But the pleasure gardens were doomed. Like most places of entertainment which depend upon the weather for their success, Cremorne suffered, as the public grew more sophisticated, from the disadvantages of the English climate. Inevitably, with the growth of the Music Hall, the richer clients drifted away. Finally, in 1877, a new licence was refused, and the handsome gates of Cremorne were closed for the last time.

The following April, Messrs. Furber and Price, the auctioneers, announced a five-day sale of the buildings, fabric and effects. The buildings, such as they were, went for nothing: they had not been constructed to endure, and six months' neglect had done them no good. 'Lying unattended to since October last, the gardens and their motley outdoor furniture present a picture the reverse of cheering . . . The winter winds have played sad havoc with the canvas coverings of the theatres and ballroom, whilst many a rent is to be seen in the panorama views which encircle the west side of the grounds.'

The gardens were unkempt and overgrown: even the beautiful trees inherited from Lord Cremorne were being sold off as 'growing timber'. The estate was to be let 'for building purposes'.

On the fifth day of the Sale, the 'Fittings, Machinery and Scenery of all the Four Theatres in the Grounds' were sold off, together with 'the theatrical Wardrobe, consisting of upwards of 6,000 dresses'.

It would be interesting to know who bought 'Four Scotch Suits with Black velvet jackets, Seven Dolly Varden Costumes', or 'Five Policemen's Tunics, four pairs of trowsers, six helmets, and a private constable's coat and cap; and 170 pairs of boots, shoes and slippers, various, in round hamper'.

Towards the close of the sale comes Lot 1084. A LARGE BALLOON, 'The Cremorne', with car, ropes, etcetera.

It was, indeed, the end of an era.

CHAPTER EIGHT

THREE EVENTS, the closing of Cremorne, the building of the Embankment, and the rebuilding of Battersea Bridge, combined to change the face of riverside Chelsea. What it gained in sophistication, cleanliness and respectability it lost immeasurably in beauty.

The name, Cheyne Walk, before the building of the Embankment, applied only to Rossetti's end. Now the whole stretch of waterside is Cheyne Walk, and, from Oakley Street (built after the destruction of Winchester House in 1830) to Milmans Street at the Cremorne end, there have been tremendous changes. Let us try and see how it looked in the 1860s.

On the western corner of Oakley Street, where today is a vast shapeless car park, pending the decision as to what form of vast shapeless building is to occupy the space, stood the Pier Hotel, completed in 1844. This cheerful Victorian pub was built on a crescent-shaped site designed to match Pennethorne's crescent on the eastern corner. The Pier wore a faintly nautical air, with its flagstaffs and balconies and striped awnings, reminiscent of Ryde or Weymouth. It was, to most people's regret, pulled down in 1968.

Past the Pier, the road curved round along the tree-lined river bank, a picturesque jumble of small shops, private houses and taverns, most of which had been there since the eighteenth century or earlier. There was the famous Magpie and Stump, with its sign hung across the road, still holding the small piece of land at the back which it had been allowed to retain in 1536 when Henry VIII took over the Manor. The little tavern, rebuilt in the eighteenth century, continued to flourish until, in 1886, it was burnt to the ground. On its site, apparently within its very walls, C. R. Ashbee built the first of three tall *art nouveau* houses in 1894, and commemorated the old inn by keeping the name and placing a carved magpie under the ground floor window. This house has now gone, but its two neighbours remain, and beyond them, today, is the large block of flats called Shrewsbury House, in remembrance of Bess of Hardwick's fine mansion. This was ruthlessly destroyed in 1813, and the materials that had gone to the making of it sold piecemeal by a speculating builder. All that remained, in the 1860s, was a small house, incorporated into a group of buildings facing the river, which may once have been a lodge or out-building of the great house. It was now one of a row of small shops. At the back of these was open ground, bounded east and west by long brick walls of Tudor origin, which are still there and are all that remains today of the original Shrewsbury House estate.

At the corner of Cheyne Row, past three Georgian houses, was an inn, the Feathers (now 49 Cheyne Walk), and on the further side the King's Head and Eight Bells, rebuilt in the 1820s. Beyond it, in the '60s, five small shops, yet another inn, The Cricketers, and a building called The Thames Coffee House, all stood, where Carlyle Mansions rise in late-Victorian majesty, with their spacious sunny rooms overlooking the river in front, and less spacious, sunless rooms at the back where servants slept, and an arrogant expanse of blank brick wall which lowers over the bottom end of Cheyne Row. But these mansion flats—and Henry James who lived in one of them—had not yet arrived: they were built in 1886.

On the far side of Lawrence Street, where the Cheyne Hospital for Children now stands, was a row of five houses, called Prospect Place, built towards the end of the seventeenth century. In the first of these, Don Saltero opened his first coffee house, which is the one referred to by Bowack when he wrote in 1705 that 'many honourable and worthy in-habitants' of Chelsea met 'every day at a coffee house near the Church'.

In this same house, from 1850 to 1854, William Holman Hunt lodged. In his studio on the first floor overlooking the river (but he kept the blinds down when he was at work) he painted 'The Light of the World', and also 'The Awakened Conscience'. Carlyle, visiting the studio, gave his views on both paintings. 'You call that thing, I ween, a picture of Jesus Christ . . . a mere papistical fancy . . . a poor mistaken presentation of the noblest, the brotherliest, and the most heroic-minded Being that ever walked God's earth. Do you ever suppose that Jesus walked about bedizened in priestly robes and a crown, and with yon jewels on his breast, and a gilt aureole on his head?' His inbred Calvinism worked itself off in a tirade which, from Hunt's account, must have lasted a long time and left both artist and critic speechless.

Of 'The Awakened Conscience', that painfully detailed portrayal of a 'fallen woman' rising from the lap of her lover, open-mouthed at the sudden discovery of her better self, Carlyle, after a long silence, pro-nounced in approving tones that 'the moonlight is well given'.

The vine which still flourishes under the windows of the Cheyne Hospital is believed to be the same plant from which Holman Hunt painted a trailing branch in 'The Light of the World'. The two houses between the hospital and the Old Church are all that remains of Prospect Place. Almost completely rebuilt, they have been left enough of their original character to remind us of the charm of this seventeenth-century row, which appears in many views of the Old Church.

Further west, between Church Street and Danvers Street, is now the Roper Garden, opened in 1964 on the site of a row of houses demolished by the magnetic mines that destroyed the church in 1941. This was Lombard Terrace, two or three early nineteenth-century houses adjoining a much older building known as the Arch House, which, in the '60s, still spanned the road at right angles to the river, and may be seen in old photographs, displaying a certain dignity as of having seen better days, but bearing the humble legend, Alldin's Coal Wharf. The archway, through which the road ran, was often a bone of contention, as there was only room for one vehicle to pass through it at a time: whoever got there first won. On one occasion the Prince Consort's carriage was obliged to wait while a tradesman's cart rattled over the cobbles into Lombard Street.

Here, the river was suddenly obliterated. Public houses and wharves crowded along the bank, making the street narrow and sunless. Lombard Street led to Duke Street (roughly where Crosby Hall now stands). The Duke was George Villiers, first Duke of Buckingham, who lived for a time in Beaufort House nearby. In Duke Street, among the taverns and cottages backing on to the river, was the Adam and Eve, which must have been a beautiful seventeenth-century inn, with wooden balconies at the back, overhanging the water.

At the junction of Duke Street and Beaufort Street, the river view opened up again and the road widened. On the left, Battersea Bridge spanned the Thames. This was, till 1887, the wooden bridge designed by Henry Holland, the architect of Hans Town, and built in 1771 for a private company headed by Earl Spencer, father of the famous Duchess of Devonshire and patron of the living of Battersea. The bridge cost £15,662 to build; it was expensive, but necessary. It was also beautiful, with its complicated timber structure and its air of fragility which was, for the first hundred years anyway, an illusion. It was a toll bridge, the charge being a halfpenny to foot passengers and fourpence for one-horse carts.

At the end of the eighteenth century, Battersea Bridge was, for the first time, lit at dusk by oil lamps, and in 1824 by gas, when its frail beauty, its appearance in the misty light of being suspended in space, was enhanced by the reflections of flickering lights which spilled down into the water. To James McNeill Whistler, being rowed below it by Henry and Walter

Greaves, Battersea Bridge stretched up into infinity, silver and gold against blue.

Beyond the bridge, the road wound on towards Cremorne. On the right stood two handsome eighteenth-century houses, which are still there: Belle Vue Lodge, on the corner of Beaufort Street (occupied, in 1829, by Luke Thomas Flood, a benefactor to the Parish, whose name is perpetuated in Flood Street); and its neighbour Belle Vue House, built in 1771, and believed to have been designed by Robert Adam. This house was in the 1860s the home of William Bell Scott, painter and poet: it had a vinery at the back, and a garden across the road running down to the river, which contained an ancient willow tree, famous enough to be marked in Thompson's Survey of 1836. Part of this old garden (which may have been a fragment of More's garden) still remains in the form of a piece of grass with an old mulberry tree, left when the Embankment was built.

After Belle Vue House are two smaller houses, built in 1777 (93 and 94 Cheyne Walk). In the first, Elizabeth Cleghorne Stevenson, who became Mrs. Gaskell, was born in 1810. She hardly had time to look out of the window at the Thames, however, for her mother died within a month of her birth, and the infant was despatched to her aunt, Mrs. Lumb, at Knutsford in Cheshire.

The houses numbered from 95 to 100 Cheyne Walk were all part of the original Lindsey House; but in the 1860s the whole stretch, from Beaufort Street to Milmans Street, was known as Lindsey Row.

The central house in the Row (98 Cheyne Walk) was the home, between 1808 and 1824, of the distinguished engineers, father and son, Sir Marc Isambard Brunel and Isambard Kingdom Brunel. The father, who left his native France during the Revolution, sailed to New York, where he practised as an architect and civil engineer. In 1799 he came to England, where his ingenuity and inventiveness were of service to the Government during the Napoleonic Wars. While he was at Lindsey House he formed a company to finance his plan for the first tunnel under the Thames, between Wapping and Rotherhithe.

Isambard Kingdom Brunel, who spent his childhood and youth at Lindsey Row, designed at the age of twenty-five the Clifton Suspension Bridge, and in later life turned his attention to ocean-going steamships. His masterpiece was 'The Great Eastern', the first steamer to cross the Atlantic, which was launched in 1859.

Architecturally, the Brunels' connection with Lindsey House was unfortunate. Mr. Peter Kroyer, in his interesting book *The Story of Lindsey House*, declares that 'Sir Marc Brunel no doubt possessed genius as an engineer; but so far as No. 98 was concerned, it would have been better had he never seen it. His alterations to the house were disastrous, particularly his removal of all the front windows and substitution of smaller ones composed of one large sheet of plate glass'. He also constructed a hideous annexe at the back, ruining the garden and obliterating the view. 'Undoing Brunel,' said Mr. Kroyer, who lived there and did it, 'proved a costly business'; but it was achieved in 1952, and the front windows restored to their original seventeenth-century size and style.

In 1863, number 7 Lindsey Row, a small unpretentious eighteenth-century house, had a new tenant, entered in the rate books as 'James Whistler'.

CHAPTER NINE

O N JULY 10, 1834, exactly one month after the Carlyles' arrival in
Cheyne Row, James Abbot McNeill Whistler, another unique
personality, who became as much a part of the Chelsea scene as the
Sage himself, was born at Lowell, Massachusetts. He came of Puritan and
military stock. When he was nine the family went to St. Petersburg where
Major Whistler was commissioned by Tsar Nicholas I to build a railway
between that city and Moscow. In 1848, after five years in the capital of
Imperialist Russia, the boy James Whistler paid his first visit to London.
His half-sister Deborah had married a young English surgeon, Francis
Seymour Haden, the son of Jane Austen's handsome 'apothecary from the
corner of Sloane Street'; and it was to the same corner house, number 64
Sloane Street, that the fourteen-year-old boy came, and from which he
caught his first glimpse of the district which he was one day to call 'my
Chelsea'.

Much water was to flow under Battersea Bridge before the unforget-
table performance which was the complete, the finished product—the
small, monocled, immaculately groomed James McNeill Whistler—
entered into his kindom on Chelsea Reach. This performance was no pose;
it was an integral part of the man; no veneer but reality. He was an artist
of the highest integrity, and it was as an artist that he built up his own
image, drawing upon his feeling for dress, his stinging wit, and also, perhaps, his failures: his attempt to follow family tradition by submitting to
a year's military discipline under Robert E. Lee at West Point, where he
failed his examination in chemistry ('if silicon had been a gas I should have
been a Major-General'); and a short-lived spell in the office of Coastal
Survey at Washington which taught him nothing but the technique of
etching maps. It was the mastery of this skill that determined him to make
use of his gift for drawing.

He prevailed upon his family to send him to Paris, where among the
artists on the Left Bank he at last found the kind of life that he had instinctively been seeking. It was *La Vie Bohème* of Du Maurier's *Trilby*, but
real, not idealized. Whistler's mistress, 'Fumette', was a spitfire gipsy
beauty who, in a rage, tore his drawings to shreds, reducing him to tears.

But the experience he gained among the artists working there—Courbet in particular—and the friendships he formed with Fantin Latour and Legros, affected all his future work.

(According to his pupil, Walter Sickert, the effect was far wider. 'Whistler,' he wrote, 'has sent the more intelligent of the generation that succeeds him to the springs whence he drew his own art—to French soil. He had the good fortune to learn painting in Paris, while the traditions of David and Ingres and Delacroix were still vivid, and his talent had the extraordinary instinct of self-preservation through the years of residence in England, never to let go again of what he had learnt.')

Paris, at the time of Whistler's sojourn there, was preoccupied with Japanese art. A little book of woodcuts by Hokusai discovered among the packings of a crate of porcelain was, incredibly, the inspiration of a movement which swept the art world. Whistler, returning to London in 1859, carried with him his enthusiasm for *Japonaiserie*, including the blue and white porcelain which became the collectors' rage, and was the source of rows and rivalry between Rossetti and Whistler—and of crafty bargaining and some shocking dishonesty on the part of Charles Augustus Howell, who, needless to say, profited from the situation.

It was natural that Whistler, who himself possessed tremendous courage, should admire the fantastic impudence of Howell—'the wonderful man, the genius, the superb liar', as he called him: 'the Gil-Blas, Robinson Crusoe hero out of his proper time, the creature of top boots and plumes —splendidly flamboyant.' 'He had the instinct,' Whistler added, 'for beautiful things.' And for this he forgave him many acts of flagrant dishonesty.

For a time, Whistler's painting was clearly influenced by Japanese art: in the early days at Chelsea he became known as 'the Japanese artist'. He had a model called Jo Heffernan, the red-haired daughter of a hard-drinking Irish sea captain. Jo, in the course of time, became his mistress, his housekeeper and the inspiration for one of his most lovely paintings, 'The Little White Girl', in which the Japanese influence manifests itself in the fan she holds, the porcelain jar on the chimneypiece against which she leans, and the sprays of blossom which decorate the foreground. This picture was painted in the first-floor room which he used as a studio at 7 Lindsey Row (101 Cheyne Walk), and it now hangs in the National Gallery. Whistler called it 'Symphony in White', a title he had already bestowed on another painting of Jo, and which he used for a third, this time of two girls, one being Jo. The critics, who liked, and expected, every picture to tell a story, disapproved of this ambiguous style of description, which, in any case, was inaccurate. 'There are many dainty varieties of tone,' wrote P. G. Hamerton in *The Saturday Review*, 'but it is not precisely a symphony in white. One lady has a yellowish dress and brown hair and a bit of blue ribbon, and the other has a red fan, and there are flowers and green leaves. There is a girl in white on a white sofa, but even this girl has reddish hair; and of course there is the flesh colour of the complexions.'

'How pleasing,' retorted Whistler, 'that such profound prattle should inevitably find its place in print! . . . Bon Dieu! did this wise person expect white hair and chalked faces? And does he then, in his astounding consequence, believe that a symphony in F contains no other note, but shall be a continued repetition of F, F, F? . . . Fool!'

Whistler was a fighter: to criticize him was to provoke him to revenge, which did not always confine itself to words. Unfortunately, his highly successful brother-in-law, Francis Seymour Haden, fell foul of him. Haden, a skilful amateur etcher, was at first stimulated by the presence in his house of Whistler, and the two spent days and evenings at work together. But the calm, conventional atmosphere of the doctor's house could not for long contain James Whistler; and after his liaison with Jo there was a breach which even his fondness for his half-sister and her daughter Annie could not heal. Seymour Haden was tactless, and possibly jealous of his brother-in-law's superior skill. In 1867, when they were both in Paris, Whistler, who had been taking boxing lessons, knocked Haden through a plate glass window. This was the end of all communication between Lindsey Row and Sloane Street.

Whistler consoled himself at Rossetti's hospitable table, where his wit won him a permanent place. Rossetti and Whistler were poles apart in their attitude to work: the Pre-Raphaelite's literary approach to painting was incomprehensible to Whistler, who never read a book. 'Why paint the picture?' he asked when Rossetti showed him a sonnet on which he was to base his next work. 'Why not frame the sonnet?'

Rossetti, though one of his poems may have been inspired by it, never painted the river at Chelsea. Whistler might be said to have had a long love affair with the Thames, which began on the muddy shore of Wapping, where he made his first etchings of barges and wharves and the delicate rigging of docked ships, discovering beauties there which no other artist had yet found.

But he owed Rossetti at least one inspiration: Whistler's butterfly signature, based on the letter W, was invented by Rossetti and adapted and elaborated by Whistler till it became a symbol of himself.

In 1866 Whistler moved to number 2 Lindsey Row (now 96 Cheyne Walk), which was the easternmost wing of the original Lindsey House. Here he remained for twelve years, and did some of his finest work. His mother, who had left America during the Civil War, was now living with him, and in this house she sat for the famous portrait, resigned, austere, with folded hands and feet firmly planted on a footstool, against the grey wall and black dado of the new studio.

The presence of his mother, dignified and aloof though she may have been, caused trouble with his mistress, who had to move out and live in lodgings. Gradually the humble, practical Jo disappeared from his life, to be replaced later on by a lady (also red-haired) called Maud, who liked to be addressed as Mrs. Whistler. Without Jo to manage them, Whistler's money affairs became more and more chaotic; but Charles Augustus Howell, who happened to be passing one evening, accompanied by three of his women ('he was like a great Portuguese cock of the poultry yard,' said Whistler; 'hens were always clucking about him') was called in to help. This sort of situation was meat and drink to Howell. He persuaded Whistler to start up his printing press and make use of the numbers of etchings he had stowed away.

'He said he would fix up the press . . . And the next morning there we all were . . . Howell pulling at the wheel and . . . grinding more ink, and with the plates under my fingers I felt the old love for it come back. In the afternoons Howell would go and see Graves the printsellers in Pall Mall and there were orders flying about, and cheques—it was all amazing, you know!'

But like all Howell stories, this one had a sting in its tail. 'One evening,' said Whistler, 'we left a pile of eleven prints just pulled, and the next morning only five were there. "It's very strange," said Howell, "we must have a search. No one could have taken them but me, and that you know is impossible!" '

Howell's finest inspirations arrived in times of financial crisis. One evening at Whistler's there was talk about the Oratory to be built at Brompton, and Whistler made a drawing of how he thought it should look. Months later, when there was a shortage of money, Howell rushed off to Attenborough the pawnbroker, returning with an astonishingly large amount of money. After some time, Whistler, passing the pawnshop, saw his sketch in the window, labelled 'Michael Angelo's first Drawing for St. Peter's'. History does not relate whether anyone bought it.

Other friends helped Whistler when he was broke. Madame Venturi, a neighbour in Lindsey Row, suggested that a portrait of Carlyle might prove profitable, and undertook to try and persuade the old man to sit. One day she arrived at the studio, accompanied by Carlyle, who by good fortune took a fancy to Whistler's portrait of his mother, seeming, as Whistler put it, 'to feel in it a certain fitness of things'. The upshot was that Carlyle agreed to be painted sitting in the same chair and in roughly the same attitude.

A few mornings later he arrived, in his long overcoat and wide black hat, seated himself and addressed the artist, to whom he was later to refer as 'the creature'. 'And now, mon, fire away!'

'That,' said Whistler, 'was not my idea of how work should be done;' and Carlyle realized it, for he added, 'If ye're fighting battles or painting pictures, the only thing is to fire away.'

Carlyle did not know how lengthy a battle would be fought before that bowed figure in the bulging overcoat, with a shawl over his knees (the studio was cold) and his hat placed on top of it, would be completed to the satisfaction of the artist. The two men had nothing in common: to Whistler the author of *The French Revolution* was a tired old man whose black clothes presented interesting problems of line and colour. To Carlyle, Whistler was incomprehensible, maddening in his refusal to work to time, inconsiderate in his finicky concentration on details which might as well be painted on a lay figure. One day, exhausted and stiff from a lengthy sitting, Carlyle descended to the hall, where he met a fair-haired child, who had just taken off her coat and hat, and ran lightly past him upstairs. He asked the servant who she was. 'That's Miss Cicely Alexander. She's sitting to Mr. Whistler.' Carlyle looked after her, wearily shaking his head. 'Poor wee lassie,' he sighed.

Whistler completed his painting of Cicely Alexander in seventy sittings, during which she was often reduced to tears of boredom, but in it he has captured like an impaled butterfly the delicacy and grace of youth.

Soon after his encounter with Miss Alexander, Carlyle retired from the battlefield, and Whistler was obliged to finish the overcoat, shawl and hat on the seated figure of old Greaves, the boatbuilder.

Whistler's taste in house decoration was years in advance of his time. His furniture was of the simplest: while Rossetti lounged or curled up like a cat, Whistler sat upright on a straight-backed chair, such as that in the Mother and Carlyle portraits. In place of Turkey carpets he used Japanese matting. Abominating the elaborate wallpapers in fashion among his contemporaries, Whistler chose plain distempered walls coloured in contrast to the painted dados and doors; and he always mixed the colours himself. In his first Chelsea studio he decorated the walls with Japanese prints, hung a Japanese birdcage from the ceiling and arranged shelves of blue and white china, interspersed with fans and pieces of lacquer. But after the Paris Exhibition of 1867 the Japanese craze became popularized and vulgarized. Whistler, in his second house, did away with fans and ornaments: the rooms, if furnished at all, were furnished with the utmost simplicity. In his third house, the famous White House, he introduced yellow walls, a startling innovation which caused Charles Augustus Howell to remark that living with Jimmy was like living inside an egg.

His taste in clothes was equally remarkable. Never for one moment—even when he was at his lowest ebb—did his appearance suggest the poverty-stricken artist. He generally wore a long frock coat of impeccable cut, black with white duck trousers in summer, and a tall silk hat with a straight brim, tilted to reveal the famous white forelock. He eschewed the lace-up boots in which Englishmen walked abroad, and invariably wore patent leather dancing pumps with square toes, sometimes ornamented with bows or rosettes. In his hand he carried a tall, slender cane, and in his eye he wore a monocle which may or may not have aided his short sight, but of which he made full use as a dramatic instrument.

Whistler, inevitably, attracted followers whom he made his slaves. The first of these were the Greaves brothers, Henry and Walter, the sons of a Chelsea boatbuilder, who, twenty years earlier, had been employed by Turner to row him about and across the Thames. In the 'fifties, the biblical painter, John Martin, who lived in the centre house of Lindsey Row, asked old Greaves to wake him up on nights when there was a stormy moonlit sky, when he would come out on to the balcony in his nightcap and make studies of the clouds. So the Greaves family—'a sort of Peggotty family', Whistler called it—had already had some connection with the world of art. The father and mother brought up their six children in the house which is now 103 Cheyne Walk, and eventually spread into number 104 as well. There was a sister known as Tinnie, who was attractive, and who sat to Whistler. The two brothers, Henry and Walter, boatmen by trade, both had artistic leanings, and gladly accepted invitations from Whistler to carry his painting things, prepare his canvases, paint his frames, help decorate his house, and generally make themselves useful, in return for which he took them to a life class in Limerston Street, where Whistler made chalk drawings of a nude model and the Greaveses sat behind him and copied what he did. Both were clever natural draughtsmen, and Walter, as his 'Hammersmith Bridge' at the Tate Gallery shows, had a streak of genius and a strong individual style; so it is debatable whether, in the long run, Whistler's influence was a benefit. But their friendship with 'the Master', while it lasted, was stimulating, and evidently provided a good deal of amusement for all concerned.

Whistler said that he taught the Greaveses to paint and they taught him to row—to row with what he called the Waterman's Jerk. They were often out on the river all night, stopping as they passed Cremorne to watch the fireworks and listen to the band, while Whistler made notes for his Nocturnes on brown paper in black and white chalk.

'He was a rare fellow for music,' Walter told the Pennells; he would hire a passing organ grinder to come and play in his front garden; and in the evening the Greaves family played for him by the hour while he danced. He was 'a rare fellow' too for card games, said Walter, and he enjoyed mimicking certain sounds—saws and rockets—which he did with verisimilitude.

It was Whistler's ambition to start a school of painting, and he evidently thought of the Greaves brothers as his pupils; but if Walter produced anything which seemed like an imitation of his work he resented it.

'Don't you see, Walter,' he wrote, 'you know how I continually invent —and invention you know is the cream of the whole affair and so easy to destroy the freshness of it. And you know that all the whole system of arrangement and harmonies which I most certainly invented, I brought you up in, so that it is only natural that I should expect my pupil to perceive all harmony in the same way—he must do it—for I have shown him that everything outside of that is wrong . . . Suppose you were to see any other fellows doing my moonlights—how vexed you would be. Well, nothing more natural than that you two should do them and quite right that the traditions of the studio should go on through the pupils—but still for instance it would be absurd now to paint another White Girl. Don't you know what I mean?'

But the Greaveses, though they imitated and admired Whistler, were not sycophantic. The three were leaning on the river wall one day, drawing the buildings on the Battersea shore. Harry looked at the Master's sketch. 'But Mr. Whistler,' he said, 'your chimneys are not straight.' Whistler turned and stared at him. 'But they are Whistler's.'

During these years at Lindsey Row Whistler was inventing and perfecting his Nocturnes. Evening after evening, he would watch the river, noting the deepening colours of sky and water, waiting for the moment when the balance of light and dark gave him the harmony, the perfect effect he wanted. Then he would stand still, 'leaning on the Embankment wall, looking. And when he had looked long, he would turn round with his back to his subject and begin to recite in a sort of chant. "The sky is lighter than the water, the houses darkest. There are eight houses, the second is the lowest, the fifth highest. The tone of all is the same. The first has two lighted windows, one above the other; the second has four." Then he would turn back to the river, correct his mistakes, and begin again. Next day he would paint his nocturne.'

Walter Greaves told the Pennells that after making his notes Whistler would paint in the studio, using quantities of medium so that the paint was as wet and thin as water colour. The canvas was often prepared with a red ground, to bring up the blues of the painting. Sometimes the nocturne was completed in an hour and a half; but if he was not satisfied he would destroy it and start all over again, perhaps many times, till he achieved what he wanted. Here was the truth behind that famous exchange in the Whistler–Ruskin libel action, as quoted by Whistler himself:

(Attorney General): 'Now, Mr. Whistler, can you tell me how long it took you to knock off that nocturne?

(Whistler): I beg your pardon? (laughter)

. . . I should have said, how long did it take you to paint that picture?

. . . As well as I remember, about a day.

. . . Only a day?

. . . Well, I won't be quite positive; I may have still put a few more touches to it the next day if the painting were not dry. I had better say then, that I was two days at work on it.

. . . Oh, two days! The labour of two days, then, is that for which you ask two hundred guineas!

. . . No;—I ask it for the knowledge of a lifetime.'

The action for libel was brought by Whistler in 1876, after a violent attack by Ruskin on one of his exhibits in the newly opened Grosvenor Gallery. The great critic, who was on the verge of a mental breakdown, ignored Whistler's portrait of Ruskin's 'dearest Mr. Carlyle' which was shown there; he passed without comment the 'Nocturne in Blue and Silver' (Battersea Bridge); but chose to vent his spleen upon the painting of a falling rocket, entitled 'Nocturne in Black and Gold', which was the finale of countless attempts to capture that vision experienced by Whistler on summer nights at Cremorne.

'I have seen and heard much of cockney inpudence before now,' wrote Ruskin, 'but never expected to hear a coxcomb ask two hundred guineas for flinging a pot of paint in the public's face.'

Whistler, in court, was supported by William Rossetti and a fellow artist, Albert Moore; he himself was in good form and scored several hits in his replies to questioning. Ruskin was too ill to appear, and was represented by a rather uneasy Burne-Jones, Frith of 'Derby Day' and Tom Taylor, the art critic of *The Times*, who could think of nothing better than to read aloud his own reviews, which had little bearing on the case. The whole thing might have been written by Lewis Carroll. The jury were clearly baffled, and decided to play safe by awarding Whistler a farthing damages and leaving both parties to pay their own costs.

For Whistler, this was a disastrous verdict. He was engaged in building himself a large studio in Tite Street, designed by E. W. Godwin, where he had planned to start his school. He had embarked on the scheme in a moment of prosperity, and was now too deeply involved to back out.

All he could do was to move into the half-finished house, where he offered his creditors champagne obtained on credit, and when the bailiffs took possession, persuaded them to wait at table while he entertained his friends. Chelsea tradesmen, offered Whistler paintings in payment of their accounts, indignantly refused. The Arts Club secretary, applying for a long-overdue subscription, replied to Whistler's suggestion that a picture might do instead, 'It is not a Nocturne in purple or a Symphony in blue and grey that we are after, but an Arrangement in gold and silver.'

The White House was a dream which never materialized. Between them, Whistler and Godwin had planned something unique, a house which imitated no period, which conformed with none of the existing fashions in elaborate decoration (the plans were only passed by the local council when Godwin agreed to design a frieze to relieve the plain front and 'keep up the tone' of the street). The walls were of white brick, the roof of green slates; windows were placed where they were needed, without regard for symmetry. It was a new and exciting experiment—and a tragic failure. Whistler went bankrupt in May 1879; bills announcing the sale of the house and contents were posted on the walls, and the following September, Whistler—who, with Howell's aid had succeeded in salvaging a few possessions from the wreck—departed for Venice. The day before he left, he mounted a ladder and wrote over his front door, 'Except the Lord build the house, they labour in vain that build it. E. W. Godwin, F.S.A. built this one.'

The portrait of Carlyle was in pawn; so was the portrait of Whistler's mother. His mother herself was in Hastings, where in 1881 she died. Whistler, accompanied by his faithful Maud, lived frugally in Venice; but this was by no means the end of his connection with Chelsea. In November 1880, he was back in London: a few months later he was back in Tite Street, where he rented a studio within spitting distance of Harry Quilter, the new art critic of *The Times* who had bought the White House for £2,700.

Much of the energy which had gone into Whistler's painting was now spent in composing polished witticisms, scorpion stings aimed, for the most part, at Quilter, whom he scornfully referred to as 'Arry, in a journal called *The World*. Hearing that the new owner was making alterations to the White House, Whistler wrote:

'Shall 'Arry, whom I have hewn down, still live among us by outrage of this kind, and impose his memory upon our pavement by the public perpetration of his posthumous philistinism? Shall the birthplace of art become the tomb of its parasite in Tite Street?'

In Whistler's view, 'Arry the philistine, if he could not appreciate the perfection of the White House, should hand it back to its creator. 'He obstinately stays there in the way, while I am living in this absurd fashion, next door to myself.'

In Venice, Whistler had made a large number of etchings: he came back to London to print and exhibit them—and to fight his enemies. The first thing he did was to make an entrance at an exhibition of etchings at the Fine Art Society. 'In one hand I held my long cane; with the other I led by the ribbon a beautiful little white Pomeranian dog; I spoke to no one, but putting up my glass I looked at the prints on the wall. "Dear me! dear me!" I said, "still the same sad old work! Dear me!" And Haden was there . . . laying down the law, and as he said "Rembrandt", I said "Ha, ha!" and he vanished'.

Whistler was carefully building up the star part he now wished to play. Wherever he went, he was careful to let it be known who he was: he wrote, he talked, he lectured; he did no great painting, but his performance of Whistler was at its zenith. He attracted new followers, principal among them the young Walker Sickert, who went daily to his Tite Street studio, watching him at work, 'and often working by him from the same sitter', even using the carefully mixed colours on Whistler's palette.

The Greaves brothers, his devoted admirers, had dropped out of his life: rowing on the Thames and dancing to the hurdy-gurdy were not in keeping with the new, more sophisticated performance. There is a sad story which illustrates how complete was the break. Walter Greaves copied the Master's style of dress; he was, as Mrs. Pennell puts it, 'a strange faraway echo of Whistler, the chief difference being that the echo was shabby and wore a red necktie'. One evening Whistler was to be the guest of honour at the Chelsea Arts Club in Church Street. He arrived— as he invariably did for everything—late: but some committee members waiting to receive him, who did not know him, saw an elderly man approaching, dressed in 'long overcoat, straight-brimmed top hat and white gloves, thought it must be Whistler, received him effusively and fluttered about him'. Then some older members appeared, to whom the mistake was obvious; but on learning that Greaves was a pupil and friend of Whistler's, they courteously invited him to stay and join the party. 'Then,' adds Mrs. Pennell, 'Whistler came, presently saw him, put up his monocle, stared at him, said nothing, and Greaves melted away.'

Walter Greaves outlived the Master by many years; lived to be claimed as a master in his own right after a show at the Goupil Gallery in 1912. There were even doubts—owing to wrong dating of some of Greaves's paintings—on Whistler's claim to have invented the nocturne. For a brief period Walter Greaves enjoyed fame, and some of his pictures sold for as much as two hundred guineas, pictures for which he would have been happy to get thirty shillings in Chelsea. But his success was short-lived: Whistler enthusiasts fought to prove that the Master was the supreme creative artist and Greaves the imitator. Though later generations have discovered in Greaves 'strange flashes of genius', he never achieved wealth or fame, but was content to remain obscure, wandering round his beloved Chelsea, making drawings of buildings dear to him that were about to be pulled down, selling his careful, loving work to small dealers for a few shillings. Many of his drawings and paintings, together with those of his brother Harry, are collected in the Chelsea Public Library, where they provide a fascinating source of information to the student of Victorian Chelsea.

Photographs of Edward Godwin make him look dull and solemn. He was evidently far from being either and was wildly attractive to women. Ellen Terry loved him passionately, and he was the father of her two children, Edith and Gordon Craig. By 1878, when he and Whistler were planning the White House, Godwin's romance with the great actress had come to an end, and he was married to Beatrix Philip, whose sculptor father[1] had a studio in Manresa Road, on the site of the Public Library. The new Mrs. Godwin dressed in the new aesthetic style caricatured by Du Maurier in *Punch*, and seen in the Grosvenor Gallery as well as in the streets of Chelsea. Tight waists and bustles were taboo, and so were the heavy, dark, upholstered garments of fashion. Aesthetic ladies wore clinging or flowing garments, floating silken scarves and low-heeled shoes; they favoured greens and yellows and dressed their hair *à la Grecque*. All this Beatrix Godwin did. She was tall, plump and pretty: Whistler liked her and gave her painting lessons.

Tite Street, in the 1880s, was becoming the fashionable artists' quarter,

[1] J. Birnie Philip, R.A. He was one of the sculptors of the Albert Memorial.

for those who could afford it. Godwin, after the White House débâcle, designed a set of studios nearby, pandering this time to the Dutch influence which was beginning to manifest itself in Chelsea architecture. On the opposite side the houses rose higher and higher, as if standing on tiptoe to get a view of the river. The highest was Tower House, also designed by Godwin. They were expensive, well built, with enormous studios: More House was built in 1882 by the Honourable John Collier, who painted 'The Last Voyage of Henry Hudson'; but he married his deceased wife's sister, was cut by his brother and sister-in-law, Lord and Lady Monkswell, who lived on Chelsea Embankment, and eventually he sold More House to Admiral Sir Edward Jephson. At Tower House Whistler, for a short time, had a studio; and Anna Lea Merritt, who called her house (now number 50) The Cottage, worked there on 'Love Locked Out'. Miss Dora Neale, of Britannia Road, Fulham, told the author in 1969 that her mother had been lady's maid to Mrs. Lea Merritt, and one of her duties had been to bath the Italian urchin who leaned, naked, against the barred door. Every day, she said, a cart arrived from the country, filled with trails of the wild roses that form part of this famous painting.

Opposite the Tower House is the handsome studio of John Singer Sargent, where—again according to Miss Neale, whose carpenter father posed to this artist—a basket of money was strung up in the hall 'so that his friends could help themselves'. No doubt they did, but Sargent could afford it.

Further up the street, on the west side, a terrace of smaller, red-brick houses was built, decorated with balconies, bay windows and terracotta bas-reliefs. Into one of these, number 16, Oscar Wilde and his young wife, Constance, moved in the summer of 1884.

Wilde and Whistler had been friends, who, naturally enough, became enemies, though the enmity did not go very deep. Whistler, invited to Wilde's wedding, sent a wire to the church, 'Am detained. Don't wait.'

While the relationship between them was that of Master and disciple, they were constantly in each other's company: each fascinated the other. But as Wilde's fame grew, the Whistler star was in danger of being dimmed by the new, flamboyant glitter. They sparred in public and in print, and many of their exchanges are famous. Wilde instinctively admired Whistler's showmanship, listened to his epigrams, and polished them up for future use. There is the story of how, after a particularly happy quip by Whistler, Oscar murmured, 'Ah, I wish I'd said that!' The monocle flashed. 'You will, Oscar, you will!'

Though he had cultivated a certain originality in his own style of dress,

Whistler abominated the extremes to which Oscar resorted. After seeing him descend from a hansom in Tite Street, in a long, tight-fitting, green velvet overcoat, frogged *à la Polonaise*, Whistler wrote, 'Oscar—how dare you! What means this disguise? Restore those things to Nathan's, and never again let me find you masquerading the streets of my Chelsea in the combined costumes of Kossuth and Mr. Mantalini.'

But the battle grew fiercer. Whistler aimed at Wilde's most vulnerable spot—his pretensions to good breeding. 'Bourgeois malgré lui,' was his summing up. Later, in a letter to the paper *Truth*, he accused him of plagiarism, and Oscar had his revenge.

'As for borrowing Mr. Whistler's idea about art,' he wrote, 'the only thoroughly original ideas I have ever heard him express have had reference to his own superiority as a painter over painters greater than himself. It is a trouble for any gentleman to have to notice the lucubrations of so ill-bred and ignorant a person as Mr. Whistler, but your publication of his insolent letter left me no option in the matter.'

But Whistler had the last word. 'O Truth!' he wrote, 'Cowed and humiliated, I acknowledge that our Oscar is at last original. At bay, and sublime in his agony, he certainly has, for once, borrowed from no living author, and comes out in his own true colours—as his own "gentleman".'

At Lindsey Row, in the 'sixties and 'seventies, Whistler's prime object and interest was painting—the ceaseless effort to translate his vision into terms of colour and design. Now, in the 'eighties, though he worked as feverishly as ever, it seemed as if his main object was to establish himself as a personality. His refusal to conform, his continual state of war with the critics, frightened off potential patrons and kept him permanently on the brink of financial disaster. When, in 1886, his Nocturne, 'Battersea Bridge', was put up for auction, *The Observer* reported that its appearance was greeted with hisses. Whistler wrote to the editor:

'It is rare that recognition so complete is made during the lifetime of a painter, and I would wish to have recorded my full sense of this flattering exception in my favour.'

But in 1891 the Glasgow Corporation, after lengthy deliberation, decided to buy the Carlyle portrait. Whistler priced it at 1,000 guineas. A pair of Scotsmen accordingly presented themselves at his studio (he was now living at 21 Cheyne Walk), their mission being to 'squeeze down' the price. They were received with the utmost courtesy, given cigarettes and tea made with rum and lemon—Vienna Tea, Whistler called it. The Scotsmen, after much humming and hawing, came to the point: they were prepared to pay 800 guineas. Whistler, in brown velveteen jacket and loose necktie, his hair curling almost to his shoulders, was the very picture of Art for Art's sake; his implication was that such a thing as money should not be allowed to enter into the negotiation. He begged them to come back next day, and he would show them the portrait of their great countryman.

They came back, and came straight to the point.

'Now, Mr. Whistler, have you been thinking any more about the price of your "Carlyle"?'

Whistler waved this aside: he had only been thinking, he said, of the pleasure of entertaining them again. More Vienna tea appeared, more cigarettes were handed. Then the picture was brought in and placed on an easel. There was a lengthy pause. Then one Scotsman spoke.

'Mr. Whistler, do you call this life size?'

'No, I don't,' said Whistler, 'there is no such thing as life size. If I put you up against the canvas and measured you, you would be a monster.'

The Scotsman tried another tack.

'The tones of this portrait are rather dull, are they not? Not very brilliant, are they?'

By this time Whistler had lost all control. 'Not brilliant!' he cried in his high-pitched scream. 'Why should they be? Are you brilliant? No! Am I brilliant? Not at all! We are not "highly coloured", are we? We are very very ordinary looking people. The picture says that, and no more.'

He got his thousand guineas.

Shortly after this, his 'Arrangement in Grey and Black'—the portrait of his mother, which he had so far refused to sell—was bought by the Musée de Luxembourg, and the artist was awarded the Légion d'Honneur, an achievement which delighted him.

He was now married, to Beatrix Godwin. She had been separated from the architect, and was freed by his death in 1886. She had long been Whistler's pupil, and his increasing interest in her had caused violent scenes of jealousy with the faithful Maud, who had for so many years shared his debts and ministered to his moods. In the end, Maud walked out, and in August 1888 Whistler and Beatrix Godwin were married at St. Mary Abbots, Kensington. The marriage was singularly happy, but in 1894 Beatrix Whistler's health broke down, and two years later she died, of cancer. She died in Hampstead, but most of their married life had been spent in Paris.

Whistler was now sixty-two. He had been devoted to Beatrix, and her loss left him purposeless, and homeless. It was inevitable, perhaps, that he should return to Chelsea. With his wife's mother and sister he went to live at 74 Cheyne Walk, a new house built by Ashbee where the fish shop in Lombard Street had stood. Lombard Street was now open on the river side, and was gradually being modernized. Number 74 had a beaten copper front door, and was the first of several Ashbee houses in the *art nouveau* style. No sooner had Whistler moved in than he began to be driven mad by the sound of hammering, which went on relentlessly as the building work on the next house proceeded.

He had no redress, and took refuge in flight, to Holland. But by now he was too frail to travel. In Amsterdam he became so ill that reports reached England that he had died, and the *Morning Post* published an obituary article, which caused the convalescent Whistler enormous delight. Needless to say, he replied, in a letter to the editor.

'. . . I must beg you, perhaps, to put back into its pigeon-hole, for later on, this present summary, and replace it with something preparatory—which doubtless you have also ready . . .

'It is my marvellous privilege, then, to come back, as who should say, while the air is still warm with appreciation, affection, and regret . . .'

He came back to Chelsea, where the hammering continued unabated. His heart troubled him: his friends noticed that he had grown suddenly old. Even his abundant curling hair with the famous white crest had lost its bounce, making his face look small and withered. He had his bed moved downstairs, to a little room beside his studio, and here, on the ground floor, he lived and worked fitfully, rolled in an old fur-lined overcoat. He had found a new model, an Irish girl with beautiful copper-red hair. At work on this painting, which he called 'Daughter of Eve', he was as endlessly patient and self-critical as on any of the Harmonies and Arrangements. Once, after a set-back, he flung down his brush and walked away from the canvas crying, 'You cannot do it, your day is done.' A moment later, he returned, saying quietly, 'You can do it, you must do it as long as you live.' He apologized to the model. 'Take no notice of me, child; I am growing an old man, and getting into a habit of talking to myself.'

Whistler died on July 17, 1903. The funeral service was at the Old Church, and Jo, his first red-haired model, was there with Whistler's illegitimate son, John, whom he always called his Infidelity to Jo. Walter Greaves, who had been refused admittance to the studio during the Master's last illness, made an etching of the small, sad procession making its short journey from house to church. After the service, the coffin was carried to Chiswick, where Whistler lies beside his wife and beside the Thames.

CHAPTER TEN

T HE MOST remarkable men I have ever known,' wrote Ellen Terry, 'were Whistler and Oscar Wilde . . . There was something about both of them more instantaneously individual and audacious than it is possible to describe.'

Even allowing for the generosity of Ellen Terry's nature, this is an arresting statement, and makes nonsense of much of the criticism of Oscar Wilde from those who found his individuality and audacity a hollow sham, the self-advertisement of a mountebank. When he first came to London, his fascination was apparent to many people, particularly women. Laura Troubridge, after her first meeting with Wilde in 1879, noted in her journal that she and her sister 'both fell awfully in love with him, thought him quite delightful'. At their next meeting, four years later, he had grown fat, which, as Byron discovered, was woefully inappropriate in a poet. The critical Miss Laura was disillusioned. 'He was very amusing and talked cleverly, but it was all monologue and not conversation. He is vulgar, I think, and lolls about in, I suppose, poetic attitudes, with crumpled shirt and cuffs turned back over his coat sleeves.'

That scornful Victorian word 'vulgar' (which Wilde himself continually employed) often crops up in descriptions of him. William Rothenstein tells us that there was 'something florid, almost vulgar', in his appearance. 'He had elaborately waved, long hair, parted in the middle, which made his forehead appear lower than it was, a finely-shaped nose, but dark-coloured lips and uneven teeth, and his cheeks were full, and touching his wide winged collar. His hands,' he adds, 'were fat and useless-looking.'

But as soon as Wilde began to talk, in that beguiling Irish voice, Rothenstein was bewitched. 'His description of people, his appreciation of prose and verse, were a never-failing delight . . .

'Tell me about so and so, Oscar, you would ask; and there would come a stream of entertaining stories, and a vivid and genial personal portrait. He was remarkably free from malice . . .'

'Wilde talked,' wrote Rothenstein, 'as others painted or wrote; talking was his art. I have certainly never heard his equal; whether he was improvising or telling stories—his own or other people's—one was content that his talk should be a monologue.'

It was as a talker that Wilde was chiefly famous when he moved into number 16 (now 34) Tite Street after his marriage. Talk, in those days, was not a means of livelihood, except for politicians, so the Wildes were hard up, but they were happy. Oscar was intoxicated with love, breaking into lyrical descriptions of the beauty of his wife, Constance: 'a grave, slight, violet-eyed little Artemis, with great coils of heavy brown hair which make her flower-like head droop like a blossom, and wonderful ivory hands which drew music from the piano so sweet that the birds stop singing to listen to her.'

He was lyrical, too, about the rather ordinary little house in Tite Street, which was transformed, inside, by the skill of Edward Godwin, who designed some of the furniture and all the decoration. Long before the 'white' craze for interior design was made fashionable by Mrs. Syrie Maugham, whose all-white drawing room at 213 King's Road was considered highly original in the 1930s, Godwin had discovered the dramatic use of white. He gave the Wildes a white front door; the hall was painted white with a high gloss, the staircase was white and the stairs were covered in whitish matting.

'I have,' wrote Oscar, 'a dining room done in different shades of white, with white curtains embroidered in yellow silk: the effect is absolutely delightful, and the room is beautiful.' This room was at the back, on the ground floor. The study was in front, facing the street. Here, the colour scheme was red and yellow. The walls were pale yellow, the woodwork enamelled in red, and on a red plinth in one corner stood a cast of Mercury. In this small room Oscar Wilde worked, on a table which had belonged to Carlyle: he admired Carlyle, and knew pages of *The French Revolution* by heart. In this small room he was alone, without an audience, and this, of all the rooms in the house, must have seen the real man. Here he kept his most precious possessions.

'It was from my father's study,' wrote his son, Vyvyan Holland, 'that hooligans stole everything they could lay hands on when he lay in prison, and the brokers were in and were completely indifferent to the treasures there. Manuscripts and books which could only have come from that room still turn up at auction sales in England and America; even some of my mother's letters to Oscar Wilde.'

The drawing room above was Constance's domain, and here Whistler—temporarily burying the hatchet—joined Godwin and decorated the ceiling in blue, with painted dragons and two brilliant peacock feathers let into the plaster. The walls of this room were buttercup yellow, and on them Whistler hung one or two of his own etchings. No doubt he was appalled when an enormous full-length portrait of Wilde by the American artist Harper Pennington made its appearance opposite the fireplace, totally out of keeping with the rest of the decor. In fact, the room was a compromise. There were blue and white curtains in a Morris design; there were black and white bamboo chairs, and other fashionable bits of Japonaiserie; there was a grand piano, painted white, bulrushes in tall Japanese vases, and small bamboo tables covered, by Constance, with the bric-à-brac beloved by ladies of the period.

Here the Wildes entertained. And it was in this room, during a reception, that Oscar's two little sons made a dramatic entrance. They were on their way to a fancy dress party, for which, at Papa's suggestion, they were to be dressed, respectively, as 'Bubbles' and 'Little Lord Fauntleroy'. Naturally, the boys despised these cissy characters, and wanted to go in sailor suits. Told to come downstairs and show themselves, they stole into their father's smoking room on the way, divested themselves of all trace of Millais's soap-blower and the Little Lord, together with everything else they had on, and marched, naked, into the drawing room. Party conversation flickered and died: even Papa was speechless. Then the boys were quickly hustled upstairs. But Wilde, his son tells us, took the hint: what happened at this fancy dress party history does not relate, but Cyril and Vyvyan were taken to a naval tailor and given suits of real naval cloth, complete with black silk scarves and knives on lanyards.

The smoking room, where they had done their defiant stripping, was at the back of the house. It was dark, and, to the little boys, alarming. The décor was vaguely Moorish, but the walls were covered in dark red and dull gold Lincrusta-Walton in a Morris design, with a black dado. There were no chairs, but low divans against the walls, carved and inlaid oriental tables, and the room was dimly lit by Moorish lanterns. The light of day was firmly excluded, for the window looked over the back of Paradise Walk. Though it may not have lived up to Wilde's lurid description of a slum in *Lord Arthur Savile's Crime*, where there were 'women with hoarse voices and harsh laughter', drunkards who 'reeled by cursing' and 'grotesque children huddled upon doorsteps', it must have been squalid, dirty, and horribly overcrowded, and the sights and sounds which reached the back windows were not pretty. Wilde, who wrote, 'One should sympathise with the colour, the beauty, the joy of life. The less said about life's sores the better,' covered his smoking room window with a wooden grating copied from a Persian design.

Oscar Wilde was attracted to Tite Street for two reasons. The first was that it was within easy reach of Oakley Street, where his mother had taken a house (number 146, it was re-numbered 87, and has now vanished). The second, and more typically Wildeian reason was that on the other side of Tite Street was Sargent's studio, and Ellen Terry was sitting to him. 'The Street that on a wet and dreary morning has vouchsafed the vision of Lady Macbeth in full regalia magnificently seated in a four-wheeler can never again be as other streets: it must always be full of wonderful possibilities.'

Lady Wilde, who had been a widow since 1876, was an extraordinary woman. An Irish patriot who in her youth had written impassioned political articles and poems under the name 'Speranza', she was unflagging in the organization of afternoon parties. Her guests in Oakley Street were received in closely curtained rooms, lit by a few guttering candles, and in the dim light their hostess presented a remarkable appearance. Like her two sons, Willy and Oscar, Lady Wilde was large and ungainly. She had a deep dramatic voice, and was heavily made up. Her clothes were invariably surprising. Sometimes her grey hair hung down her back, and her dress was pure white; in another, more majestic, mood, she would appear in purple brocade, her head crowned with a gilt laurel wreath. She wore a great deal of heavy, clanking jewellery and her bosom was plastered with large brooches. She was kind, and took great trouble about introducing her guests to one another, giving each a short biography in whispered, telegraphic précis. Oscar, remembering this, wrote in *Dorian Gray*, 'Poor Lady Brandon treats her guests exactly as an auctioneer treats his goods. She either explains them entirely away, or tells one everything about them except what one wants to know.'

But he adored his mother, and made a point of attending her receptions, where his presence undoubtedly attracted more guests. In fact, in the 1890s when his success in the theatre made him in demand here, there and everywhere, Lady Wilde's receptions languished and died. She accepted the situation philosophically, ceased to paint her face, and threw open the curtains to let in the daylight. Her social success no longer mattered: it was enough that she was the mother of Oscar Wilde. 'He is always working and the world will not let him alone. No one in London is so sought after as Oscar.'

Wilde smoked a great many cigarettes: he smoked in his bath, he even smoked in bed, which cannot have pleased his fastidious wife. He was supposed to smoke in his smoking room, and here no doubt he did smoke with his friends, the air thick with tobacco fumes, the oriental tables laden with decanters and glasses. But it was in his ground floor study, to the innocent accompaniment of tea and bread and butter, that one afternoon in 1891 he received Lionel Johnson the poet, who brought with him a young man, Lord Alfred Douglas. From that moment, the direction of Wilde's life altered. The part he had played in Tite Street, of wage earner, dutiful if erratic husband and affectionate father, was suddenly re-written.

Perhaps, by now, he was bored with his marriage; perhaps, inevitably, Constance's limitations would not have stood the strain of Oscar's success. Sir William Rothenstein, who went to see the Wildes in 1893, was favourably impressed by Constance. 'She wasn't clever, but she had distinction and candour. With brown hair framing her face, and a Liberty hat, she looked like a drawing . . . by Walter Crane. I knew little,' he adds, 'of the difficulties which were beginning between Wilde and his wife: they seemed on affectionate terms; he delighted in his children; only I felt something wistful and a little sad about Mrs. Wilde.'

Constance Wilde was no fool: she was practical and direct, but possibly tactless. There is, for instance, the story that in the middle of a dinner party when Wilde was launched on an amusing anecdote, she suddenly interrupted him with, 'Oh, Oscar, did you remember to call for Cyril's boots?' Even if apocryphal, this illustrates an impression received by one guest that, like that of Mr. and Mrs. Dickens, this was not a marriage of true minds. But both were ready to make concessions. Constance obediently displayed her husband's far-fetched designs for aesthetic costume. Mrs. Belloc-Lowndes described her at a private view at the Grosvenor Gallery 'in a green and black suit and hat which recalled coloured engravings of eighteenth-century highwaymen. It made,' she added, 'a considerable sensation.'

Constance also allowed herself to be consulted on matters of taste in dress and decor. She trained herself to be a good hostess to Oscar's friends, and though hers may sometimes have bored her husband, he was by nature a good host, and scintillated as brightly for the curate's fiancée as before the most distinguished personages in Constance's Visitors' Book, which held the signatures of Sarah Bernhardt, Ellen Terry, Henry Irving, Whistler, Swinburne, Ruskin—an all-star cast of the artistic and theatrical firmament.

Their two little boys were very attractive, and Constance took a pride in them. They were allowed to mix with the guests at their parents' Sunday receptions—an unusual thing for English children at this time— and evidently (apart from the fancy dress escapade) behaved prettily. The top floor of the house was the boys' domain, and consisted of a night nursery and a day nursery, with a bathroom in between. The day nursery contained two large, built-in platforms, about a foot from the ground and four feet deep, running along two sides of the room. Here the little boys marshalled their armies of lead soldiers, set up forts and placed cannons in strategic positions, and fierce wars were waged with peas as shot.

When Papa came up to the nursery, there was fun for all. 'He had so much of the child in his nature,' wrote his son Vyvyan, 'that he delighted in playing our games. He would go down on all fours on the nursery floor, being in turn a lion, a wolf, a horse, caring nothing for his normally immaculate appearance.'

He would also tell stories, from writers that he admired, such as Jules Verne and Stevenson, or his own fairy tales, shortened and simplified. 'Cyril once asked him why he had tears in his eyes when he told us the story of "The Selfish Giant", and he replied that really beautiful things always made him cry.'

'It is the duty of every father to write fairy tales for his children,' he told Richard Le Gallienne. 'But the mind of a child is a great mystery,' he continued. 'For example, a day or two ago, Cyril yonder came to me with the question, "Father, do you ever dream?" "Why, of course, my darling. It is the first duty of a gentleman to dream." "And what do you dream of?" asked Cyril, with a child's disgusting appetite for facts. Then I, believing of course that something picturesque would be expected of me, spoke of magnificent things. "What do I dream of? Oh, I dream of dragons with gold and silver scales, and scarlet flames coming out of their mouths, of eagles with eyes made of diamonds that can see over the whole world at once, of lions with yellow manes and voices like thunder . . ." So I laboured on with my fancy, till observing that Cyril was entirely unimpressed, and indeed quite undisguisedly bored . . . I said, "But tell me, what do you dream of, Cyril?" His answer was like a divine revelation: "I dream of pigs," he said.'

Out of doors, the boys, with other children of the neighbourhood, were out and about daily, bowling hoops and riding tricycles along the pavements. Mrs. Jacqueline Hope-Nicholson, who still lives in Tite Street, remembers 'being furious with Cyril because he wouldn't let me ride his tricycle on the Embankment'. In the Royal Hospital Gardens, Cyril and Vyvyan made friends with some of the Chelsea Pensioners, who allowed the boys to dig in their gardens, and invited them to their rooms for tea out of thick mugs and slabs of bread and butter and cake. They were entertained with stories of the battlefields, and one old man, who was nearly a hundred, told them that he had been a drummer boy at Waterloo, and had sailed home in the same ship as the Duke of Wellington.

The boys were healthy and happy, enjoying omnibus rides down the King's Road, or up Sloane Street in the 'Halfpenny Devil', a one-horse bus which plied between Sloane Square and Knightsbridge. It had no conductor, only a driver who stopped for passengers, or at the pulling of the bell-cord. The fare was one halfpenny, which you were asked to place in a box. Unfortunately, the public took advantage of this arrangement, and so many buttons were found in the boxes that the Halfpenny Devil had to be taken off the road.

Constance Wilde must have fought to preserve an atmosphere of normality about the household, even when its foundations were rocked by the first intimations of disaster. For three years, between 1892 and 1895, Wilde was earning large sums of money through the success of his plays; and during those years his life was governed by his infatuation for Lord Alfred Douglas. The story is too well known to need detailed repetition. In April 1895 Wilde's action for criminal libel against the 'Screaming Scarlet Marquis', Douglas's father, failed, and the Marquis was acquitted. On the same day, Wilde was arrested at the Cadogan Hotel, refused bail and lodged in Holloway Prison till his first trial on a charge of sodomy, at the end of April. The jury disagreed, and Wilde was released for two weeks on a bail of £5,000, which, with great difficulty, was raised among his friends.

Constance remained in the background; though an occasional mention of her reveals what she must have been suffering. Ignorant of the very meaning of the 'unnatural practices' of which her husband had been accused, she is described as having said, 'He has been mad the last three years.' And so indeed he must have seemed. She must have grown to dread the very name of Lord Alfred Douglas, and yet she steeled herself to dine in public with him and her husband two nights before the Queensberry trial. 'She was very agitated,' wrote Douglas, 'and when I said goodnight to her at the door of the theatre there were tears in her eyes.'

Wilde's life at Tite Street was over. During his fortnight's bail he went —after being refused by a number of hotels—to Oakley Street, where his foolish, drink-sodden brother and drama-loving mother must have made life almost intolerable, and from whence he was rescued by his friend Ada Leverson, who invited him to stay with her husband and herself at Courtfield Gardens (having first obtained the consent of their servants). Oscar's friends implored him to leave the country before the second trial, but his brother Willie told everyone, 'Oscar is an Irish gentleman; he will stay and face the music.'

He stayed; and the whole of fashionable London turned from him in horror. Gently nurtured ladies, who had not the faintest inkling of what the crime was of which he was accused, found themselves unable to pronounce his name. The words 'Oscar Wilde' were like a shameful disease which could not be mentioned and must at all costs be stamped out. And stamped out the name was, from playbills and programmes, at the theatres where *An Ideal Husband* and *The Importance of Being Earnest* were being performed. Actors went on acting, audiences went on applauding and laughing, while between them was a conspiracy to believe that the author, like Bunbury, did not exist. But the game could not be kept up. The theatres closed; Wilde's books were withdrawn from circulation. Royalties on all his work abruptly ceased.

At his second trial, in May 1895, he was found guilty and sentenced to two years' imprisonment with hard labour—a savage sentence for a man of his calibre. The judge who pronounced it, Mr. Justice Wills, by a strange quirk of fate, was Wilde's neighbour in Tite Street (number 46), and no doubt saw the boards going up at number 16, advertising the sale of the entire contents.

On the day of the sale, the house, wrote William Rothenstein, 'was filled with a jostling crowd, most of whom had come out of curiosity; the rest were dealers, mostly local people, who had come to pick up bargains. And bargains there certainly were. Bundles of manuscripts, books, pictures and prints and bric-à-brac went for almost nothing. I bought a picture by Monticelli for eight pounds, which later I was able to sell to Colnaghi to help Wilde.'

The two boys had already been asked to leave their school, and now they and their mother were hurried out of the country, and eventually found refuge, under an assumed name, in Switzerland. Vyvyan and Cyril, who had not been back to Tite Street, complained at the loss of their toys. Their armies of lead soldiers, the fort that their father had laboriously mended, the cannons and trains and railway lines—all the nursery paraphernalia which Oscar had bought with such enjoyment and played with so enthusiastically had, in the rush of flight, been left behind. When the boys asked for them, Vyvyan Holland wrote, 'We could not understand why it upset my mother, since of course we knew nothing about the sale. It was only when I saw the catalogue, many years later, that I realised why my mother had been upset. Lot no. 237 was "A large quantity of toys".' They went for thirty shillings.

There is a story that while Oscar Wilde was staying at Oakley Street between the two trials, a veiled lady drove up one evening in a cab, and silently handed in a huge bunch of violets with a horseshoe bearing the words 'For Luck'. The 'veiled lady' gives the story an authentic touch of Victorian drama; the offering is reminiscent of those received by actresses on first nights, but in this case the situation was charged with a more heartfelt emotion. The lady behind the veil was Ellen Terry, of whom Oscar had once written:

> With thee I do forget the toil and stress,
> The loveless road that knows no resting place,
> Time's straitened pulse, the soul's dread weariness,
> My freedom, and my life republican!

His poetic imagination had been stirred by her beauty when, fresh from Oxford, he watched her with Irving.

> She stands with eyes marred by the mists of pain,
> Like some wan lily overdrenched with rain.

He pleased her with the phrase 'wan lily', which, in her memoirs, she says 'represented perfectly what I tried to convey'. 'I hope,' she adds, 'I thanked Oscar enough at the time.'

Many people have written about Ellen Terry, searching for words to convey the inexhaustible supply of magic which she dispensed, a magic which even in old age did not desert her. Her great-nephew, Sir John Gielgud, knew her as an old lady, 'bowed and mysterious, under the shadow of a big straw hat, covered in scarves and shawls, with a big bag and two or three pairs of spectacles, like a godmother in a fairy tale'. And he adds, 'With her lovely turned up nose and wide mouth, and that husky voice—a "veiled voice" somebody called it once—and her enchanting smile, no wonder everyone adored her.'

She had the sort of beauty that was fascinating and elusive to painters, and she moved in the world of artists and designers during that revolutionary period of the 'seventies and 'eighties. She knew Chelsea well: she knew Rossetti; and, through Edward Godwin, the father of her children, she knew and admired Whistler. His tribute was to present her with a set of Venetian glass—'too good for a world where glass is broken,' she said—and to send her daughter Edie a miniature Japanese kimono.

Walter Sickert, unknown and poor, adored her from afar, and, on a first night, spent his all on a bouquet of roses, which he flung, weighted with lead, from the gallery. They fell, with a heavy thump, on to the stage, narrowly missing Irving. According to William Rothenstein, who was there, 'a loud Ha! Ha! rang through the house. Whistler had observed the scene'.

Dr. Phene's house

Photo: Bignell

Mr. Peter Jones, linendraper, numbers
4–6 King's Road

Peter Jones's new building

BUSINESS PREMISES
KINGS ROAD & SYMONS STREET.
CHELSEA
Messrs PERRY & REED. Architects

A tea-party in Cheyne Walk. Water-colour by Henry Tonks

Augustus John. Chalk drawing
by himself, *c.* 1901

Demolition in the 1960s

Photos: Bignell

Chelsea Students

But it was not till 1904, when her children were grown up and she herself (she was born in 1848) no longer young, that she came to live in Chelsea. Her house, number 215 King's Road, still stands, one of a pair built in 1720. It is a charming old house, occupied in 1771 by Dr. Arne, the composer of 'Rule Britannia'. Its front is of mellow brown brick with red brick dressings and the front door has a hood supported by curly brackets. Inside, the walls are panelled and there is a pretty Georgian staircase. Edward Craig, Ellen Terry's grandson, who spent nearly two years at 215 King's Road when a small boy, clearly remembers how it used to look.

His grandmother's furnishings, he says, were a mixture of pleasant things, 'rather as one might find in an artist's house today'. Much of the furniture had been designed by Godwin, whose taste, says Mr. Craig, 'was greatly influenced by Japanese simplicity and Ellen naturally inherited this taste from him. This resulted in Japanese matting being put down wherever she could, and her great love of a certain type of blue material which she used in the downstairs rooms for window curtains, sofa covers and partition curtains. This material she found that she could get in Brittany. It was a very coarse blue linen used by fishermen out there, and she discovered that when it had been washed a number of times and a little starch had been put in the water, it became a lovely light blue with a sheen on it like a well worn pair of jeans'.

Ellen Terry's long experience in the theatre had taught her how simple materials could, with skill, be transformed into things of beauty. One of these blue curtains was used to divide the ground floor dining room from a small room used as a study. 'Upstairs on the first floor,' says Edward Craig, 'was a lovely old panelled room with folding doors that led into the room behind, and here the curtains were eighteenth century yellow and cream striped silk. One wall was covered in bookshelves and the rest of the room had rather pleasant pieces of furniture, including a fine Dutch inlaid bureau. The rest of the furniture was bits and pieces that she had picked up here and there as she travelled around England. She was always buying chairs and bits of china, and as she had a number of little cottages that she had picked up for very small sums in various parts of England, she was always able to house her bits of furniture in one or another, and at the same time use them as store houses from which she could extract pieces that she felt a desire to have near her up in London.'

This account, so accurately remembered by a man who is himself an artist and theatre designer, gives a clear picture of the sort of home that Ellen Terry made inside that old house.

Dame Sybil Thorndike, who has lived in Chelsea since 1921, has a memory of visiting Dame Ellen, who was by this time in her seventies. 'I remember her being very chatty—Lewis was with me—she loved him and said that I was a lucky gal to have him always with me to keep me on the straight path—in the theatre she meant—not necessarily in private life! I remember her looking enchanting and very vague—I think it must have been "Grand Guignol" time, for she liked hearing about the different sorts of parts we were playing. I think she had that wondrous bag which was never separated from her, and which I remember at Smallhythe so well . . .' This bag, mentioned also by Sir John Gielgud, was an important prop: it was evidently very large, made of well-worn leather and fastened with a padlock.

Ellen Terry was closely guarded by her daughter, Edith Craig, and the blindness which assailed her in old age was already manifesting itself before she left Chelsea; but she was undaunted. Dame Sybil says, 'I think it was in Chelsea that she escaped watchful eyes and was found in the midst of the traffic on an island, and was taken home like a naughty little girl with a twinkle in her eye.'

Chelsea was the poorer for her loss when, in 1920, she was obliged to move away. Oscar Wilde, after seeing her drive down Tite Street, felt that that street could 'never again be as other streets'; Sir Charles Wheeler, who came to Chelsea as a youthful artist, describes how, for him, she momentarily transfigured the King's Road.

'I saw her only once,' he writes, 'but was struck by the gaiety, grace and charm of this ageing, but still lovely actress, as she left her house in the King's Road near Glebe Place and got into an open motor car. She wore a large hat with a veil placed over it . . . and tied beneath the chin. As a harmony in grey she might have been painted on canvas by Whistler. But she was real enough, and, equipped against dust and wind, drove off merrily, as I remember, that late afternoon, westwards along the King's Road into the golden glow of the setting sun.'

CHAPTER ELEVEN

THE KING'S ROAD today has a name as familiar as Broadway or
Montmartre; but it is only within a very short space of time that it
has become internationally famous. Even in Chelsea, up to the end
of the nineteenth century it was relatively unimportant, except as a bus
route, and the few shops it contained were useful and unpretentious,
scattered at intervals among nursery gardens and private houses. Since
then, it has been through many vicissitudes, and it consists today of a
heterogeneous jumble of architecture, from Edwardian Billiard Saloon
Rococo to twentieth-century Tudor, while some modestly attractive early
nineteenth-century house-tops raise their eyebrows in astonishment at the
dimly-lit boutiques which have taken possession of their ground floors.
Pleasant terraced houses with lime trees and paved front gardens have
given way to high modern college blocks; and the old Chelsea Palace,
where George Robey appeared (and always went for a drink afterwards at
the Wellington, to the delight of the locals in the bar), has been pulled
down. This theatre, built in 1902 on the site of Wilkinson's Sword Factory,
was chiefly a variety house, and many of the big stars of Music Hall were
billed there, world-famous names like Sir Harry Lauder, Vesta Tilley,
Little Tich, Gracie Fields, till the Cinema, the Second World War and
Television combined to put all Music Halls out of business. In 1957
Chelsea Palace was bought by its conqueror, Granada TV, and turned
into a studio. After a few humiliating years this travesty of a theatre was
demolished, and will be replaced, in the course of time, by office blocks.

The odd thing is that, in spite of all the changes, the demolitions and re-
buildings, a few old houses remain. The oldest are numbers 229 and 231,
two tiny houses, now shops, which date from about 1620, before the
King's Road was made. They were probably labourers' cottages, built on
the Glebe land which ran southwards towards the boundary of Shrewsbury House, and facing that way, so that they are now perforce turned
back to front in order to open on to the King's Road. Number 229 was,
until quite lately, a tobacco and snuff shop, which (like several others in the
district) claimed Carlyle as a customer, and where a plaque of his head is
still kept as a reminder of his patronage.

Number 231, now a picture dealer's, is said to have been a tavern during Charles II's reign, where the king once took refuge from the crowds watching a pageant. It was occupied in the 1830s by a family named Middleton, and in 1877 was opened as a picture framer's by J. Middleton, under whose name the business was carried on, first by himself, and later by his son-in-law, until the latter's death in 1968. The original cottage is still intact; built of brick and timber, with beams across the low ceilings. There is one room above stairs, and a basement below, paved in slabs of slate laid directly upon the earth. This room, which for years had no ventilation and was reeking with damp, is now lit by the original seventeenth-century window, which was found and replaced by the present tenant, Mr. Nicholas Martine. These old houses, the property of the Church Commissioners, are under threat of demolition. It is to be hoped that they will be saved, if only as a reminder that there was a Chelsea before there was a King's Road.

'An old Inhabitant', writing in 1900, remembers the King's Road in the 1820s, when it was a country road 'with a toll gate on the N.E. side of Sloane Square', and tells us that in those days Paradise Row and Cheyne Walk were the most thriving parts of the village, as nearly all its business was concentrated on the river bank, where the breweries were, the wharves and docks, and the men who caught and sold fish. And, in spite of all this activity, he assures us, 'nearly all the best families lived in Cheyne Walk or Paradise Row'.

Nevertheless, one or two discerning people chose to build their homes away from the riverside, among the fields and lanes which bordered the narrow highway.

To get a glimpse of how the King's Road once looked, one should approach it from Manresa Road with eyes directed across the thoroughfare and to the left. Here, to the east of Glebe Place, stand four old houses with front gardens, one of them Ellen Terry's home for sixteen years. The house on the corner of Glebe Place, number 217, is a little younger than the pair beyond: it was built about 1750. Number 213, lived in now by Sir Carol and Lady Reed, is similar in design to Ellen Terry's house. Beyond it, on the corner of the King's Road and Oakley Street, is Argyll House (so called because the fourth Duke spent the last year of his life there between 1769–70). It was built in 1723, for a gentleman called John Perrin of whom nothing is known beyond the fact that he must have had good taste. His monogram is on the main gate. He engaged a Venetian architect, Giacomo Leoni, to design the house, of which Leoni later wrote:

'Upon the King's Road between Chelsea and London this little House of my invention was built for Mr. John Pierene [sic]. The Kitchen, Buttery and other Offices are within the Basement. The Apartments are of a size, suitable to a private Family. The Door in front is Doric, with two columns and two half Pilasters. The ornaments of the Windows are all of Stone, as is also the great Cornice; the rest is grey Brick, which in my opinion sorting well with white Stone, makes a beautiful Harmony of Colours.'

The architect was justly proud of this house, which remains today almost as he saw it. Its Italian conception must have attracted Emilie Venturi, the friend and admirer of Mazzini, for she moved here from Lindsey Row, where she had been neighbour to Whistler, and, as we have seen, persuaded Carlyle to be painted by him.

During the nineteenth century, many of the old houses remained, and others were built, still dwelling houses, not shops; and the road was still half countrified, with one or two houses standing back in their own grounds, and cottages with palings and little gardens in front. For so long it had been a private road, the King's private road, that for years after its emancipation in 1830, when it became a public thoroughfare, it was still unprepared to receive so much attention from the public, and still narrow and awkward for traffic. On Derby Days, when every sort of vehicle from a four-in-hand to a coster's donkey cart poured along it, there were endless altercations and traffic blocks, and no doubt red faces and a good deal of shouting, as wheels became entangled and frightened horses kicked.

In the nineteenth century the King's Road contained a number of taverns, which gradually became converted into Victorian pubs: at the western extremity was the World's End, in the eighteenth century a wooden building of great age. Then there were the Man in the Moon, the Globe, and the Rose and Crown, on the north-east corner of Church Street, which is now the Cadogan Arms. Farther down, past a private lunatic asylum for ladies, which stood between Church Street and Bramerton Street, and on the far side of Oakley Street, was the Six Bells, patronized by Whistler and other artists. It was eighteenth-century in origin, rebuilt in 1900; and before then had no particular claim to beauty, except at the back, where there were a bowling green, a fountain, an old mulberry tree, and a row of little trellised arbours, part of an eighteenth-century tea garden.

Opposite the Six Bells was, and still is, the Old Burial Ground, given to the parish by Sir Hans Sloane, enlarged by Lord Cadogan in 1790, and now a pleasant green garden shaded by lime and plane trees—a peaceful oasis in the midst of the perpetually busy street. After the completion of

St. Luke's Church in 1824 this ground was no longer used for burials, and became a garden for the Workhouse (now St. Luke's Hospital). In the nineteenth century the old men in their scarlet caps and the old women in their blue cotton gowns might be seen taking the air there among the tomb-stones. Several notable people were buried there, including John Baptist Cipriani, the artist and founder member of the R.A., and John Martyn, F.R.S., the famous eighteenth-century botanist who married the daughter of Chelsea's Rector, Dr. John King, and lived for many years in Church Street.

On the edge of the Burial Ground there was once a pump, famous for its sparkling, transparent water. People came from far and wide to draw a bottle-full. Then, according to the 'Old Inhabitant', a local wag started the rumour that a human tooth had been pumped up into someone's bottle. Macabre thoughts of the pump's proximity to the graveyard sprang to mind. 'It then began to dawn on the authorities,' he writes, 'that the beautiful clear water might not be quite so wholesome as people imagined —and the handle of the old pump was chained up.'

Further down, on the other side of the King's Road—on the site of what is now Radnor Walk—a house stood back from the road with a carriage drive in front, and grounds which ran almost the whole length of the present street (Smith Terrace was not yet in being). This property was known by the grand and rather misleading name of Manor House. About 1836 an enterprising Mr. Smith turned it into a Tea and Recreation Garden—a humble Vauxhall. It was open after dusk, lit with coloured lamps, and furnished with all the right accompaniments to al fresco entertainment: winding paths, secluded arbours, classical statuary, a shrubbery and a fountain. There was music and dancing; and, for the less romantically minded, Flexman the clown was engaged to do his break-down dance.

It was cheap and enjoyable, a good evening's outing for the family— and flourished till Cremorne put it out of business.

Opposite the Manor House was a seventeenth-century building which still survives, behind its incongruous triumphal arch, and is now a club. It was originally a pheasantry belonging to Box Farm, which stood next to it, on the site of the Classic Cinema. This farmhouse was built in 1686, and owned in the nineteenth century by a family named Evans (probably connected with the Evans of Evans' Farm on the Cremorne Estate, who had been granted right of common by Queen Elizabeth I). Box Farm was pulled down in 1900, and the last owner was Mr. Pullam Markham Evans.

He gave his second name to Markham Square, which stands on the site of an orchard belonging to the farm. Next to it, in the nineteenth century, were two of Chelsea's best known nursery gardens, Davey's and Colville's. Between them ran a lane charmingly called Butterfly Alley, which is now Anderson Street, leading to Sloane Avenue. The gardens are immortalized in a poem entitled 'Flowers and Fashion' by Samuel Jackson Pratt, which begins:

> Where smiling Chelsea spreads the cultured lands,
>   Sacred to Flora a pavilion stands,
> And yet a second temple neighb'ring near
>   Nurses the fragrance of the various year.
> Of Davy this, of Colville that, the care,
>   While both the favour of the goddess share.

On the south side of the road, where Chelsea House, the residence during the eighteenth century of the Cadogan family, once stood, is an imposing building now known as the Duke of York's Headquarters. The Duke of York was George III's second son, a good soldier, who unfortunately aided and abetted his mistress, Mary Ann Clark, in selling commissions, which brought his career as Commander-in-Chief of the Army to an abrupt end. This was in 1809; but in 1801 his popularity was still high when he laid the foundation stone of the Duke of York's School, as this building was originally known. It stands at right angles to the King's Road, its classical portico facing west. On the front, beneath the Royal Arms, was inscribed 'The Royal Military Asylum for the Children of the Soldiers of the Regular Army'. There were spacious grounds in front of the building—now used as sports grounds and playing fields—and the soldiers' children must have led a healthy life. At first both boys and girls were accepted, but in 1823 the girls were removed to Southampton, whether a result of misbehaviour or as a matter of convenience, it is not known.

On Sundays, the boys marched to Chapel. Beyond this was a girls' school, where in 1772 the Rev. John Jenkins addressed the pupils on 'Female Education and Christian Fortitude under Affliction'. It was still a school in the nineteenth century, and it is possible that such windows as gave on to the Military Asylum contained clusters of female heads watching the smart soldier boys drilling and marching on the other side of the railings. The building was bought in 1842 by the National Society for the Training of Schoolmistresses, and became known as Whitelands Training College. It had a yearly May Day Festival, inaugurated in 1881 by John Ruskin. Amid traditional Olde English festivities, the chosen Queen of the May received a gift from bearded Mr. Ruskin in person, and signed copies of *Sesame and Lilies* or *The Seven Lamps of Architecture* were eagerly accepted by a select number of her friends.

We have by now moved down the King's Road nearly to Sloane Square without noticing a single shop. Such shops as there were during the nineteenth century were unimposing, but useful; dairies, butchers, greengrocers. There was a bakery where Beeton's, established in 1913, still sell home-made bread and cakes; and the ovens in their basement bear Queen Victoria's monogram. There was evidently, in the 1860s, a chemist's shop (probably at the corner of Park Walk); which is described in *A Book with Seven Seals*.

But shops, in the middle of the nineteenth century, were few and far between in the King's Road. More trade was done in the side streets; and Marlborough Road, now Draycott Avenue, was a very busy shopping centre. It was here that two young men, newly arrived in London from distant parts to seek their fortunes, each independently set up business. One was named Thomas Crapper, the other, Peter Jones.

Crapper came first. In 1848, at the age of eleven, he walked to London from Thorne, near Doncaster, in search of a job. He found one with a Master plumber in Robert Street (now Sydney Street), Chelsea. He was paid four shillings a week, and lodged in a nearby attic. He was a bright boy and quickly mastered the mechanics of his trade; and he arrived in the plumbing business at a time when Londoners were becoming uneasily aware that there was room for improvement in the drainage of their city.

In 1861, when London had just installed its first two main sewers, Thomas Crapper, now aged twenty-four, set up in business as a Sanitary Engineer. His premises were at 50, 52, and 54 Marlborough Road, a two-storey stucco building with a yard and a brass foundry at the back, through an archway. 'Sanitary Engineer' was an imposing title, indicative of the revolution that was taking place. Chamber pots and earth closets were still considered adequate for small London houses (Thompson's map of 1836 shows earth closets behind all the houses in Cheyne Row and Paradise Walk; Carlyle did not install a water closet till 1870). Although they had been in use since the beginning of the century, water closets were apt to go wrong, causing floods, and needing constant attention from the plumber. Thomas Crapper made it his business to know all that there was to know about their workings, and then invented a water closet of his own: 'Crapper's Valveless Waste Preventer,' he advertised. 'Certain Flush with easy Pull.'

Orders poured in. In due course Crapper found himself appointed Royal Plumber. His first order, in the 1880s, was to install drainage at Sandringham, which had been bought some twenty years earlier, presumably without drainage, for the Prince of Wales. In the course of time this inspired plumber became the proud possessor of four Royal Warrants: to Queen Victoria, to Edward VII, and to George V, both as Prince of Wales and as King.

During the 'eighties Crapper received, and carried out, a commission to install 'a removable armchair upholstered in Royal blue velvet', designed to fit over the water closet in Lily Langtry's house in St. John's Wood whenever a royal visit was expected. As well as being an expert sanitary engineer, Thomas Crapper was something of an artist. His china pans—the early ones enclosed in mahogany and raised, like thrones, up steps—were decorated with flowers and given the names of Chelsea streets. It was in Chelsea that he found his vocation, and he lived in Chelsea all his working life.

In 1907 the firm moved to 120 King's Road, a three-storey Georgian mansion; and there it remained till 1966, when it was taken over by John Bolding and Company and the familiar shop front facing Royal Avenue disappeared for ever.

On March 3, 1872, *The Times* reported:

'FALL OF A HOUSE. About three p.m. yesterday the drapery co-operative store at 163, Marlborough Road, occupied by Mr. Jones, Draper, fell down, and several persons were buried in the ruins. The Inspector of Police, with a detachment of the B Division, and Dr. Reutsch, the district surgeon, were promptly in attendance, and by their assistance Mrs. Jones and a workman were extricated from the basement. Charles Freed, an apprentice, aged sixteen, was also, after some difficulty, dug out, and removed to the surgery of Dr. Reutsch. Every effort was made to his restoration, but he was dead. The premises were undergoing repair at the time of the accident.'

The *Chelsea News*, a day later, printed dramatic headlines: 'Fatal and Deplorable Results from the Falling of a House in the Marlborough Road. Roof Fell In. Mrs. Jones Buried in Debris.'

Mr. Peter Jones, away on business, came back to find his 'Co-operative Drapery Shop' a heap of rubble, his wife in a state of collapse and his first venture as his own boss threatened with disaster. He was not yet thirty. Five years earlier, Peter Rees Jones had come to London from Newcastle Emlyn in Wales, to seek work, as many Welshmen did at this time, in the drapery business. He brought with him £14 in gold which he hoped to keep in reserve against a rainy day. He lost no time in getting a job, and was taken on as an assistant at Tarn's Emporium in Newington Causeway. A year later, hoping to better himself, he moved to Messrs. Stagg and

Mantle, a high class establishment in Leicester Square. In 1871 he moved to Chelsea, where he rented two shops, numbers 163 and 165 Marlborough Road, and knocked them into one.

It was this operation which led, a year later, to the disaster reported above. At the inquiry following the accident, it was discovered that 'in order to make the two shops into one it was necessary to put up a "Cressemer" beam to support the upper part of the front of both houses. It was intended to support that beam by means of iron pillars . . . It appeared that the "Cressemer" . . . had been left utterly without the ordinary supports and that in consequence of that fact the beam being 34 feet in length it had snapped in the centre . . . While the iron pillars were being waited for,' states the report, 'the accident happened.'

A new firm of builders had been engaged to install these pillars, and the foremen in charge were anxious to prove that the death of the unfortunate apprentice, not to mention the attendant calamities, were not due to negligence on their part. But the Coroner, Dr. Diplock, thought otherwise, and returning a verdict that 'the deceased expired from the effects of injuries received during the fall of certain houses in the Marlborough Road, Chelsea, he gave it as his opinion that Messrs. Bradden and Salter, the foremen . . . who were employed superintending the work connected with the fallen houses, are deserving of censure, they being two inexperienced men, for taking work of this description'.

Altogether, it was a bad business. It must have taken some courage on the part of young Mr. Jones to set in hand the rebuilding of his ruined shop, to reassure the three frightened shopgirls, who had managed to escape through a window at the back, to rescue what remained of his stock, and to assist the recovery of his wife, Mrs. Blanche Jones, who had been flung down the basement stairs and half buried in debris.

But determination and hard work prevailed. The Co-operative Drapery Establishment arose once more, between C. Burls, Boot and Shoe Maker and W. H. Coton, Pork Butcher, re-opened and flourished. Then, in December 1877, an advertisement appeared in the *West Middlesex Advertiser*.

'Ladies are invited to recommend their Servants and Club Tickets to JOSEPH COX, "the People's Draper", no. 163 and 165, Marlborough Road, Brompton, being by Common Consent the Cheapest House in the Neighbourhood for Drapery, Hosiery, Haberdashery, Flannels, Blankets, etc., etc.'

Mr. Peter Jones had moved up in the world. In fact, he had moved to Sloane Square, where he rented numbers 4 and 6 King's Road.

These shops had previously been occupied by Lambe Brothers, linen drapers, and were in a good position, so it is surprising to learn that the customers were mostly of the artisan class. Evidently the gentry, for the most part, shopped in London, and Mr. Jones's neighbours in 1877 were in a small way of business: his establishment stood between George Wain, Grocer, and A. Livingstone, Boot Warehouse. On the corner of King's Road and Sloane Square, was a public house, the Star and Garter. Further up the road was another linen draper, Mrs. Caroline Powell, so there was competition, which was probably an added stimulus to the energetic Mr. Jones.

The draper's shop described in *A Book with Seven Seals* must be the counterpart of, if not the very shop kept by Mr. Peter Jones, and it is worth quoting the authoress's memory of being taken there as a child.

Mamma and the two little girls travelled by omnibus from Oakley Street to Sloane Square, where they alighted, to find Mr. Peters, the linen-draper, 'standing behind the glass door of his shop, looking out for customers. He bowed low with a gratified smile, as he held it open for them to enter . . .

' "Good afternoon to you, Ma'am, very pleased to see you," said the gratified man. "Walk this way, and what may it be our pleasure to serve you with?"

. . .'Three high cane-bottomed chairs were pulled forward, on which Mrs. Danvers and her little daughters seated themselves for the afternoon. It was not the custom in those days to go from one counter to another for what they required. Everything asked for was brought forward by the young man who served; trembling under the watchful eye of Mr. Peters, who hovered near at hand to see that the Parson's wife was waited on to the best advantage. He regarded Mrs. Danvers as one of his most distinguished customers . . .'

And so, seated on their high chairs, Mamma and the children carefully chose muslin for party frocks, red and white flannel for underclothes, warm tartan wool stockings for Sundays and grey ones for weekdays, ribbons for sashes and bows, white openwork stockings and white kid gloves.

When, at last, everything had been bought, Mrs. Danvers rose from her chair, 'which Mr. Peters pulled back from beneath her with a bow, before preceding her to the entrance, where he opened the door with another bow, wishing them a Happy New Year, and they emerged into comparative darkness from the gas-lit street'.

'Mr. Peters' deserved to succeed. In his first year at Sloane Square, the turnover was £18,000. By 1884 he was employing a staff of one hundred and fifty, and had enlarged his shop by taking on two more houses; during the next ten years he succeeded in acquiring a further ten. By this time his premises had been rebuilt and presented an imposing appearance. An article in *The Builder* describes the shop, which must have been hideous, 'built of red Mansfield Stone and red Fareham bricks . . . the roofs covered with German green slates'. But a local account considers the buildings 'of harmonious design and handsome appearance, rising to a height of five storeys and crowned by a turret from which rises a flagstaff that is quite a landmark in the vicinity'.

Inside, the Costume and Mantle Department, upstairs, was 'very elaborately fitted with walnut and ebony cases, decorated with carvings of natural foliage. The premises,' adds *The Builder*, 'were the first of their character to be lighted with electricity.' Mr. Jones believed in moving with the times. Evidently, no expense had been spared: he was now attracting customers from the new grand houses in Cadogan Square and Cadogan Gardens, and no doubt had his eye on Eaton Square and Belgravia as well.

Peter Jones was a family man, and took a fatherly interest in the welfare of his employees. The apprentices lived in a hostel over the shop, and there were also residential quarters for assistants, with a library, a piano, and billiard tables. Mrs. Florence Nye, a hundred years old in 1968, was in her youth apprenticed to the millinery department, and in an interview described her experiences. The food, she said, was good: so good that during the school holidays the two Jones sons were sent to eat with the apprentices. Mrs. Peter Jones spent most of her time at the shop, as did the Jones family dog, which liked to follow Mrs. Nye (then Miss Addis) when she went out delivering hats to customers. Mrs. Jones put a stop to this: it did not, she said, look businesslike. So Miss Addis (without the dog) went to Buckingham Palace, to deliver hats for the Royal children. She was evidently happy in her job, and the only time she fell foul of Mr. Jones was when she cut off her long thick hair. The next girl to cut her hair off, he declared, would be fired.

Lady customers liked everything sent, and no difficulty was made about this. There were two deliveries daily. Eighteen horses were stabled in Rawlings Street, and there were nine vanmen, each in charge of two horses. They lived in a house beside the stables and started work at seven in the morning, cleaning horses, harness, and van. At nine the first horse was harnessed, and each man made thirty to forty deliveries, arriving back at about two. They started on the second delivery at five, and were back by nine, when the horses were unharnessed, stabled and fed. After this, presumably, the men were fed and stabled. They earned twenty-five shillings a week, and worked every day (there was no early closing); on Sundays they had to pay two visits to the stables, to look after the horses. They did not, apparently, complain. It was a steady job, with a good boss, who took a personal interest in both men and horses.

But in 1903, the boss fell ill. The shop managed without him for a while; but lacking his inspired direction and meticulous care it began to go downhill fast. Customers, quick to notice a change, went elsewhere. In 1905, saddened by the failure to survive without him of all that he had built up in thirty years of industry, Peter Jones died. The following year, Mr. John Lewis, another Welshman, who was already established in Oxford Street, decided to buy the business. The price was £22,500, and Mr. Lewis, who never wasted money on cabs, walked from Oxford Street to Sloane Square with twenty thousand-pound banknotes in his pockets. Messrs. Peter Jones, Ltd., became his property, and is now a prosperous part of the enormous John Lewis empire.

By the end of the nineteenth century Chelsea had ceased to be a riverside village: farms and fields and nursery gardens had almost without exception given way to streets. Many fine and elegant houses had been designed in the 'seventies and 'eighties, and the sort of architecture which Osbert Lancaster calls Pont Street Dutch manifested itself in several areas (its features 'a fondness for bright red brick, a profusion of enrichments in that most deplorable of materials, terra-cotta, and a passion for breaking the sky-line with every variety of gable that the genius of Holland had produced, and a good many that it had not'). C. R. Ashbee, less flamboyant in taste, was designing his own type of *art nouveau*—described by the press, for some extraordinary reason as 'Queen Anne'—with exaggeratedly high-pitched roofs, numbers of high narrow casement windows with small panes, a deliberate lack of symmetry and a great deal of beaten copper and wrought ironwork. Two good examples of these, numbers 39 and 41 Cheyne Walk, still remain, number 41 with a splendid *art nouveau* lamp and a peacock over the front door.

The newly built Chelsea Embankment provided, in the 1870s, two tempting stretches of river frontage, divided by the Apothecaries' Garden, between Cheyne Walk and the Royal Hospital; and here the tall elaborate red brick and stucco buildings which amply housed the prosperous Victorians and their servants were planted, enjoying the river view once open to the old houses in Paradise Row. Norman Shaw, R.A., who designed Cadogan Square, was the architect of two of these riverside mansions,

Clock House (1879) and Swan House (1875), the latter built on the site of the Old Swan inn, and now the headquarters of Securicor.

But as well as these expensive, carefully designed edifices, there were rows and rows of terraced houses, quickly, plainly and uniformly built, without bathrooms or indoor sanitation. Some, with bay windows and small back gardens, had aspirations towards gentility; others were just 'workmen's dwellings'. Chelsea was a part of London now, and Chelsea's poor shared the discomforts and squalid conditions of the poor in all big towns. Photographs taken towards the end of the century of some Chelsea streets and alleys are depressing: poverty and ugliness brood over the dirty, smoky, shabby houses. The shops look drab and uninviting. Always one or two men stand about leaning against walls or lampposts. Perhaps they have just come to look at the photographer: perhaps they are not out of work, but they look it. Everything around them seems to need a clean-up and a fresh coat of paint. Even the advertisements for 'Iron Jelloids' or 'The Daily News' are dull and ugly.

All this may be due, in part, to the generally murky appearance of London suburbs at this period, and the dark, depressing clothes worn by both sexes. But there is no doubt that a great deal of poverty lurked in the back streets and alleys of Chelsea, and that though England between the Jubilees was enjoying a period of prosperity, there was a sharp division between the privileged classes and the poor. An old man, a builder's labourer, told the author that as small boys he and a friend used to walk from World's End to Hans Crescent in wintry weather, to sweep the snow from the doorsteps of the rich houses there and in Cadogan Square, and thought themselves lucky if the butler gave them a penny. If the cook invited them down to the basement for a cup of tea, it was a red-letter day.

In Chelsea, there was a complete cross-section of society, in which the poor were well represented, even among the artists and writers, of whom there now were many. The less successful were living in damp and verminous shacks, where they pooled their earnings and paid rent when they could. Even as lately as the 1960s, an occupant of a studio in Manresa Road was known to subsist chiefly on soup made from used-up hambones collected from a kind-hearted butcher.

By the end of the century, Chelsea was the acknowledged artists' quarter of London. 'Of course you will settle in Chelsea,' said Whistler to young William Rothenstein when he came back from Paris in the 'nineties, and Rothenstein unhesitatingly agreed. 'The men who counted most for me lived there—Sickert, Steer, Ricketts and Shannon.'

Rothenstein admits that he was disappointed with the long King's Road

—'a shabbier Oxford Street, with its straggling, dirty, stucco mid-century houses and shops.' But he, like many another artist before and since, was captivated by the riverside and its beautiful houses, by the Physic Gardens and The Vale.

'The Vale,' he writes, 'was then really a vale.' This turning off the King's Road, opposite Paultons Square, was then a cul-de-sac and contained only four houses, surrounded by trees, all of which appear in Thompson's map of 1836. To the north was a large paddock, belonging to Chelsea Park, where stags roamed at large, kept by an eccentric Mr. McGuire. In the end the stags died, or had to be removed, but Mr. McGuire, nothing daunted, replaced them with plaster replicas.

At number 1 The Vale, William de Morgan and his wife Evelyn, a painter in the Pre-Raphaelite tradition and sister to the famous Mrs. Stirling of Battersea House, lived for twenty-two years. Their house was a pleasant early nineteenth-century one, creeper-covered at the back, with a pretty porch leading into the garden. Number 2, on the other side, was between 1886 and 1890 the home of Whistler, and it was here that a famous row took place between Maud, his mistress of many years' standing, and his future wife, Beatrice Godwin. Whistler firmly shut the door on both ladies, leaving them to settle things out of doors, and the quiet of The Vale was shaken by their uninhibited exchanges. Very soon after this, Whistler and Beatrice were married, and after a short time in The Vale moved to 21 Cheyne Walk.

Number 2 became the workshop and home of two artists, Charles Ricketts and Charles Shannon, who set up the Vale Press here, producing masterpieces of book production. In their early days at The Vale they were both hard up, and meals were precarious. Oscar Wilde, who admired and liked both these handsome men, often spent evenings at The Vale, dining on cheap London eggs washed down with cheap London beer. Years later, after his release from prison, he inquired of Rothenstein how Ricketts and Shannon were.

'I told him that Ricketts and Shannon had now become prosperous; Shannon especially was selling his pictures and getting portraits to paint. Oscar appeared surprised. "The dear Valeists rich!" Then, after a moment's reflection, he said, "When you go to sup with them, I suppose they have fresh eggs now!" '

PART FOUR

'I CHANGE, BUT I CANNOT DIE'

CHAPTER ONE

ITS INHABITANTS have always liked to talk of Chelsea as a village: they still do. And indeed, among the artists and writers who came to live there there was a free and easy friendliness, a lack of ceremony, which was unlike town behaviour. The idea of Chelsea, which was by 1900 a thickly populated urban district, being called a village, seems on the face of it ridiculous; but the description testifies to the spirit of the place. You could live there on a small income, and there were small, villagey shops. You could buy a house for as little as £150 freehold. According to Mr. F. G. Ferebee, who bought one, a six-bedroomed house in Limerston Street cost £250.

For the more prosperous citizens with their large families and numerous servants there were tall, basemented brick mansions. Some of the dreariest are the grey, prison-like houses in Elm Park Gardens. In Oakley Street there are more cheerful examples, designed by Dr. Phene, F.R.I.B.A., who also planned the charming classical design of Margaretta Terrace.

This curious and rather mysterious character lived in Chelsea for over fifty years. A scholar and antiquary, he came of an ancient French family which had owned, among other estates, the Château de Savenay on the Loire. This was unfortunately destroyed by the Vendéans, but Dr. Phene resolved to design and build its counterpart, which he called Le Renaissance du Château de Savenay, on the corner of Oakley Street and Upper Cheyne Row. He owned a large piece of land here, which had once belonged to Cheyne Manor,[1] where he planted avenues of rare trees imported from Holland. He had a theory about trees in towns, believing that they purified the air and prevented the spread of epidemics. In 1851 he planted trees on both sides of Oakley Street: and this interesting innovation caused the Prince Consort to inquire about Dr. Phene's theory, which so favourably impressed him that he ordered trees to be planted in South Kensington outside the new Museum.

Dr. Phene dug in his garden, where, in the early nineteenth century, a Mr. Shailer had grown lavender and produced the first moss rose; but

[1] See page 29.

the learned Doctor's digging was archaeological, and he was rewarded by finding part of the underground passage from Shrewsbury House and a Roman skull. He filled the garden with things that he had dug up from other places and the walks were lined with rather ugly statues. Then, in 1901, he began to build his Château. It took a long time. 'Dr. Phene,' announced a newspaper, 'is taking the very greatest care that the building in Oakley Street, when completed, shall be as near a counterpart of the Loire Château as possible.'

The Doctor lived on the opposite side of Oakley Street, and was able to watch the progress of his house. Five years after work started, in January 1906, a newspaper announced, 'It will be some months before the building is completed, but after seeing the designs we believe that Dr. Phene has every reason to feel that, when it is finished, he will have constructed a building unlike anything else in Europe.'

It was certainly unlike anything else in Chelsea. Through the scaffolding fascinated onlookers could see that the front was literally plastered with writhing figures, heraldic beasts, caryatids supporting balustraded columns, armorial bearings, gods and goddesses and portrait busts of the English Royal Family. It was a staggering sight. The house was painted red, the pillars and balustrades yellow, picked out with gold, a colour scheme which must have been remarkable among the sober hues of Oakley Street.

At last the scaffolding was removed, and Dr. Phene was photographed, standing on the steps of the château, a small, dapper, bearded figure, displaying satisfaction in the materialization of his dream. He was elderly, and a bachelor, but now it was rumoured that he was about to marry: the house was being prepared to receive his bride. But mysteriously, unaccountably, the wedding never took place: perhaps the house had been too long a-building and the lady had grown tired. Local legend has it that the bride died on her wedding day, and the doctor turned away forever from the red and gold château. Dickensian stories grew up of the untouched wedding breakfast, festooned with cobwebs and overrun by mice and rats; imaginations were given full play, and the château behind its padlocked gates stood empty, its brave incongruous colours fading, till, in the 1920s, it was mercifully demolished. Only its garden wall, running along the north side of Upper Cheyne Row, remains.

Another odd story of a house which became a folly belongs to a later period. In 1930, on the site of Shrewsbury House, a new mansion, number 42 Cheyne Walk, was built, designed by Sir Edwin Lutyens. It was the wedding present of Lord Revelstoke to his daughter, the Hon. Calypso

Baring: a dream house of silver-grey and vermilion brick, with a white stone portico, and large windows looking down the long drive, through trees to the river. At the back there were a tennis court, an ancient mulberry tree and beyond the gardens a grove to provide an air of mystery. Inside, the house was given everything that money, taste and ingenuity could provide, and a profusion of bathrooms that caused local wags to declare that there were more baths in this one house than in many Chelsea streets. There was a nursery wing, decorated with wit and originality. But no tiny feet pattered across those well planned nurseries. After only a few months the house was abandoned. Now it is hard to believe that it ever existed; but Miss Athene Seyler stoutly asserts that she and her husband, Nicholas Hannen, dined there with Miss Gertrude Lawrence, who, she says, had rented it for a time. There is no record of another tenant, and in 1934 the *Evening News* announced that 'Number 42, Cheyne Walk Chelsea, one of the most luxurious mansions built in London in recent years, is to be pulled down and replaced by a block of flats'.

Perhaps there was someone to mourn the passing of this beautiful house, but today nobody seems to have heard of it: it is as if it had never been.

On Sunday afternoons, in the years just before the First War, well-fed, well-dressed fathers, top-hatted and tail-coated, would step from their front doors in Oakley Street or Cheyne Gardens and usher their sons and daughters across the Albert Bridge and into Battersea Park, where, taking the air with others of their kind, they would sometimes pass their King, dressed exactly as they were, ushering his daughter and sons along the same gravel walks, while Mamma, presumably, rested at home. Decorum, respectability, and a fading aroma of roast beef pervade the scene, which is nostalgic because we know it to be the end of an era.

It was a strange period of transition: the hideous taste and the prosperity of Victorian and Edwardian England still survived, but Mrs. Pankhurst rallied supporters from a balcony in Glebe Place, and Suffragettes with banners marched down the King's Road. Ragged children still ran barefoot in the back streets of Chelsea, but people still believed in heroism, and wept when Captain Scott, who lived in Oakley Street, died nobly in the Antarctic.

In 1911 Henry James discovered Chelsea. His secretary, Theodora Bosanquet, was sharing a flat at 10 Lawrence Street with a friend, and offered her employer two rooms at the back where he might work on his autobiography while he stayed at his London club. 'Chelsea,' she wrote later, 'began to make its appeal to him before long. He walked about and made little purchases in the shops. He liked talking to the people; he liked the kind of village atmosphere that he found there . . . And then he found a delightful flat round the corner at Carlyle Mansions . . .'

Number 21 Carlyle Mansions became the great novelist's London home on January 5, 1913.

'This Chelsea perch,' he wrote to his friend Edward Warren, 'the haunt of the sage and the seagull, as you so happily term it (though I feel scarcely more like one of these, than like the other) proves, even after brief experiment, just the thing for me.'

He liked his two front rooms, looking over the river, and chose the westerly one for his writing. He was pleased, too, that, 'just at hand, straight across the River, by the ample and also very quiet Albert Bridge, lies the very convenient and in its way also very beguiling Battersea Park'.

On April 15, 1913, he reached his seventieth birthday, and his friends chose to celebrate it by presenting him with his portrait, to be painted by Sargent. After the inevitable misunderstandings and hurt feelings, a formidable list of distinguished subscribers—writers, artists and actors—signed a birthday letter which James acknowledged 'with boundless pleasure' before beginning his sittings to his fellow American in Tite Street.

The portrait was completed in ten sittings and Henry James was delighted. It was, he said, 'Sargent at his very best and poor old H.J. not at his worst; in short, a living breathing likeness and a masterpiece of painting. I am really quite ashamed to admire it so much and so loudly—it's so much as if I were calling attention to my own fine points. I don't alas, exhibit a "point" in it, but am all large and luscious rotundity—by which you may see how true a thing it is'.

He was sorry that the sittings were over—'J.S.S. being so genial and delightful a *nature de grand maître* to have to do with, and his beautiful high cool studio, opening upon a balcony that overhangs a charming Chelsea green garden, adding a charm to everything.'

James had always been Anglophile: the outbreak of the 1914 war confirmed, if they needed confirming, his love and loyalty. In 1915 he became naturalized.

'The odd thing is that nothing seems to have happened and that I don't feel a bit different,' he wrote to Edmund Gosse '. . . The process has only shown me virtually what I *was*.'

He felt deep sympathy for England's part in the war, and chafed because he was old and ill and could do nothing active. He was concerned about the plight of the Belgian refugees, a large contingent of whom were centred at Crosby Hall, and in a monograph described their sufferings and the welcome given to them by the people of Chelsea. After his death in 1916 Edmund Gosse wrote that 'when the war with Germany broke out he ceased to be merely the idol of an esoteric group. He became a soldier; he belonged to England. No one has suffered more in spirit, no one was more tensely agitated by the war than Henry James . . .'

Gosse was the friend who, shortly before James's death, brought the news that he had been awarded the Order of Merit for his services to literature. Lying in bed with closed eyes, the Master was apparently unconscious. 'Henry, they've given you the O.M.' Gosse whispered, bending close. There was no sign of life, and Kidd, the maid, murmured that he was too far gone to understand what was said. After Gosse had left, James opened his eyes. 'Kidd,' he said, 'turn off the light to spare my blushes'

'A marvellous monument transplanted,' Henry James wrote of Crosby Hall. In 1910 this beautiful sixteenth-century building was carried, piecemeal, from its original site in Bishopsgate, and re-erected on Cheyne Walk. It was the banqueting hall of Crosby Place, the home of Sir John Crosby, a rich wool merchant. In 1483 it was occupied by Richard, Duke of Gloucester, who became King Richard III; on her arrival in England Catherine of Aragon was feasted there by the next owner, a goldsmith named Sir Bartholomew Reed, Lord Mayor of London, and in 1523 Sir Thomas More bought the lease for £150, but it is unlikely that he ever lived there.

Crosby Place was evidently uncomfortable: nobody stayed there long, and by the end of the eighteenth century pieces of it were being removed and sold. In 1831 the site was advertised for sale, but nobody bought it; and in 1839 Elizabeth Fry held a bazaar 'of Works and Books in aid of Female Prisoners and Convicts' in Crosby Hall. Despite efforts to rescue it, the place fell on evil days, and in 1868 it became a restaurant. Forty years later the Chartered Bank of India, Australia and China bought the site for offices. They were persuaded to have the hall carefully demolished, each stone and beam numbered, and thus, under the direction of Mr. Walter Godfrey, the architect who was later to reconstruct the Old Church, Crosby Hall was rebuilt in Chelsea. The building as it stands today is incorporated in an International Club House and Hall of Residence for University Women. From the outside the design is a hotch-potch of styles, but the fine old hall has been preserved, with its magnificent oriel window and elaborately carved ceiling—'a marvellous monument transplanted.'

The 1914 war took many of the younger artists, and those who came back were eager to get started again. George Thomas, the sculptor son of

Havard Thomas, Professor of Sculpture at the Slade School, returned from the army to his family home in Glebe Place and began work in a studio in Upper Cheyne Row. On the death of his father he was appointed to succeed him at the Slade. This young sculptor, whose work was full of promise, died a few years later as a result of war injuries, one of many whose lives and careers were cut short.

But many survived. Chelsea in the 1920s became literally infested with artists—painters, designers, sculptors, potters—working in all sorts of places: wooden huts and corrugated iron sheds, garrets and cellars. After the empty war years it was a renaissance: an exciting period in which a new generation of artists was being born. One of these—a sandy-haired youth with beguiling blue eyes and boundless enthusiasm—was Charles Cundall.

This distinguished Academician with his still youthful air lived till lately in a studio cottage in Cheyne Row, one of the last of the Chelsea artists of the 1920s to remain in Chelsea. He is famous for his beautiful silvery landscapes, several of which are hung every year at Burlington House. His studio was always open to his friends, and on Tuesday evenings he was to be found seated in the middle of the room, surrounded by easels and canvases, doing his football pools. He had no system and said he knew nothing about football, but he was always hopeful, making splendid plans for what he and his friends would do when he hit the jackpot. Perhaps one day he will.

A Lancastrian born in Manilla, Cundall won the Henry Grant Scholarship to the Royal College of Art in 1912, and migrated to Chelsea, where he rented a loft over a stable in Whiteheads Grove for seven shillings a week. In the 1914 war he joined the Royal Fusiliers, returning with a wounded right hand and an army grant of £90 a year. He set out to teach himself to paint with his left hand, and to finish his interrupted training at the Royal College. He had to live on a shoestring; but he was young, and alive, and painting again—and he had met a girl, a fellow student called Jacqueline Pietersen, who was known as Pieter.

In 1923 Cundall held his first exhibition, at the Leicester Galleries: he and Pieter decided to get married if he made £150 out of it (his average price was £30 a picture). He made £200.

The Cundalls shared the studio in Whiteheads Grove. Sometimes one of them sold a picture and they celebrated by dining out at the Good Intent in the King's Road. The dinner cost one and sixpence each. Beer was fivepence a pint, and sometimes they walked to the Café Royal to drink in style. Life for young artists in Chelsea may have been precarious, but it was endlessly stimulating: living was cheap, and there were plenty of others as poor as you. Pieter, like many other girls, made her own clothes. Chelsea girls did not follow the ugly fashions of the 1920s but dressed like Augustus John pictures, designing themselves gaily coloured cotton or woollen dresses with fitting bodices and full, flowing skirts. They wore buckled shoes (it was *Beggar's Opera* period) and sometimes large black felt hats. The King's Road in summer was like a flower garden, but the flowers often smelt of turpentine. Artists' Colourmen were as predominant as boutiques are today: paint was in the air.

So was grease-paint. Chelsea attracted some of the more distinguished and discerning of the theatrical profession. Sybil Thorndike and her husband Lewis Casson had a house in Carlyle Square, and her brother Russell lived in Oakley Street. Athene Seyler and Nicholas Hannen lived in Manor Street, where Mr. Hannen, who had trained as an architect, had the vision to pick a Regency cottage and modernize it. 'Manor Street,' said Miss Seyler, 'was of course all cottages with little gardens in front. On the Swan Court side there were two little shops in cottages—one a draper's with a little counter in the front parlour, and the other an antique shop kept by a Miss Toogood, who also had her wares in the sitting room.' This was in the 1920s. 'All the cottages in Manor Street had outside loos including ours. But we had a covered passage to ours,' Miss Seyler added with some pride. Trams lurched and groaned over Battersea Bridge and up Beaufort Street at this time; and by holding up your hand you could stop a bus at any point in the King's Road.

The Chelsea Arts Club was by this time an established institution: it had been formed in 1891 with the idea of providing artists with a centre where they could enjoy good company and good food at reasonable prices. The idea came from Thomas Stirling Lee, a sculptor, and the club's first premises were at 101 King's Road, now the Chenil Gallery. George Clausen, Philip Wilson Steer, Walter Sickert and James Whistler were all founder members; also Fred Pegram and W. H. Townsend, Art Editor of *Punch*. Of course Whistler should have been made President; but he was by this time so quarrelsome that nobody dared to nominate him. In 1902 the club moved to its present quarters, a low rambling old house with a beautiful garden, in the upper part of Church Street.

According to the original rules only men professionally connected with some branch of art could join. Many distinguished artists have sat at the long, well scrubbed white-wood table in the dining room, where Sargent, asked to make a speech, could only dig his fork into the table, mutter 'Thanks, thanks', and sit down. There was always a large open fire in the billiard room-bar, the holy of holies, where even today women are not allowed, although they have invaded the rest of the club, to the indignation of many of its members.

(The Chelsea Arts Club inaugurated the Chelsea Arts Ball, held at first in Chelsea and then at the Albert Hall till it became too riotous and had to be stopped. It was in intention a great artistic event, and every year the décor was designed by a famous artist: Augustus John, Stephen Spurrier, Alfred Munnings, Charles Wheeler, all contributed, and some of the costumes were magnificent. Breakfast next morning at the Club was an institution and had a calming effect after the ardours of the Ball.)

Among numerous distinguished artists who belonged to the Club was Henry Tonks, Principal of the Slade School, who with his cold blue eye and colder voice struck terror into female students when he stalked round the life class. ('Can you *sew*?' he is said to have demanded of one poor thing after a glance at her untalented effort.) Tonks lived in The Vale (his house is still there) and his greatest friend was Philip Wilson Steer, who lived in Cheyne Walk. Tonks's painting of Steer at home, attending a tea party given by his housekeeper to her cronies, hangs at the Slade, and shows his delicate touch and brilliant sense of character.

Steer was often at the Club; indeed, for about fifty years he was to be seen there, silent—like Sargent, he had no gift of the gab—and with a passion for chess. Charles Cundall remembers him there, playing chess, in his favourite chair, at his favourite table, with a box of fifty cigarettes beside him. 'He was a big man, afraid of draughts, used to sit hunched up over the fire.'

Wilson Steer is a fascinating character, a genuine piece of Chelsea. He lived at 109 Cheyne Walk from 1898 until his death in 1942, attended for much of that time by his housekeeper, Mrs. Raynes, who had been his nurse. She was a Welshwoman, and gave her whole love to him from the day of his birth, when his mother became seriously ill. She never altered in her manner towards her charge, and when he was an elderly and distinguished painter would still address him as if he were a small boy. 'Well, well!' she would exclaim, finding him at work. 'Daubing away! Daubing away!' Steer had a great respect for her, and alleged that when praised for her cooking of a pudding she declared, 'There's art in everythink, even in painting pictures.'

Steer's house, which overlooks Turner's reach, was built about 1790. The morning room, the scene of Tonks's tea party painting, is to the right of the front door, and the large beautiful room on the first floor, which has three windows overlooking the river, was Steer's drawing room, and also his studio. He never liked the roof-top studio which he built on soon after he went there, but kept it as a lumber room. He needed one, for the house was stuffed with things. He was an inveterate collector, of coins, of china and pottery, of bric-à-brac and pictures. He liked junk too, and used to go round the Chelsea junk shops in search of pretty trifles which in those days you could pick up for very little.

A gentle, humorous, reserved man, he was beloved and greatly esteemed by his friends. 'Do be careful,' Sickert wired him on learning that Steer had been knocked over by a car while shopping at World's End. 'Do be careful—I have no desire to be the greatest living painter.' But when, just after he received the Order of Merit, Steer, still in Court dress, answered the door to a dealer who said that he had come to buy masterpieces at the painter's own price, 'I don't paint masterpieces,' said Steer, and shut the door. 'Painting is a job like any other,' he told a journalist in a rare interview, 'something one has to do between meals.' Public honours alarmed him: he would not hear of a knighthood, and only accepted the O.M. under pressure from his friends. 'Steer,' wrote Tonks, 'is the simplest man I have ever met. He must be pleased he has been a success. I think everyone can enjoy that pleasure, but anyone with a mind at all is able, by that very mind, to see into the far country he has not reached.'

He was beloved by his students at the Slade, where his dread of catching cold was a source of amusement. He always wore old-fashioned high collars against draughts, and his excuse for not attending formal dinners was the 'risk' of changing into evening dress.

After the death of Mrs. Raynes (her portrait by Steer is in the Tate) he was looked after for the rest of his life by 'Flo', a girl from Fulham whose full name was Florence Hood, and who had been chosen long before and trained by Mrs. Raynes. Flo faithfully served 'Father', as she called him, for thirty-four years, keeping his house like a new pin and taking care of his cats. These were important characters, and were all called Mr. Thomas. The first, a black and white, died in 1906, and was succeeded by a magnificent tabby, who ruled the household for eighteen years. He appears as a kitten in Steer's painting 'The Muslin Dress'. A chair was kept for him at table opposite his master's. If anyone sat in it he would leap on to the table and stare at the offender till Steer was obliged to say, 'I'm afraid you are sitting in Mr. Thomas's chair.' In 1924 Mr. Thomas died of influenza. The last Mr. Thomas died during the Second War, and was not replaced. He too was a large striped tabby, who used to hunt seagulls on the mud-flats opposite the house, and who accompanied his master on shopping expeditions to the World's End.

In 1935 Steer began to go blind. He was characteristically philosophic: it was just as well, he said; most people painted too many pictures. When the war came, his sight was very dim; but he endured the air raids stoically, sitting up all night in his cellar, fully dressed with his hat and coat so that if the house were hit he wouldn't keep the wardens waiting by fumbling for his clothes. 'Flo,' said his doctor, 'sat with him in a space about 4 feet by 10 feet. Impossible to imagine anything more uncomfortable, but neither he nor Flo complained.' One of his friends suggested that it was not fear that sent him down to the cellar, but the fact that for the first time in his life, in that air-tight hole, he was out of a draught.

Chelsea suffered badly, probably because it was on the river and between two power stations. The worst night was that of April 16, 1941, when for nearly eight hours 450 German bombers attacked south and central London, and magnetic mines, Hitler's first 'secret weapon', were dropped. One of these fell on the Royal Hospital Infirmary; a second and third demolished Chelsea Old Church and the row of houses to the west of it. The church was a ruin: only the More chapel was left standing. Steer was, for the first time, badly shaken. 'I have not had the heart,' he wrote, 'to view what remains of the Old Church.'

But the raids went on, and he endured, supported by Flo. Nearly blind, with little left of all the things that had brought him joy, he held on, cheered by letters from his friends and an occasional visit. Nothing would induce him to leave Chelsea. He died in the early morning of March 18, 1942. The strain of those sleepless nights had taken its toll.

Dame Ethel Walker was Steer's neighbour; she lived beyond the houseboats, in what was known as the slummy end of Cheyne Walk; but this woman of genius paid no attention to externals and was oblivious of creature comforts. Her studio, like Steer's, was on the first floor, and reflected the changing light from the Thames; but there was no Mrs. Raynes, no Flo, to cosset her; only a 'char' of whom Ethel Walker said, 'She only stays on with me because she's always hoping that one day she may lay me out.' She once remarked, 'I have only to look into the eyes of a horse to love it, but when I look into the eyes of most human beings round me I absolutely detest them.' Her sole companions in later life were her cats, whom she fed on steak and milk. She herself ate little, but she supped every night on rice pudding. 'We all saw it all day,' writes her niece Rachel Fourmaintraux, 'simmering on a trivet beside the open fire in her sitting room (which was also her studio) at Cheyne Walk, and woe betide any visitor who, in helping to put coal on, should drop ashes into the beloved pudding.'

As she grew old she became tortured with arthritis, which twisted her hands. 'When she walked,' writes Nicolette Devas, 'she tottered and swerved out of control, and her gestures were jerks. Her painting hand trembled. I was amazed each time I watched the brush, clasped like some offensive weapon, mix the paint on the palette, vaguely, rather as if it was pig's swill, and then travel over the canvas with tender precision.'

In 1900 she became the first woman member of the New English Art Club, and George Moore so admired her work that he offered her the use of rooms in his Ebury Street house as backgrounds to her paintings. She did some of her best work there, making good use of Moore's fine old furniture and mirrors. All true art, she said 'must surprise and delight'. The first visit of the Diaghilev Ballet to Covent Garden, just before the 1914 war, surprised and delighted Ethel Walker, who went night after night and sat in the gallery with Epstein and other artists. She was ravished: Nijinsky became her inspiration and she never forgot the rapture of those nights at the first Russian Ballet.

In 1949 Augustus John, who tremendously admired Ethel Walker's work, asked her if she would agree to a joint exhibition. This was held at the Lefevre Gallery: her last show, and the summing up of her life's work. John was distressed because the critics gave more space in their notices to his work than to Dame Ethel's: but it was only after her death in 1951 that she gained full recognition. In the Les Bas Collection shown at Burlington House in 1963, she was represented by sixteen works. 'Ethel's works,' writes her niece, 'held their own, even next to a wonderful Bonnard, "Le Bol de Lait". They were a revelation to a younger public to whom her work was comparatively unknown . . .' Two of her large paintings, 'The Zone of Love' and 'The Zone of Hate', hang today in a place of honour at the Tate Gallery.

Augustus John has won a greater fame than any other Chelsea artist since Whistler. He was, like Whistler, a star performer, and the part he played was a showy one which probably hid the real man from all but his intimates. 'It was difficult to get close enough to Augustus,' wrote Nicolette Devas, who grew up with his children, and loved him. He complained, she said, of loneliness, 'but people were frightened to talk to him; shy and sensitive inside his protective shell, he often snapped and snarled sarcastically'.

He had a studio in Mallord Street, and later at 33 Tite Street. Sometimes he was to be seen striding down the King's Road, an unmistakable figure, tall, broad-shouldered and bearded, with a bandana knotted round his neck and a wide-brimmed felt hat. His eyes, says Sir Charles Wheeler, were like those of a bull. People stared and made way for him as today they would for a pop star. This was the passage of a god.

Chelsea emerged from the war battered, dirty, with gaps in her streets. There were many empty houses whose owners had left London, many others requisitioned by the Borough to house bombed-out families. The first years of peace saw a tremendous influx; artists returning in search of studios, deserted houses being opened up. The war had brought a great friendliness among the diminished population: Chelsea, under fire, had shrunk into itself. Pubs and clubs like the Pier and the Pheasantry had been crowded, the same people congregating there night after night. Now there was a tendency to withdraw, to settle into home life again, to put up new curtains and do a bit of redecorating. Only the young needed to be out and about. And it was the young who began to take possession of the new, post-war Chelsea.

CHAPTER TWO

PEOPLE FLOODED back after the war, and developers were soon casting predatory eyes over vulnerable spots, planning blocks of 'luxury' flats. Fortunately there were still some people who cared passionately about Chelsea's history—and her future. The Chelsea Society, founded in 1927 by Reginald Blunt, that ardent defender of old Chelsea, got ready to do battle.

Its new Chairman was Basil Marsden-Smedley, whose name is now memorable in the annals of Chelsea. He had loved and served the Borough since he came to live there in the 1920s, and for two years running, in the crucial years after the war, he was Mayor. Marsden-Smedley was a familiar figure, limping round the old streets (he was stricken by polio when he was sixteen), pausing to look at some detail of a building, or to consider the well-being of a tree. Trees were to him members of the community, and he spent much time and energy saving and safeguarding the beautiful trees—plane, ash, chestnut—which spread their branches over Chelsea streets and squares. His quiet forceful spirit pervaded the Borough during the period of change immediately after the war. With Richard Stewart Jones he carried through the plan to rebuild the ruins of the Old Church against what seemed insurmountable opposition from the Diocesan Authorities. In 1946 he succeeded in saving Turner's house, which had been badly knocked about. Later, many of the old studios were threatened: land was becoming immensely valuable and these shabby buildings were, in the view of planners, a waste of space. To Marsden-Smedley every studio was precious, a part of Chelsea's tradition: if the artists were to go, he believed that the place would lose its character for ever.

But even he could not prevent the eviction of artists from Trafalgar Studios in Manresa Road, or the demolition of King's Parade, that charming terrace of Georgian houses, with paved front gardens bordered with lime trees, which ran along the King's Road between Dovehouse Street and Carlyle Square. They were pulled down to make way for the new Fire Station, and for the College of Science and Technology, a purposeful-looking tower block, soon to be crammed with students.

Change was in the air. New buildings were needed, and Planning

Authorities armed themselves with powers of compulsory purchase; each plan was conceived without relation to the others or to the neighbourhood as a whole. In Basil Marsden-Smedley's view, there was only one remedy: a single Planning Authority must be given the power to decide what buildings, private or public, should go up, and what must be demolished. He died with this vision unfulfilled.

The Chelsea Set was a name much bandied about in the press, though no one in Chelsea could explain precisely what it meant. 'I think,' said Mary Quant, 'that it grew out of something in the air which developed into a serious attempt to break away from the Establishment. It was the first indication of a complete change of outlook.' There certainly was, as she suggests, something in the air: something which was felt by the young, a need for a new way of life. This was reflected by a sudden flowering of new talent in the theatre, which stemmed from Chelsea's Royal Court.

This playhouse had once, under the inspired direction of Vedrenne and Granville Barker, been the birthplace of plays by a hitherto unappreciated dramatist, George Bernard Shaw. In 1955 Dame Edith Evans unveiled Shaw's bust in the foyer, and as if stimulated by this reminder, the theatre took on a new lease of life. In April 1956, the English Stage Company opened their first experimental season, under the direction of George Devine.

It is interesting, looking through their Record of Productions, to observe how hard this company, or rather the Director and his associates, must have worked. There was no permanent company of actors; each play was separately cast, and seldom ran for more than a week. Many of these were maiden efforts by unknown writers; and Devine and his readers must have waded through immense quantities of scripts before each advance list of productions was decided upon. John Osborne, Arnold Wesker, Harold Pinter, N. F. Simpson, were some of the new names given places on these lists. The theatre even put on extra plays, without scenery, on Sundays, in its tireless search for new techniques and new talent. And few theatres can have made so many discoveries. The most startling, because the most widespread in its impact, was the company's third production, a play called *Look Back in Anger* by an unknown writer and actor, John Osborne. A new character was born, the Angry Young Man.

The young men now beginning to throng the King's Road coffee bars may have been angry; for the most part they were in search of something to be angry about. Some grew beards and joined Ban-the-Bomb marches; some painted a little, some learned to play the guitar in a sketchy way. In the course of time, those young men and women who seriously wanted to be creative artists moved away to find work, and somewhere cheaper to live. Those who came to Chelsea attracted by a spurious *vie bohème* grew tired of the problems created by living, jobless, in a shared bed-sitting room, in a house honeycombed with bed-sitting rooms, and having to wash up in a restaurant or decorate somebody's flat if they wanted to eat. Eating, after all, was necessary, however angry one felt about the Establishment.

The first King's Road coffee bar was started by Alexander Plunket-Greene and Archie McNair, two talented young men with enough money to be adventurous. Plunket-Greene, with his handsome looks and sudden enthusiasms, was a born trend-setter: his ideas caught on. His great-grandfather was Sir Hubert Parry, who composed the music of 'Jerusalem'; he inherited a talent for the trumpet, a passion for jazz, and enough enterprise to buy, with McNair, a house on the east corner of Markham Square and start a restaurant, Alexander's, in the basement. Plunket-Greene was friendly with a girl called Mary Quant, a young ex-art student who lived in one of the countless bed-sitting rooms in Oakley Street. Mary had ideas about clothes, and within a few weeks they opened Bazaar, the shop that caused a revolution in fashion. It opened with a party outside in the forecourt, under a striped awning. Bazaar was an immediate, staggering success; it became for the young the focal point of the King's Road, the embodiment of the new 'something in the air'. It was natural that others should follow the lead given by Plunket-Greene and Quant, natural, too, that their ideas should be imitated and become commonplace. Boutiques and coffee bars began to open up wherever King's Road shopkeepers could be persuaded to move out. 'More Old Shops Make Way for Boutique Boulevard' announced the *Chelsea News*, recording that Ward the Florists, who were a link with the old market gardens on the King's Road, had moved away. 'Is King's Road, Chelsea, one day to become a long chain of boutiques?' asked the columnist.

The answer came more quickly than anyone could have believed. Rents went up, and old-established family businesses moved out. One after another, the small shopkeepers were obliged to go and their premises were given new fronts which opened on to darkened interiors emanating pop-song and festooned with garments, suitable apparently for either sex. Because of the prevalence of shop-lifting, some are lined with mirrors and have notices warning customers that they are being watched.

With its Discothèques, Boutiques, coffee bars and jazzed-up pubs, the King's Road became, in the space of a year or two, a sort of international fairground, its pavements jammed with Americans and Europeans agog for souvenirs by which to remember that they had seen Swinging Chelsea. It is a curious fate for a road which never, in all its long life, aspired to be anything more than a means of getting from one place to another, and whose shops aimed only to provide Chelsea people with their daily needs.

The anachronism is that this same Chelsea is now part of the Royal Borough of Kensington. Shortly before Basil Marsden-Smedley's death in 1964 the two boroughs were amalgamated. 'The Chelsea Society,' said Marsden-Smedley, 'will now be more important than ever. Chelsea will have no other voice with which to speak.' It needed to be a loud voice, to be heard over the din in the King's Road.

The artists were moving out. By the mid-sixties, Chelsea studios were too expensive for all but the well-established and successful, and many of these were leaving too, deploring the changes that had come about. For residential Chelsea, since the war, has become smart.

It is true that, between the wars, a few 'society' people chose to live there: from 1928 to 1936 Mrs. Syrie Maugham reigned at number 213 King's Road, and gave fashionable parties in her famous all-white drawing room, while Lady Sybil Colefax gave even grander and more celebrity-studied parties at Argyll House next door. The last of these was in June 1936, and the guests included King Edward VIII and Mrs. Simpson, the Winston Churchills and Noel Coward . . . Higher than that, Mrs. Maugham, you cannot go.

But living in Chelsea for these ladies was an adventure: there was still a raffish bohemian spirit about a place where at any moment one might still find oneself in a slum, or at least in a very shabby-looking back street.

Now in the 1950s these back streets were being cleaned up. Dear little houses in Chelsea became tremendously fashionable among the young and newly married, and there was a craze for Regency architecture. Enterprising landlords, reckoning anything between 1800 and 1860 suitable, bought up terraced houses, tore their insides out and modernized them, gave them clean white fronts and brightly coloured doors, and sold them at a handsome profit. The dear little houses, as they changed hands again, became dearer, and still dearer. Some, of course, were well built, and withstood the shock of modernization; and as, all the time, values were going up, buying a house in Chelsea was not only a fashionable thing to do, it was a good investment.

The face of Chelsea is now very clean and pretty. The houses have never been so well-groomed, so immaculately painted, or decorated with such a variety of burgeoning window boxes. The beautiful old houses in

Cheyne Walk and Cheyne Row, in Old Church Street and Lawrence Street, Paultons Square and St. Leonard's Terrace are carefully preserved and probably better looked after than in all their long lives. Chelsea is, for the most part, infinitely more prosperous and less hand-to-mouth than it used to be. Yet to some extent, though gaining so much, it may be losing what matters: its character.

EPILOGUE

MY DOG Toby and I proceeded slowly along Cheyne Walk, returning from one of our potterings round old Chelsea. It was a warm Saturday afternoon, and there was hardly a soul about; but as we approached Oakley Street I saw a young man standing in the middle of the pavement, looking as if he had lost his way. He wore a Carnaby Street tie and carried a small knapsack.

'Excuse, please, where is Chelsea?' he asked. Perhaps he was Italian.

'Where . . .' I looked at him blankly. He hastened to explain.

'I seek,' he said, gesticulating, 'the 'eart of Chelsea.'

'Why,' I replied, anxious to promote international relations (and also, perhaps, to share my knowledge), 'you are in the middle of it!'

'Here?' He sounded unconvinced.

'You could hardly be more in the middle of it,' I assured him. 'Just behind you . . .' he glanced round hopefully, 'was Henry VIII's red brick house with its gardens where Princess Elizabeth and her brother Edward played, and where, later, Queen Catherine Parr secretly met her lover.'

'Is so?' he replied, politely.

'And here is a link with the past,' I continued. 'Just round the corner, in Oakley Street, lives the present Duke of St. Albans. Now, he is the descendant of Nell Gwynne's son by King Charles the Second, "A pretty boy", Evelyn called him (he must have taken after his mother)—and *he* lived for a time in Paradise Row, which was a street of old houses just up there, on the way to the Royal Hospital.'

'Is so?' he repeated. I saw that I was not cutting much ice.

'Or if it's literary history you're after,' I said, 'why, this very path we're standing on was trodden by countless literary feet. Dante Gabriel Rossetti . . .' I hoped that the name might ring a bell.

But he was shaking his head.

'I seek,' he said, 'the 'eart of Chelsea. Today.'

His meaning was all too clear.

'You mean the King's Road?'

His face lit up.

'The King's Road, S.W.3! I am sent it on a postcard. Yes, please, that is what I seek.'

I directed him. He scuttled happily away and was soon out of sight round the corner.

But is there a Chelsea still which is not the King's Road, which has not only a heart but a spirit? Where is Chelsea, the Chelsea whose fame grew from century to century, spread abroad by the people who fell under the spell of this 'Hyde Park on the Thames'? It is still on the Thames, though separated from it by an ever-increasing flow of traffic. It still has a beauty of water and sky, and the remains of a nostalgic antiquity.

A place belongs to the people who live there and takes its character from them; and it is her people who have brought greatness to this place. What other district in London can boast such an array of talent, such a collection of rare characters? Scientists and divines, writers, painters, actors, kings and queens, a saint and a sage, and countless others, known and unknown, have contributed to Chelsea's fame. The cinematograph was invented in the King's Road, Gordon of Khartoum lived in Beaufort Street, Sir Alexander Fleming in Danvers Street. Miss Jo Oakman lived for years in one dark room which smelt of cat, in order to go on painting views of Chelsea. George Malcolm, the harpsichordist, lives in Cheyne Walk, Mick Jagger and the Rolling Stones have left; and Dr. Charles Burney was organist at the Royal Hospital for twenty-three years, and 'never wished to change the place of his abode'.

These facts may be fortuitous, but they are worth remembering while searching for the heart of Chelsea.

BIBLIOGRAPHY

I have made use of manuscripts, maps and press-cuttings at Chelsea Public Library, including 'An Account of the Parish and Rectory of Chelsey in the County of Middlesex' by Dr. John King, D.D. (1694–1732), the Journal of Edmund Howard, and the volumes of *Chelsea Miscellany*.

I have also consulted the following books:—

Thomas Faulkner: *A Description of Chelsea and its Environs*. London 1810.

John Bowack: *The Antiquities of Middlesex*. London 1706.

The Rev. Daniel Lysons: *The Environs of London*. London 1792.

Randall Davies, F.S.A.: *Chelsea Old Church*. London 1904.

— *The Greatest House at Chelsey*. John Lane 1914.

Alfred Beaver: *Memorials of Old Chelsea*. London 1892.

Reginald Blunt: *Handbook to Chelsea*. London 1900.

— *Paradise Row*. London 1906.

— *In Cheyne Walk*. London 1914.

— *The Wonderful Village*. London 1919.

The Rev. A. G. L'Estrange: *The Village of Palaces*. London 1880.

The L.C.C. Survey on London (1909–27) Vols. I–IV.

Rosamund J. Mitchell and M. D. R. Leys: *A History of London Life*. Longmans 1958.

G. B. Stuart: *A Road-Book to Old Chelsea*. London 1914.

Thomas Croker: *A Walk from London to Fulham*. London 1860.

Eleanor Davies: *In Remembrance*. London 1909.

Henry Kingsley: *The Hillyers and the Burtons*. London 1895.

An Old Inhabitant: *Rambling Recollections of Chelsea as a Village*. London 1901.

Anon.: *A Book with Seven Seals*.

Raymond W. Chambers: *Thomas More*. Cape 1935.

William Roper: *Life of Sir Thomas More*. Ed. Hitchcock. London 1935.

Martin Hume: *The Wives of Henry VIII*. London 1905.

Daniel Benham: *Memoirs of James Hutton*. London 1856.

Peter Kroyer: *The Story of Lindsey House*. Country Life 1956.

The Diary of Samuel Pepys.

The Diary of John Evelyn.

G. R. de Beer: *Sir Hans Sloane and the British Museum*. O.U.P. 1953.

E. St. John Brooks: *Sir Hans Sloane*. Batchworth Press 1954.

Letters of Horace Walpole. Ed. Cunningham. London 1891.

Letters of Saint-Evremond. Ed. Hayward. Routledge 1930.

Captain C. G. T. Dean, M.B.E.: *The Royal Hospital, Chelsea*. Hutchinson 1950.

Lord Hervey: *Memoirs of the Reign of George II*, Vol. I.

Derek Hudson: *Holland House in Kensington*. Peter Davies 1967.

C. P. Moritz: *The British Tourists*. 1798.

J. P. Kenyon: *The Stuarts*. Batsford 1958.

The Ambulator, or Stranger's Companion. 1782.

Memoirs of William Hickey. Ed. Peter Quennell. Hutchinson 1960.

Elizabeth Blackwell: *A Curious Herbal*. 1739.

Dorothy Stroud: *Henry Holland*. Country Life 1966.

The Rev. A. G. L'Estrange: *The Friendships of Mary Russell Mitford*. London 1882.

Laman Blanchard: *The Life and Literary Remains of L.E.L.* London 1841.

D. E. Enfield: *L.E.L. A Mystery of the Thirties*. Hogarth Press 1928.

Disraeli Letters (to his sister, February 1832).

The Letters of Jane Austen. Ed. Chapman. O.U.P. 1932.

Autobiography of Leigh Hunt, Vol. II. Ed. Inkpen. London 1903.

Edmund Blunden: *Leigh Hunt*. Cobden-Sanderson 1930.

The Letters of Thomas Carlyle. Ed. Norton. Macmillan 1886.

Letters and Memorials of Jane Welsh Carlyle. Longmans 1883.

J. A. Froude: *Thomas Carlyle: A History of his Life in London*. Longmans 1885.

Jane Welsh Carlyle: *Letters to her Family*. Ed. Huxley. Murray 1924.

— *Letters Selected by Trudy Bliss*. Gollancz 1950.

Thea Holme: *The Carlyles at Home*. O.U.P. 1965.

The Diaries of William Allingham. Ed. Mrs. Allingham. London 1907.

The Letters of Charles Dickens. Macmillan 1903.

W. Justin O'Driscoll: *A Memoir of Daniel Maclise*. London 1871.

G. D. Leslie, R.A.: *The Inner Life of the Royal Academy*. Murray 1914.

Bernard Falk: *Turner the Painter*. Hutchinson 1938.

A. J. Finberg: *Life of J. M. W. Turner, R.A.* O.U.P. 1961.

W. Holman Hunt: *Pre-Raphaelitism and the Pre-Raphaelite Brotherhood*. Macmillan 1905.

Helen R. Angeli: *Pre-Raphaelite Twilight*. Richards Press 1954.

T. Hall Caine: *Recollections of Dante Gabriel Rossetti*. Cassell 1928.

H. Treffry Dunn: *Recollections of Dante Gabriel Rossetti and his Circle*. London 1904.

Gale Pedrick: *Life with Rossetti*. Macdonald 1964.

Rosemary Glynn Grylls: *Portrait of Rossetti*. Macdonald 1965.

Ellen Terry: *Memoirs (The Story of My Life)*. Gollancz 1933.

Lewis Carroll Diaries. Ed. Green. Cassell 1953.

W. Graham Robertson: *Time Was*. Hamish Hamilton 1938.

G. C. Williamson: *Murray Marks and his Friends*. John Lane 1919.

Dante Gabriel Rossetti: *Letters*. Ed. Doughty and Wahl. O.U.P. 1965.

Oswald Doughty: *Rossetti: A Victorian Romantic*. O.U.P. 1960.

E. R. and J. Pennell: *The Life of James McNeill Whistler*. Heinemann 1908.

— *The Whistler Journal*. Lippincott 1921.

James Laver: *Whistler*. Faber 1930.

Philip Henderson: *William Morris*. Thames and Hudson 1967.

Edward Burne-Jones: *Memorials of Edward Burne-Jones*. Macmillan 1904.

Edmund Gosse: *The Life of Swinburne*. Macmillan 1917.

Henry Adams: *The Education of Henry Adams*. Constable 1919.

Humphrey Hare: *Swinburne*. Witherby 1949.

R. Emmons: *The Life and Opinions of W. R. Sickert*. Faber 1941.

J. M. Whistler: *The Gentle Art of Making Enemies*. Heinemann 1890.

Hesketh Pearson: *The Man Whistler*. Methuen 1952.

Jaqueline Hope-Nicholson: *Life Amongst the Troubridges*. Murray 1966.

William Rothenstein: *Men and Memories*. Faber 1931.

The Letters of Oscar Wilde. Ed. Hart-Davis. Hart-Davis 1962.

Vyvyan Holland: *Son to Oscar Wilde*. Hart-Davis 1954.

Hesketh Pearson: *The Life of Oscar Wilde*. Methuen 1946.

Richard Le Gallienne: *The Romantic Nineties*. Putnam 1925.

John Gielgud: *Early Stages*. Macmillan 1939.

H. A. Taine: *Notes on England*. Trans. Hyams. Thames and Hudson 1957.

W. Acton: *Prostitution, considered in its Moral, Social and Sanitary Aspects, in London and other Large Cities*. London 1870.

Sir Charles Wheeler: *High Relief*. Country Life 1968.

W. M. Reyburn: *Flushed with Pride*. Macdonald 1969.

John Lewis House Magazine (John Lewis Archives).

Osbert Lancaster: *Pillar to Post*. Murray 1938.

H. Montgomery Hyde: *Henry James at Home*. Methuen 1969.

D. S. MacColl: *Philip Wilson Steer*. Faber 1945.

Nicolette Devas: *Two Flamboyant Fathers*. Collins 1966.

Mary Quant: *Quant by Quant*. Cassell 1966.

W. and A. E. Wroth: *The London Pleasure Gardens of the Eighteenth Century*. 1896.

Molly Sands: *Invitation to Ranelagh*. Westhouse 1946.

Frederic Drewitt: *The Romance of the Apothecaries' Garden at Chelsea*. London 1922.

INDEX

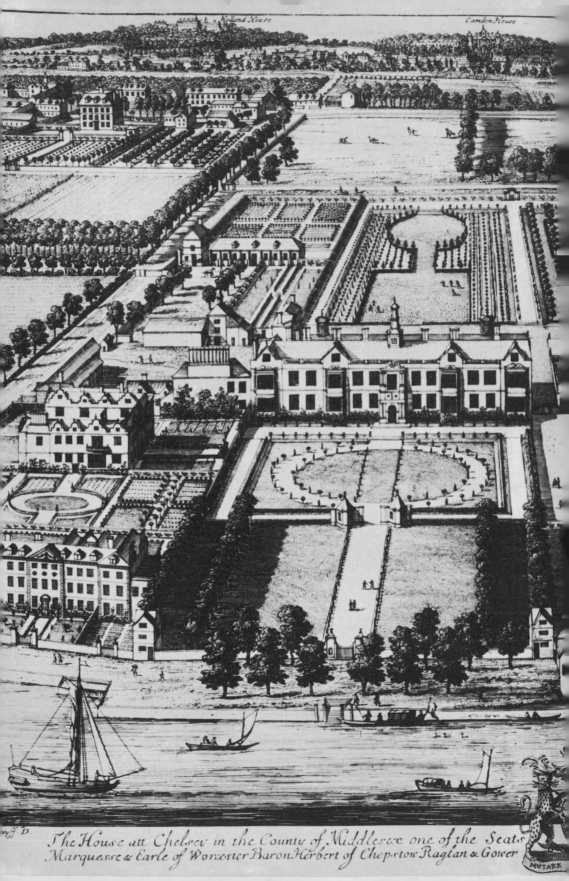

Holland House   Camden House

The House att Chelsey in the County of Middlesex one of the Seats
Marquesse & Earle of Worcester Baron Herbert of Chepstow Raglan & Gower

MUTARE